D1234287

THE STRUGGLE FOR GERMANY

NORTH SEA

BALTIC SEA

SWEDEN

DENMARK

DEN.

DEN.

KIEL

SCHLESWIG HOLSTEIN

ROSTOCK

LÜBECK

MECKLENBURG

HAMBURG

Elbe R.

Weser R.

BREMEN

OLDENBURG

NIEDER-SACHSEN

BRANDENBURG

POLAND

HANNOVER

BERLIN

Elbe R.

SACHSEN

MÜNSTER

THE RUHR BASIN

ESSEN DORTMUND

Rhine R.

Ruhr

DÜSSELDORF

ANHALT

LEIPZIG

KASSEL

HESSEN

COLOGNE

BONN

DRESDEN

SACHSEN

THURINGEN

KOBLENZ

FRANKFURT

BELGIUM

NETHERLANDS

LUX.

RHEINLAND PFALZ

SAAR

SAARBRÜCKEN

Main R.

PRAHA

CZECHO-SLOVAKIA

MANNHEIM

NÜRNBERG

KARLSRUHE

BAVARIA

FRANCE

Rhine R.

WÜRTTEMBERG

AUGSBURG

Donau R.

BADEN

MUNICH

A U S T R I A

SWITZERLAND

ITALY

GERMANY
ZONES OF OCCUPATION

UNITED STATES   GT. BRITAIN

RUSSIA   FRANCE

AIR LIFT

BOUNDARIES OF GERMAN STATES

The Struggle for

GERMANY

By DREW MIDDLETON

THE BOBBS-MERRILL COMPANY, INC.

Publishers

INDIANAPOLIS • NEW YORK

COPYRIGHT, 1949, BY DREW MIDDLETON

PRINTED IN THE UNITED STATES OF AMERICA

First Edition

PREFACE

THE intention of this book is to demonstrate that Germany is the most important single problem of American foreign policy and that the fate of the world may rest on the direction which Germany takes.

There are no easy answers to the internal problem in Germany or the struggle for Germany's future. One of the major detriments to clear political thinking in our time is the habit, which we have caught from the totalitarians, of thinking in terms of black and white. This book will not tell you whether Germany is "democratic" or "Fascist" or "Communist." Nor will it tell you conclusively the direction Germany will take in the future. It will, I hope, demonstrate the penalties of failure and the rewards of success in Germany. Ultimately, whether we succeed or fail in Germany depends on the people of the United States.

What I have tried to do is tell how the struggle for Germany has been fought thus far and how I believe it will go in the future.

My personal connection with Germany began on a September afternoon in 1944 when, just after we had crossed a narrow bridge, a shell burst in the field adjoining the road.

"Here we are in Germany," said the sergeant, "and they don't seem glad to see us!"

From 1939 to 1945 as a war correspondent first for the Associated Press and then for the *New York Times* I was at the

Baker 7 Taylor 216

9FSI

27941

receiving end of German nationalism. In France, Belgium, Holland, French North Africa and finally in Germany, I saw enough of war as the Germans fight it to inspire a deep loathing of any political system which converts men into the beasts I found them to be. But, as a Christian, I have never believed that an eye for an eye and a tooth for a tooth is the solution of our problems.

I was in Germany from May of 1945 until March of 1946. In May of that year I had the good fortune to be sent to the Soviet Union to study and report on another authoritarian system. Inevitably some of my impressions of Russia have found their place in this book.

In April of 1948 I returned to Germany. I have worked there ever since as Chief Correspondent in Germany for the *New York Times*. But the views in this book are my own.

Most of this book is based on my own findings in Germany and my work at three meetings of the Council of Foreign Ministers, at Moscow and London in 1947 and at Paris in 1949. Where it has been necessary I have drawn figures from the official publications of the Office of Military Government (U. S.) such as Report 175 of the Information Services Division.

I am indebted to various officials of both American and British Military Government and to numerous members of the city government of Berlin and the Parliamentary Council for the assistance they gave me in locating relevant material and revealing their own personal wishes.

The struggle for Germany is emotional as well as mental. Many of the men, German, American, British and French, whom I interviewed in Germany, felt strongly on the subjects we discussed and in a number of cases held views diametrically opposed to mine. Yet I met with the greatest courtesy from everyone, from General Clay to Willy Agatz, the Communist leader in the Ruhr.

Again, this book offers no solution. Basically it is an inquiry into how far we have gone in our struggle for Germany and what lies before us. If in the end it offers a few suggestions to those who will continue the struggle, I will be satisfied.

—DREW MIDDLETON

Berlin
August 24, 1949

THE STRUGGLE FOR GERMANY

N O SOONER HAD THE CURTAIN fallen upon the final convulsions of a dying Germany in May of 1945 than it rose again upon the first act of a longer but equally important drama, the rebirth of Germany. No one knows what form the new Germany will take. But we know there will be a new Germany and that the question of whether it faces east or west is of vital importance to the world.

States, like men, are conditioned by environment. Understanding of the German problem is impossible without understanding of the Germany of 1945-1949. Much of the nonsense talked about a German comeback is due to the fact that too many people think of the Germany of 1945 in the terms of the Germany of 1918. They have underestimated or discounted not only the physical destruction wrought upon Germany by five years of war but the cumulative effects of enormous casualties in two world conflicts, the psychological effects upon the German people of war in Germany, on the ground and in the air—sustained bombing, complete and utter defeat four years after Germany had reached a pinnacle of power it had never before attained—and, finally, occupation and partition.

Germany will come back. But when the effects of war and defeat twice in a third of a century are weighed against the industry, virility and courage of the Germans, it is extremely doubtful that Germany will come back all the way. I do not think Germany will ever again achieve the pre-eminence in Europe and the power for evil she won in 1914 and 1939. This will be due first to her own exhaustion from two wars and second to a less parochial reason: the rise to a disputed world leadership of the United States and the Soviet Union, empires that dwarf Germany. Germany's future potential for evil—or good—will be as a makeweight in the contest between these powers, not as a decisive factor in itself.

Returning to Germany and the German problem, let us refresh and perhaps appall ourselves with a view of Germany as she was in May of 1945 as the curtain rose on the latest act in the long life of the German tribes. For unless we have a clear view of the Germany in the hour of defeat, we cannot understand the Germany of today and tomorrow.

Here was destruction and chaos in a degree never before known in the world. An intricate, highly organized society had been disrupted. The invasion of Germany from west and east, heralded in the west by prolonged and intensive bombing, had brought about not only the complete defeat of the German armies but the ruin of a state. This we have forgotten. The Germans have not forgotten it, for there are few Germans living today who are not reminded of it every day of their lives. (The destruction and disruption in which the Germans found themselves then are the primary reasons why the Germany of today differs so greatly from the Germany of 1922.)

There are those who, viewing the first faint stirrings of German nationalism in 1948, were quick to say, "We'll have it all over again. History repeats itself." How can history repeat itself under conditions so different?

For whereas in 1918 the Western Allies had occupied only

a narrow strip of territory in western Germany, and the physical structure and the forms of local government endured, albeit under great strain, all of Germany was occupied in 1945, the physical plant upon which the state was based was destroyed, damaged or at a standstill, and the processes of normal economic and political life had ceased to function. Germany no longer existed as a state.

The Germany of that day was silent and broken. Allied planes flew low over the Ruhr. In the sunshine lay the huge plants that had fed the armies of the Kaiser and Adolf Hitler with guns and ammunition. Nothing moved on the ground. Locomotives and cars lay on their sides rusting in the sun. Great gaps had been rent in the factories so that from the air one could discern the torn and twisted machinery that lay within. Other plants had been burned out. Strangely, many of the tall factory chimneys remained. A wisp of smoke appeared from one or two. It was the only sign of life in that dead landscape.

And when the airplane turned from its steady buzzing over the factories and flew over the areas where the workers had been housed, there were more acres of destruction.

All that summer and for many months thereafter various Allied commissions poked and pried through the rubble of the German cities or pored over the reports kept by the Germans on the extent of bomb damage. Meanwhile the casual traveler journeying through a land hammered by an almost incredible weight of bombs was impressed not only by the destruction done to industry, which was great, but by the manner in which bombing had disrupted communications, dispersed the population and deadened the resistance of a brave people.

There is an argument that bombing, long-range strategic

bombing on the pattern of the United States Air Force and the Royal Air Force in the second World War, cannot be a decisive weapon and that German industrial production rose steadily until 1944. This may be true if the result of strategic bombing is measured only by its effect on actual industrial production. My own impression in 1945 was that the effect was far greater than can be calculated by the tonnage of bombs dropped on X number of factories and the rise or fall of production in commodities Y and Z. This effect has carried over to today; not only did it vitally influence the course of the war but it will influence vitally the future of Germany. It would be madness to discount the influence of five years in a concentration camp on a normal adult; it is folly to overlook or underestimate the influence of five years of bombing on the Germans and the physical structure of Germany.

The physical ruin of the country was the thing that struck Americans first in 1945. This was true both when one visited Hamburg or Cologne or Kassel or Munich and when one went out into the countryside. Here if farmhouses and barns were largely intact, the farm machinery was broken or gone. German agriculture is not extensively mechanized; what machines had existed in 1939 had fallen into disuse due to lack of gasoline and spare parts. Gone too were the horses which had been taken by the Wehrmacht and which supplied the traction power in the bulk of the German infantry divisions.

In the midst of pleasant farming country one often found scars of war which seemed all the worse in contrast, a huge bridge destroyed, a railroad train lying twisted and broken in a field beside the tracks, a village which had been the scene of a rear-guard action and which had been flattened as a consequence.

Closely connected with this physical ruin was the dispersion of the population. Bombing had driven Berliners south into Saxony, Westphalians northeast into Schleswig-Holstein. Millions of Germans had fled westward from the path of the Russian armies. Until 1946 the roads were dotted with small groups of people returning home, their few belongings piled high on small wooden carts called with bitter humor "the new postwar *Volkswagen.*"

At night the cities and larger towns were dead. By day they stirred feebly in the sun. The only movement across the broken land was the march of armies, the driblets of Germans walking back toward their homes and the vast, pathetic aimless movement of millions of Poles, Russians, French, Rumanians, Italians, Norwegians, Danes and every other nationality in Europe, all lumped under the useful but distasteful name of displaced persons.

But pervading everything else was the destruction. Some of it has been "cleaned up" today. But most of it remains. It will affect the rebirth and growth of the German state directly because of the enormous setback it has administered to one of the most highly integrated economies in the world, and indirectly because the effects of five years of bombing have changed the German people. To them as perhaps to no other Europeans bombing is synonymous with terror and hardship. The German Communists know this and have advised their Russian masters. Today in western Germany one of the strongest points in Soviet propaganda is that the Western Powers are preparing not merely a new war, but "a new bombing terror."

In 1945 when the guns became silent there was something else which struck Americans: the absence of young men.

Perhaps we will never get precise figures on German casualties in the second World War. Colonel General Jodl, former chief of staff of the Wehrmacht High Command, said in
May of 1945 at Flensburg that most of the German Army's
records had been lost earlier that year. He estimated, however,
that the army, navy and air force of the Third Reich had
lost over three million dead in the war.

Subsequent estimates have placed the number of military
dead at 2,100,000 and the number of "missing" at 2,900,000.
The estimate for civilian dead killed by bombing or in the
fighting during the invasion of Germany is put at half a million. My own impression from German police chiefs in half
a dozen cities and towns is that the figure was higher.

In the first World War, Germany, less Austria, lost 1,773,-
000 killed. Thus in two wars in a third of a century Germany
has lost certainly nearly five million and perhaps seven
million killed plus an indeterminate number of severely
wounded.

The cumulative effect upon Germany of these two great
blood baths is one of the factors that makes the Germany of
1949 far different from the Germany of 1922. Even though
the prisoners taken by the Western Powers have been repa-
triated, Germany still is desperately short of young men, not
only in agriculture and industry but in politics. One of the
most depressing aspects of the gathering at Bonn which, as
the Parliamentary Council, wrote the constitution for the
West German State was that it included very few men under
forty or forty-five years old.

In the *Land* governments of western Germany there is a
similar shortage of young men. The Germans who are assisting at the rebirth of their country in the west are for the

most part elderly men with little knowledge of or interest in the remnants of the generation that Hitler sent to the battle-fields.

This condition will continue for a long time. In the next ten years the West will have to deal with two classes of Germans: the elderly civil servants and petty politicians who have come to the fore during the occupation, and young, inexperienced men who have come to manhood since 1939.

Conspicuously missing in German society today are the young engineers, doctors, lawyers, civil servants, businessmen who might be providing a lead for the former soldiers, sailors and airmen of the Third Reich. Thousands of them died in action or in captivity. But many thousands more, plucked from their professions by a totalitarian state and molded into officers of that state, never have returned to their old jobs even though they have survived the war. War and soldiering have made them unfit for anything else. Here is one parallel with 1922: they form a dangerous potential of the worst kind of German nationalism.

Physical destruction and the loss of life were two factors which affected Germany more than anything else in the summer of 1945. With the passing of four years, occupation and partition, two other consequences of defeat, have attained an almost equal influence over the mass mind of Germany. They are responsible in some ways for the revival of various types of German nationalism since early in 1949. But they are also responsible for a further weakening of German unity and national morale.

"Occupation," a Frenchman told me in 1944 when General Eisenhower's armies were sweeping eastward across France, "tears the guts out of a country."

This seems to me to be as true in Germany as it was in France. Granted the loss of millions of the ablest and bravest Germans in the war, the will of the remainder has been sapped by occupation. And partition, by depriving the Germans of a unified country, has denied the people anything more tangible than slogans on which to base their national life.

The importance of occupation and partition as incentives driving the Germans toward a new nationalism cannot be discounted. But up to the present my impression has been that these two factors have delayed and weakened the Germany of the future rather than strengthened it.

These are all tangible factors difficult but not impossible to measure in everyday terms. Destruction means the shattered tenement of yesterday and the one-room apartment for the whole family of today. Casualties mean the empty space at the workbench or in the harvest field. Occupation takes the form of the foreign soldier in the street. Partition is the solidly guarded frontier of the Soviet Zone of Occupation running from the Bight of Lübeck in the north to the village of Adorf in the south where Czechoslovakia bulges into Germany.

But beyond these factors is the psychological effect of defeat upon a people. Observers of international affairs still note the effect upon the French of the much less complete defeat suffered by France in 1940. The German defeat of 1945 was much more complete, it was accompanied by a greater disruption of normal life, far greater bloodshed and preceded by a long period of very heavy bombing. No national character is proof against such overwhelming psychological attack.

When in the summer of 1945 I wrote that Germany in defeat seemed to be a country where the men had no honor and the women no virtue, I was roundly assailed in the United

States. Those at home who had loved Germany in the past and held hopes for her democratic future could not, of course, understand what defeat on a hitherto unimagined scale did to morals as well as the morale of a nation.

In that summer very few Germans saw farther ahead than the coming winter. All the standards had fallen. The national slogan seemed to be "eat, drink and be merry and damn the expense to your honor or your virtue." The Germans did not believe "tomorrow we die." They believed something far more hopeless; that tomorrow would be worse than today. So it was not surprising that millions of Allied soldiers found Germany a combination of brothel and black market.

The psychological climate of Germany in the first three years after the war was one of negation. Some called it hopelessness, some said the people were numb, some said they were apathetic. This condition endured until the early summer of 1948 when it began to disappear under the influence of various events which produced some sort of hope in Germany's economic and political future. We will discuss these later. At the moment, however, it is well to remember that the apathy is still very strong in Germany and that the psychological consequences of defeat still remain.

When the physical and the psychological results of the defeat of 1945 are fully realized, I think it is impossible for anyone to view the German problem of today as similar to the problem a quarter of a century ago.

CHAPTER TWO

I

IN 1945 THE FOREMOST CONSIDERA-
tion, in the minds of the Western Powers at least, was to prevent the Germans from ever again becoming powerful enough
to bid for world leadership. Beyond that they looked hazily
for some formula which would transform the most warlike
of European nations into a peaceful, parliamentary democracy. To obtain the first of these objectives, they had already
invaded Germany from the west and south, blasted its cities
and occupied it from the Baltic to the Alps. To obtain the second they had thousands of plans, charts and theories, much
good will and hope.

The curtain which had gone down on the defeat of the Germans had found a purely military cast in the center of the
stage sharing the applause. The smiling and affable Eisenhower. Montgomery like an eager fox terrier. Spaatz and
Harris grimly contemplating the fruit of their labors with
strategic air power. The curtain that rose the day after defeat already found the soldiers and the airmen giving way to
the builders and the planners. Clay and Robertson, the military governors to be, grew in stature as the combat soldiers
wandered off to accept the plaudits of the crowd and bicker
over credit for the triumph.

Behind the leaders who were soldiers of construction rather
than destruction was a vast motley host: army officers and
welfare workers, civil servants and businessmen on the make,

theorists with this and that plan for "reforming" the Germans, amateur empire builders from the Middle West alarming in their ignorance and professional empire builders from Whitehall equally alarming in their cynicism. All these set to work on the prostrate body of Germany.

They were handicapped at the beginning by the fact that although everyone, general and private, American, Briton or Frenchman, knew what kind of Germany he did not want, no one knew what kind of Germany he did want. Across the Elbe the Russians must have hugged themselves with glee. For out of Marxist mythology and the iron realities of the moment there was a plan.

Oh, the West had plans too. Dozens of them. But each reflected the country or special group which produced it and each emphasized the negative side of the problem: the desire to keep Germany down. Engineers of the three Western armies surveying the German scene with a chilly and nonpolitical eye opined this might all be very nice, but was it intended to keep Germany a desert in the midst of Europe and, if so, who would pay to keep its people alive?

Having seen at first hand the terror and destruction and brutality of the Nazi regime from Belgium in 1940 to Holland in 1945, I was, in 1945, strongly convinced that a German desert might be a good idea. What changed my mind in the next three years was the impression gained in western Europe that a German desert now meant a general European desert and a general European war later. And, of course, in the meantime I had been in the Soviet Union for a year and had been profoundly impressed by the enormous potential strength of that country and the potential power for evil which resides there, as indeed it does in all tyrannies.

In the summer of 1945 the only people not consulted about their future were the Germans. Actually even if this had been possible at the time, it would have produced very little. In 1945 the Germans wanted to be left alone; they had had enough of national aspirations and world politics. Under the terrible stress of a chaotic situation the German society broke up for a while into cities and towns and villages. The Germans not only denied their future, they denied their past.

Let us look at the other peoples as they considered the German problem in the summer of 1945. France wanted a weak Germany, a position she since has held with unwavering persistence for four years. The United States wanted a weak Germany but was beginning to doubt, ever so slightly, whether this would be to the economic or political advantage of Europe and eventually of the United States. The British wanted a somewhat stronger Germany and imposed a touching faith in socialism's ability to keep the German tiger quiet. The Russians wanted Germany. They still do.

In studying the German question there is one point concerning the plans of the Soviet Union which should be kept in mind. The Russians thought it would be easy.

It is clear now that the Soviets underestimated the bitterness which the actions of the Red Army had aroused in Germany and overestimated the swing to the left which they expected in Germany.

"What else can Germany do but swing into the camp of the Soviet Union?" a Russian officer asked me in Berlin in the winter of 1945-1946. "It is obvious that any country emerging from the terrible regime of the Fascists will naturally move as far away from that sort of rule as is possible. And there are great numbers of Germans who never lost their admiration for Communism and who will lead the rest of the people toward a true democracy."

To this officer, whom I cannot name because he is still alive and, as far as I know, flourishing, it was as simple as that. His belief, I am sure, reflected the opinions of his superiors both in the army and in the Political Bureau in Moscow. We have become accustomed to thinking of the latter as a group of infallible zealots, largely due to the Communist propaganda line which never admits a mistake. Nevertheless plenty of miscalculations and misjudgments have been made since 1945. And even though the Russians in the Kremlin are long-term planners, it seems obvious that in 1945 they failed to seize their opportunities and win the maximum gains from the chaotic, bewildered Europe that wearily staggered to its feet to face the peace. The Russians, had they acted wisely in Germany and restrained the excesses of their army, would have laid foundations then of a truly representative Communist Party in the Soviet Zone. As it was they did nothing but deepen the feeling of hatred and fear of the Russians which Dr. Goebbels had inculcated in his charges from 1941 onward. During that first summer after the war the Germans were politically apathetic. The only topic that roused them from this apathy was the mention of the Red Army.

That summer the Germany which endured until the first months of 1948 took shape. The French established themselves in the smallest of the four Zones of Occupation. The armies of the two principal Western Powers, the United States and Britain, receded slightly, giving up Thuringia to the Soviets in the south and a section of the Baltic coast in the north. The Russians have conveniently forgotten that in the final battles inside Germany the Western Powers occupied far more land than the Red Army.

The zonal boundaries which endured until the establishment of Bizonia in western Germany were set. Theorists and administrators now began the long, almost fruitless struggle to combine and correlate the German policies—or what passed for German policies—of four countries, all of them, in the hour of victory, intensely nationalistic. Inside the German boundaries the German state, now split into four segments, no longer existed. Here and there feeble stirrings were evident. But these upon investigation usually proved to be attributable to one German's energy and industry rather than to any communal effort.

At Frankfort where United States Headquarters were situated and at Bad Oeynhausen where Montgomery commanded, thoughtful administrators were thinking of the coming winter and the prospect of hunger, disease and general misery. In those days no one wanted to cushion the shock of defeat or spare the Germans the suffering they had imposed elsewhere. But there was a growing realization that unless "something is done" Germany would become a public charge on the world.

What that "something" was to be no one knew. For soldier and civilian alike were faced with differences in policy and disputes over method. "Damn it," harried officers would say, "you can't let these Krauts starve!" And if they were answered, "they let plenty of other people starve," they scowled and said it was no answer. Perhaps it wasn't. It was, however, the answer that plenty of people were ready to give.

Before we re-examine the plans for Germany of the four Occupation Powers and the great struggle that grew out of these plans, the effect of Germany on the occupation forces should be mentioned. To some degree it has affected policy in Germany just as the effect of the occupation is influencing the Germany which is taking shape today.

The Russian soldier was not the only soldier to be impressed by Germany. Ivan Ivanovitch was impressed because Germany was so unlike Russia: so clean, so well-ordered, so advanced. G.I. Joe liked Germany because, as he frequently said, "these people are a lot like us; they know the same sort of dope about cars and stuff. They're on wheels, see."

Joe's reaction certainly pleased a number of American officers who had never been wholly convinced that the United States was fighting the right people. It also frightened a large number of observers who were prone to give undue weight to Joe's conversation.

And, once the fighting was over, Joe found the Germans most friendly and accommodating. He does not find it so true today, but this was in 1945 when the Germans, having no boots to kick anyone with any longer, licked the boots of the conquerors.

At Nürnberg early in 1946 I used to talk two or three times a day to a sergeant of the guard at the courthouse where the International Military Tribunal was listening to the long, ghastly catalogue of German war crimes. One night as I left the courthouse I met him carrying a knapsack.

"Going over to see my girl," he said. "Always bring them some food. The old lady cries and the old man gets out a bottle of schnapps. And my gal, hell, boy, I never seen anything like her! She's only sixteen, but God damn, she knows *everything,* you know what I mean."

I said he seemed to be pretty fond of the family.

"I sure am," he said. "I come all the way from Omaha Beach and we had plenty of tough fighting. But now it's over, these Krauts, they seem like our sort of people. A lot nicer than the French, cleaner and they work harder."

He lowered his voice. "You sit up there every day and listen to that stuff, don't you?" he asked. "Golly, I read some of it in the *Stripes* and I find it damned hard to believe. People like my girl and her folks can't act like that. Maybe a few of them top Nazis did get out of line. But I don't think these people are like that, can't be."

Contact with the Germans in their homes, instead of in tanks or stukas, had this effect upon large numbers of the Occupation Forces. The Germans had slightly less success in winning the British and the French over to the idea that they were at heart a race of kindly householders who had been victimized by a sharp confidence man named Hitler.

The Germans had another effect on the higher command of the Western Powers. Although many a general "fell" for the easy life and the easy women which were his in 1945, the primary effect was made by the industry and ability of the Germans. When late that summer the Americans and British began to work on restoring the communications of western Germany, the engineers and administrators were enormously impressed by the Germans with whom they worked. They found them industrious and able, willing to work long hours for a pittance, cheerful and obedient.

Americans are a race of doers. To scores of officers and civilian officials the Germany of 1945 presented not a political problem but a technical challenge. They did not want merely to get things working again; they wanted to get them working better than they had been before. They labored with enthusiasm and skill. Their political understanding of the situation may have been negligible in a large number of cases, but they brought to their job unswerving devotion and great technical ability. A directive, such as the one given subsequently to the Anglo-American Coal Directorate in Essen which said in essence, "maximize coal production," was all they needed to spur them on toward their goal.

When, during their labors, they met Germans of equal ability (although careful, in most cases, not to parade it), men who would work as long and as hard as they would, they were impressed. Thus both G.I. Joe and the expert administrator from Washington or the area commander were unconsciously moved toward admiration for the Germans, and this development, in turn, had an enormous effect on the making of American policy in Germany as opposed to the making of American policy in Washington.

Germany in 1945 was not the Germany of 1918. Scourged and blasted by bombs and shells, its manhood almost decimated, its cities in ruins and its fields empty, it lay under the heel of conquerors. But the conquerors were themselves divided, and as the divisions widened, the Germany of the future slowly began to take shape.

The policy of the United States toward Germany has oscillated between a "hard" and a "soft" peace. In the beginning, during the last years of the war, the objective was a harsh settlement. Midway through 1946 sentiment both in Washington and Germany began to swing toward a less restrictive peace and a considerable measure of German recovery. In both instances, however, the principal governing factor was relations between the United States and the other Occupying Powers. The United States hoped in 1944 and 1945 to govern Germany in harmony with the other Occupation Powers. When through the intransigence of first France and then Russia this proved impossible, the United States had to hammer out its own German policy. Russia replaced Germany as the potential emeny.

Inevitably policy reflected the state of relations with the Soviet Union and, since the Soviet Union maintained the political initiative in Germany until late in 1948, the American policy was a defensive, negative one. The United States knew what it did not want in Germany; both Washington and the Office of Military Government in Berlin were less clear about what they did want.

But tracing the course of American policy as it has been written in Washington and molded by events in Germany brings us back to the original concepts formulated during the closing years of the war. And these, like so many other plans made during that happy period, all have the same weakness. They counted on a reasonable amount of co-operation from the Soviet Union.

Throughout the war earnest men in Washington and London had discussed plans for what would be done with Germany once the war was over. But it was not until after the meeting of the Foreign Ministers of the United States, Great Britain and the Soviet Union in Moscow in September 1943 that the European Advisory Commission was set up to insure co-operation among the Allies in matters arising from the defeat of Germany and her satellites. The Commission originally was composed of representatives of the three principal Allies. Later a French representative was added.

The first formal high-level discussion of policy toward Germany between President Roosevelt and Prime Minister Churchill occurred at the Quebec Conference in September 1944. No reports on the talks were published and it was asserted that they were merely preliminary to consultations with the other Allies.

The talks were important in one respect. They marked the debut in the formation of German policy of the Morgenthau Plan drawn up by Mr. Henry Morgenthau, then Secretary of the Treasury and a man of commanding vision and good will. The plan, although never adopted, has exercised a profound and continuous influence on American thinking on Germany and in Germany and upon the Germans. In a curious way occupation officials in the first years of the occupation became known as pro or anti-Morgenthau.

But the approach to the German problem was to be a co-ordinated one of the three principal Allies. American thinking on Germany was to be co-ordinated with that of the Soviet Union and the United Kingdom. When President Roosevelt left for Yalta and the conference which took place in February of 1945, three months before the German surrender, many still believed that such co-ordination was possible. When we review the various policies in Germany, this fact should never be forgotten. For in Germany, as elsewhere, a fundamental misconception of Russian aims cost us dear.

The communiqué issued at the close of the Yalta Conference described the bare bones of the future Allied administration in Germany and the broad objectives of the occupation.

The military forces of the three Powers and France, if she so desired, would each occupy a separate zone of Germany. Co-ordinated administration and control were to be provided through a central Control Commission consisting of the Supreme Commanders of the Occupying Powers with headquarters in Berlin.

The objectives of the occupation were stated in two paragraphs.

It is our inflexible purpose to destroy German militarism and Nazism and to insure that Germany will never again be able to disturb the peace of the world. We are determined to disarm and disband all German armed forces; break up for all time the German General Staff that has repeatedly contrived the resurgence of German militarism; remove or destroy all German military equipment; eliminate or control all German industry that could be used for military production; bring all war criminals to justice and swift punishment and exact reparation in kind for the destruction wrought by Germans; wipe out the Nazi Party, Nazi laws, organizations and institutions; remove all Nazi and militarist influences from public offices and from the cultural and economic life of the German people; and take in harmony such other measures in Germany as may be necessary to the future peace and safety of the world.

It is not our purpose to destroy the people of Germany but only when Nazism and militarism have been extirpated will there be hope for a decent life for Germans and a place for them in the comity of nations.

A review of these ringing affirmations shows that although the three nations were in accord on what they would not allow in Germany, very little was said about what form they wanted Germany to take. It is probable that in this period only the Russians knew what they wanted.

The communiqué also recognized the justice of Germany's being obliged to make compensation in kind "to the greatest extent possible" for damage caused to the United Nations in the war and announced that an Allied Reparation Commission would be established in Moscow to consider the extent and methods of reparation.

A protocol, which remained secret for two years, recorded an agreement on the form of reparation to be imposed. Subsequently its provisions were modified and amplified by the Potsdam Agreement.

The Yalta Protocol provided that reparations were to go to those nations which have borne "the main burden of the war, have suffered the heaviest losses and have organized victory over the enemy," and that reparations in kind were to be exacted from Germany in three forms.

First, removals, within two years from the surrender or the end of organized resistance, from the national wealth of Germany both inside and outside her territorial boundaries, of industrial equipment, machine tools, ships, rolling stock, German investments abroad and shares of industrial, transport and other enterprises in Germany.

These removals were to be carried out chiefly for the purpose of destroying the war potential of Germany.

The second form of reparations was to be annual deliveries of goods from current production for a period which at that time was unfixed.

Finally there was the use of German labor.

The protocol had another important passage. It stated that the Russian and American delegations had agreed that the Moscow Reparations Commission "should take in its initial studies as a basis for discussion the suggestion of the Soviet Government that the total sum of the reparation in accordance with points (a) and (b) [the first two forms of reparation] should be twenty billion dollars and that 50 percent of it should go to the Union of Soviet Socialist Republics."

The British opinion was that until the Commission had studied the question no figure of reparations should be mentioned.

American diplomats subsequently regretted the agreement of the Russian and American delegations. For, far from accepting ten billion dollars merely as "a basis for discussion" of future reparations, the Russians took it as an agreement that the Soviet Union would receive that amount in reparations. The atmosphere of future meetings of the Council of Foreign Ministers became more than usually acid whenever Vyacheslav Molotov, the Soviet Minister of Foreign Affairs, his eyes shining and his plump body braced, shouted that the Americans at Yalta had promised the Soviet Union ten billion dollars of reparations and now were going back on that promise.

As Yalta ended the great armies poised on the borders of Germany moved in for the kill. By May it was all over and unconditional surrender achieved.

For several weeks after the surrender, the administration of Germany was carried out by the armies and their Military Government detachments which happened to be in occupation when the fighting ceased.

By a declaration signed in Berlin by the four Allied Commanders in Chief on June 5, 1945, the United States, British, Russian and French governments assumed supreme authority in Germany, including all the powers possessed by the German government, the High Command and any state, municipal or local government or authority.

Simultaneously two further joint official statements announced the division of Germany into four defined Zones of Occupation with Berlin occupied by forces of each of the four Powers and the establishment of the Allied Control Council and other control machinery. The functions of the council were laid down in the first two clauses of the statement.

1. In the period when Germany is carrying out the basic requirements of unconditional surrender, supreme authority in Germany will be exercised, on instructions from their Governments, by the British, U.S., Soviet and French Commanders-in-Chief, each in his own zone of occupation, and also jointly, in matters affecting Germany as a whole. The four Commanders-in-Chief will together constitute the Control Council. . . .

2. The Control Council, whose decisions shall be unanimous, will ensure appropriate uniformity of action by the Commanders-in-Chief in their respective zones of occupation and will reach agreed decisions on the chief questions affecting Germany as a whole.

The European Advisory Commission, the Yalta Conference and the Declaration of Berlin all illustrate United States policy in relation to general Allied policy. But there were other factors influencing American thinking on Germany although relations with the other Allies, especially the Soviet Union, were the governing factors. There were, for instance, the influence of public opinion in the United States, the economic and political state of Europe and Britain and the rapid reduction in strength of the American Occupation force. All these tended to complicate and confuse a policy which, despite joint avowal with our Allies of broad objectives, remained, in its administration, obscure to many.

"What's our policy in Germany?" asked a Military Government officer in Bavaria in 1945. "Brother, I don't know. Maybe the big wheels in Frankfort can tell you. They snow me under with all sorts of papers. How 'm I going to read them when I'm doing forty-eleven different things to get this burg running again?"

This sort of confusion was general among many of the lower-echelon Military Government people early in the occupation. It reflected, if not confusion, differences of opinion on policy and its administration. And of course it was the harried Military Government officer who received, in triplicate, the end products of this confusion.

For it seemed that even then the United States was beginning to ask itself: just how hard is a hard peace?

Rereading the Morgenthau Plan today gives one a curious feeling of return to those hopeful days of 1944 when men of good will believed that the defeat of Germany and Japan would open a new era of good feeling in international affairs based on co-operation between the great Powers of East and West. Those who entertained such hopes, and I believe such people existed in the Soviet Union as well as in the West, have seen them smashed by the iron reality of the Russian grab for power in the European vacuum. But they were hopes which seemed to many intelligent men well founded and they guided many men who were thinking beyond the war into the peace.

The Morgenthau Plan was a radical plan because it provided for the death of a state, Germany, and the creation of two autonomous independent states, one in the south comprising Bavaria, Württemberg, Baden, and some smaller areas, and a new North German state made up of a large part of the old states of Prussia, Saxony, Thuringia and several smaller states.

The Ruhr, the industrial areas surrounding it, the Kiel Canal and all German territory north of it were to be made an international zone to be governed by an international security organization to be established by the United Nations, the plan stipulated.

But before this partitioning there was to be considerable alteration of Germany's frontiers. France would get the Saar and the adjacent territories bounded by the Rhine and the Moselle. Part of East Prussia and southern Silesia were to go to Poland.

This wholesale rearrangement of the geography of Europe was not, however, the most important and most criticized part of the Morgenthau Plan.

Here is what the memorandum summarizing the plan which President Roosevelt took to the Quebec Conference in September of 1944 had to say about the Ruhr and its industry in the future:

Here lies the heart of German industrial power. This area should not only be stripped of all presently existing industries but so weakened and controlled that it can not in the foreseeable future become an industrial area. The following steps will accomplish this:

(a) Within a short period, if possible, not longer than 6 months after the cessation of hostilities, all industrial plants and equipment not destroyed by military action shall be completely dismantled and transported to Allied Nations as restitution. All equipment shall be removed from the mines and the mines closed.

(b) The area should be made an international zone to be governed by an international security organization to be established by the United Nations. In governing the area the international organization should be guided by policies designed to further the above stated objective.

Morgenthau opposed reparations in the form of future payments and deliveries. His plan envisaged that the transfer of existing German territories and industrial assets would satisfy the nations despoiled by Germany in the war.

Nothing in the plan, as it is summarized in the memorandum mentioned above, so betrays the difference of political climate between the world of 1944 and that of 1949 as the final article which reads as follows:

Although the United States would have full military and civilian representation on whatever international commission or commissions may be established for the execution of the whole German program, the primary responsibility for the policing of Germany and for civil administration in Germany should be assumed by the military forces of Germany's continental neighbors. Specifically, these should include Russian, French, Polish, Czech, Greek, Yugoslav, Norwegian, Dutch and Belgian soldiers.

Under this program United States troops could be withdrawn within a relatively short time.

The author of this plan envisaged the Germany of the future as a largely rural country. "Germany's road to peace leads to the farm," wrote Mr. Morgenthau in 1945. Agriculture was to be supplemented by a few light industries to process farm products and supply the needs of the population. Basically the author of the plan felt that Germany could never again be trusted with heavy industry and cited not only the destruction of Europe by the products of that industry but the manner in which German cartels, export subsidies, special kinds of currencies and clearing agreements had supported the German economic warfare of the previous ten years.

The Morgenthau Plan never was accepted as United States policy but it had an astounding virility. Even those who rejected most strongly its provisions for the elimination of German industry were influenced by the Secretary of the Treasury's wise and sober account of the rise of German industrialism between the wars and took steps to see that some of the abuses which had fostered that rise were prevented from recurring in the first postwar years.

Many of the most foresighted believe today that, should the flow of American dollars into Germany suddenly be cut, German industrialists and businessmen would be forced to resort to some of those practices which helped build the industrial might of the Third Reich.

The plan had another influence. Many of the civilian and military officials who took over the administration of the United States Zone of Occupation in 1945 were former Treasury Department employees. They believed most heartily in the plan evolved by their chief. When United States policy began to shift toward a somewhat softer peace than envisaged by Mr. Morgenthau, these officials served as a counterweight against those officials who because of fear of the Soviet Union or other reasons wanted to rebuild Germany.

Why was the Morgenthau Plan never accepted? I have pointed out that it was thought out in the brave days when the West looked hopefully toward the East for collaboration in the postwar world. The failure of that collaboration to develop and the development instead of the expansionist policy of the Kremlin would in any case doom a plan based on the theory of continued collaboration. Who would run Germany today if, as Mr. Morgenthau suggested, its occupation had been left up to Germany's continental neighbors led by the Soviet Union and including Poland, Czechoslovakia and Yugoslavia?

Another weakness lies in the fact that no matter how strong

the intentions may be, it is impossible to denude a country entirely of industrial wealth. Mr. Morgenthau's plan was to close the coal mines of the Ruhr. This would have meant a considerable hardship to Europe. But beyond that, closing the mines does not remove the coal from the ground. While it remains there someone is liable to come and get it. Wars have been fought for smaller prizes than the coal fields of the Ruhr. Politics is the art of the possible; the Morgenthau Plan did not come within the boundaries of the art.

Yet today when any hope of implementing the Morgenthau thesis has been banished by the ugly facts of Russian intransigence there are those who proclaim proudly, "I'm a Morgenthau man; I believed in that plan." It is a lost cause today, but like all such causes it has its attraction if only because once in the midst of world-wide slaughter it appeared to offer a promise that such slaughter would come no more.

The first general order on United States policy and administration in Germany was the famous Directive Number 1067 of the Joint Chiefs of Staff sent to General Dwight D. Eisenhower in April of 1945, the month before the German defeat.

This document on the surface was one which called for a "hard peace," and Eisenhower, and General Lucius DuBignon Clay, who came to Europe that spring to act as Deputy Military Governor, both believed in that sort of peace. The document did not go as far as the Morgenthau Plan and it contained phrases and clauses which might be exploited, as some of them were, to temper the harshness of the directive as a whole. Nevertheless at that time there was no disposition to do this, although, as I have said, there were already questions being asked by the French and the Belgians and the Dutch as well as in our own Military Government about the effect that the envisaged reduction of German industry would have on the economy of northwestern Europe.

Those who think United States policy moved too quickly or too slowly in the spring of 1945 should remember that one of the primary objectives of all the Powers when the Germans capitulated was to catch and try those who had been responsible for the tragedy of the preceding years.

General Clay in his first press conference in Paris on May 16, 1945, emphasized this point when he promised he would make the German war criminals pay for their crimes and then "begin to worry about the long-range problems and the final treatment and regeneration of Germany."

Clay had as his principal assistants two men who, with him, were to exercise a maximum effect on United States policy in Germany, Ambassador Robert D. Murphy and Brigadier General William H. Draper. Murphy, who had been a political adviser to Eisenhower in the Mediterranean, served in that role in Germany under both Eisenhower and Clay. Draper, a combat officer in the Pacific, came to Germany as head of the Economics Division of Military Government. General Draper had been associated with the Wall Street house of Dillon, Reed and Company. This connection proved a boon to the Russian propagandists in their efforts to prove that Germany was to become a colony of Wall Street.

In this, as in much of their propaganda, the comrades approached the ludicrous. General Patton, I was told in Stalino in the autumn of 1946, always had dealt "easily" with the Germans because he was a director of Standard Oil.

JCS 1067 was on the face of it a very harsh document. Yet it included those phrases and clauses which might be used to ameliorate it. During the summer of 1945 when it was the

basis for American rule in Germany there was constant bick-
ering between those who wanted a harsh interpretation and
those who sought a somewhat milder line. I was myself much
inclined toward the former point of view since I had not then
realized, as I should have done, that Germany is not an
island but part of Europe. My excuse is that for five and a
half years I had watched the war, sometimes at very close
range, and the defeat of Germany and destruction of her
military power had come to be the only objective.

The political direction of JCS 1067 was toward the decentralization of Germany. The administration of affairs in Germany, it ordered, "shall be directed toward the decentralization of the political and administrative structure and the development of local responsibility."

It should be remembered that there was no thought of dealing with any German government and the feeble imitation of
one presented by Admiral Doenitz was eliminated, albeit
somewhat tardily, at Flensburg in May of 1945.

The directive did not give the geographical outline of the
various zones; these were not finally fixed until after the Potsdam Conference; nor did it make any attempt to follow the
Morgenthau Plan suggestions for the establishment of separate states and the internationalization of the Ruhr. For this
it was much criticized. Yet it was not a long-term policy
statement on the future of Germany. It was merely a directive
under which the United States Military Government could
work.

The only centralization to be allowed in Germany, the directive stated, was to be that necessary for control of essential
public services such as railroads, communications and power,
finance and foreign affairs and distribution of essential commodities. This modest objective also was sharply criticized

as moving United States policy toward a commitment on the restoration of a central German state. Events proved that even this small degree of centralization was prevented first by the French and then by the Russians.

The basic objectives of Military Government in Germany as set forth by the directive were simple. "The principal Allied objective in Germany is to prevent Germany from ever becoming again a threat to the peace of the world," said the directive.

Among the essential steps toward achieving this objective, it said, was "the industrial disarmament and demilitarization of Germany, with continuing control over Germany's capacity to make war and the preparation for an eventual reconstruction of German political life on a democratic basis." Economic control, the directive advised, was instituted to achieve these objectives. Moreover, it added, the Allies had no intention of allowing the Germans better living conditions than the people of the surrounding countries.

The controls on the German economy, the directive said, were to be imposed only to the extent necessary to accomplish these objectives, provided that controls were imposed "to the full extent necessary" to achieve the industrial disarmament of Germany. No steps were to be taken "looking toward the economic rehabilitation of Germany" or to "maintain or strengthen the German economy."

General Eisenhower was ordered to "prohibit and prevent production of iron and steel, chemicals, nonferrous metals (excluding aluminum and magnesium), machine tools, radio and electrical equipment, automotive vehicles, heavy machinery and important parts thereof" *except for certain purposes.* Here was an important modification.

Paragraph 5 of the directive stated that economic controls

were to be instituted not only to achieve the objective of disarming Germany but "also as they may be essential to protect the safety and meet the needs of the occupying forces and assure the production and maintenance of goods and services required to prevent starvation or such disease and unrest as would endanger these [occupation] forces."

Thus the prohibition was balanced by a clause which gave an opening, however slight, to those who favored the recovery and rehabilitation of Germany.

In 1945 there were many bitter arguments as to how much of the German economy could meet the requirements of the occupation forces and keep the German society "just ticking over," as the phrase went then. And here a new influence was encountered. The war against Japan was still in progress when Military Government was established in June of 1945, and it was claimed that a number of German factories would be kept in production to assist the American war effort in the Orient. I never saw any specific directives on this score, but my diary shows that the importance of sending German supplies to the Pacific was impressed on me by a number of officers who seemed inordinately willing to keep the wheels going in Germany. Evidently they had the idea that United States production was incapable of defeating Japan!

Today the pleas made in 1945 by many able and intelligent officers for enough German production to ward off disease and starvation have an odd ring. But if the reader will refer to the last chapter, it will be evident that these dangers were real. Moreover, in the chaotic condition of the country at the time, there was a real opening for Communist infiltration. At the time raising what was termed "the Communist bogeyman" amused the newly arrived civilians from the United States; they were still living in the rosy glow of optimism over future international relations. Still in Frankfort, Munich and a half-dozen other cities in the summer of 1945 the Communist Party was most active and, on the whole, well led. Had chaos continued it might have laid the foundations for much greater strength than it boasts at present in western Germany.

The directive also stated that economic controls were to be imposed to the full extent necessary to achieve the industrial disarmament of Germany. Moreover it stated it was the policy of the United States Government to "effect a dispersion of ownership and control of German industry."

Reading JCS 1067 today leaves the inescapable impression that from the point of view of Germany's future economy there was still no general agreement in Washington. The document is on the surface an instrument for a "hard peace." But it does contain loopholes which would enable a Military Governor who wished to rebuild Germany a chance to lay the foundations for that reconstruction.

Yet casting back to my own notes during that period I find no sign that there was a plot to restore Germany as the Communists and their left-wing echoes have claimed. There was a good deal of slipshod thinking about the German problem and a marked failure to face the fact that a factory put into operation to make agricultural equipment, so that the Germans would be able to harvest their crops, could, if stringent controls were not instituted, be used to make light tanks in some future world catastrophe.

Moreover the American impulse to "get things working," which I have mentioned earlier, ran full blast without much attention being paid as to whether the production or service to be restored was in accord with the general objectives.

I have stressed the economic rather than the political side of JCS 1067 because in the period between the end of the war and the opening of the Potsdam Conference politics were dead in Germany. The Communists were busy, the Social Democrats who had been overwhelmed with the Communists in the Nazi tidal wave of the early 1930's had begun to revive and the Christian Socialists were busy in Bavaria. However, none of the parties was making any real impression on the mass of the German people, nor did they for some months to come, and in general the orders of the Occupation Forces were carried out with that submission which seemed all the more strange in view of the bitter fighting which had marked the last year of the war.

It was a strange period. Despite the weaknesses of Allied policy there was confidence that when the United States, Great Britain and the Soviet Union next met, some sort of common policy for Germany would be worked out. Moreover it was time to make a final alignment of the Zones of Occupation and to pay attention to the insistent claims of France for a recognized share in that occupation.

And although there were many on the western side of the fence who already were beginning to doubt how much actual co-operation would be forthcoming from the Russians, whatever was settled at an international meeting, everyone was willing to try. The deep pessimism that held the American and British policy makers in thrall during the Moscow and London meetings of the Council of Foreign Ministers was not yet in evidence.

So the long summer days went past. The Allies prepared for Potsdam. The Germans, almost forgotten quantities in the involved equation of a peace settlement, thought about the next meal.

JCS 1067 gave the United States Government's views on

what it did not want in Germany. But beyond the rather cloudy reference to "an eventual reconstruction of German political life on a democratic basis" there was no sign of what the United States did want in Germany. This negative approach was to be a weakness in American policy that endured for years and still plagues our occupation.

2

At that period the Germans were a minor factor in the occupation. Yet under the first impact of occupation certain tendencies began to develop.

Perhaps the most remarkable of these from the standpoint of the Western Occupation Forces was the stunned submissiveness of the Germans. The people who had fought so long and so hard that it had taken the combined might of the United States, the British Empire and the Union of Soviet Socialist Republics to defeat them appeared in the first months of victory as meek and acquiescent. For months before the surrender there had been predictions about the resolution and strength of the German underground which would fight the Occupation Powers once German resistance in the field was over. An undergound in the sense of the Norwegian or Greek underground never developed.

Equally startling to those who in prewar days had been impressed by the strength of National Socialism was the speed and ease with which the German people divested themselves of all connections with the Nazis. Fortunately, written records are more durable than German memories and the Occupation Powers were able to learn from them how deeply implicated some of the most violent postwar Nazi-haters had been.

Almost overnight the signs and symbols of the creed disappeared. By autumn of 1945 one could drive from Hamburg to Munich without seeing a single one of the various insignia in which the National Socialists had delighted.

"Swastikas?" a German said in Hameln that summer. "We tore them down as soon as we could. They were forced on us. We were never Nazis here."

Thus spoke millions of Hitler's supporters in the hour of defeat.

The submissiveness and the eagerness of the Germans to repudiate "der schöne Adolf" and all his works had a considerable influence in the summer when the administration of American policy was shaking down. The British and French, who knew more about the Germany of 1934-1945, were less easily fooled, but in the American Zone there were quite a number who could not believe that the smiling, bowing peasants, the pretty, easy girls and motherly women could be connected with Dachau and Sachsenhausen.

There were many ready to believe "there's no fight left in these people" and to scoff at fears that Germany might rise again. The danger of German revival to the heights of 1939 was undoubtedly remote but not because German nature had changed.

At any rate there were scores of honest and earnest Military Government officials who could not understand why the harshest sections of their orders must be carried out and consequently carried them out in a halfhearted fashion.

The Germans had another weapon as well. That summer saw the start of the German campaign to divide the Allies.

In this, of course, they were aided by the Russians who already were showing tendencies toward instransigence and whose army in eastern Germany had acted just about as badly as the German Army had in Russia.

But the mass of the United States Army and Military Government knew very little about what the Germans had done in the Ukraine and they were appalled, and justly so, by what they heard of Russian actions in Germany. In those days correspondents were prone to ascribe such stories to the insidious propaganda of the Germans. The circulation of the stories certainly was propaganda. But I am convinced that the stories were true.

The Russians were not the only object of the campaign. The Americans were flattered and told how they had saved the British and the French. The British were praised and regaled with stories of American and French cowardice in the war. The French were offered the theme of European unity against the islanders of Britain and American barbarism.

None of this was immediately important. The submissiveness, the denial of Nazism and the taletelling about the other Allies had no immediate effect. But in the United States Zone at least they strengthened the feeling that these people who seemed so kindly, who loved children, dogs and beer were not so bad after all and that there was really no reason to be harsh with them. There were plenty of graves from Stalingrad to Calais and from the North Cape to Alamein to prove the contrary and plenty of bone ash at Dachau, but time passes and men forget.

**CHAPTER
THREE**

R USSIAN REFLECTIONS ON THE Potsdam Conference must be bathed in a golden glow. For around the conference table from July 17 to August 2, 1945, Soviet foreign policy scored its last great victories on Germany. Never again were the Russians to find the West so accommodating. Never again did a few hours' negotiation produce such impressive dividends in material and territory. Granted the debt which the West owed, or thought it owed, to the Soviet Union for its services in the war, the Potsdam Conference not only paid a great deal of that debt but threw in an exorbitant amount of interest.

Until Potsdam the plans of the United States, the Soviet Union and Great Britain followed the same general lines. After Potsdam the plans of West and East diverge.

In retrospect Potsdam was the last great Russian diplomatic success. Certainly it was the last international conference at which a Russian delegation was present where an atmosphere of cordiality and mutual confidence prevailed. For the great reversal of Soviet propaganda and policy against the West did not begin until late in 1945. Because of this some critics have opined that something the West did at Potsdam infuriated the Russians and "turned" them against the United States and Great Britain. This betrays a fundamental misconception of the Communist attitude toward the West. The capitalist world, and the socialist world of Great Britain, have always been regarded as enemies by the Communists. The degree of enmity does not vary. We were as much enemies in 1941 when the Soviet Union needed our help so desperately as we are today. The difference was that in 1941 the realists in the Kremlin realized they must modify the outward indication of their enmity. They did, and the aid they received helped them drive the Germans out of the Soviet Union.

But the disillusionment which the Soviet Union implanted in the minds of many earnest and honest Americans and Britons, who had admired Russia for her struggle, when the propaganda machine was turned full blast against their countries, may, in the end, prove a more deadly weapon to Russia and Russia's cause than the panzers of Hitler. In the last four years Russia has not only betrayed her own revolution, she has weakened and betrayed the cause of the working classes all over the world by identifying that cause with a tyrannic imperialism which trumpets equality and democracy while it smashes independence and freedom in Europe and Asia.

After thirty years the Communist state has very nearly succeeded in expunging from the minds of men the hopes it roused throughout the world thirty years ago.

At Potsdam the Russians got their rewards. When Joseph Stalin, Harry S. Truman and Winston Churchill met in the town the Prussian kings had adorned, their ostensible purpose was to determine the broader questions of Allied policy for Germany in line with the previous agreements at Yalta. It is noteworthy that during the conference Churchill and Eden, the most experienced and wary Western representatives, were replaced by Clement Attlee and Ernest Bevin,

Prime Minister and Foreign Secretary of the new Labor Government in Britain.

The "whys" and "hows" of the secret conference at Potsdam are best left to the participants. The results betray, however, just how cleverly and forcefully the Russians put and won their case. All the same, the Russians were not satisfied by the results of their victory and the next two years found them attempting with monotonous persistence to expand the gains already won on the pretext that such expansion was called for in the agreements reached at Potsdam.

These agreements were recorded in a protocol, and the policy to be followed during the occupation of Germany was more precisely defined under the heading "The Principles to Govern the Treatment of Germany in the Initial Control Period."

According to this document the purposes of the occupation were:

(1) The complete disarmament and demilitarization of Germany and the elimination or control of all German industry that could be used for military production.

(2) To convince the German people that they had suffered a total military defeat and that they could not escape responsibility for what they had brought upon themselves, since their own ruthless warfare and the fanatical Nazi resistance had destroyed German economy and made chaos and suffering inevitable.

(3) To destroy the National Socialist Party and its affiliated and supervised organizations, to dissolve all Nazi institutions, to ensure that they are not revived in any form, and to prevent all Nazi and militarist activity or propaganda.

(4) *To prepare** for the eventual reconstruction of German

---
* Italics mine.

political life on a democratic basis and for eventual peaceful
co-operation in international life for Germany.

The political section also included specific provisions on
the abolition of military and quasi-military organizations,
disarmament, denazification, the judgment of war criminals,
the control of education, the reorganization of the judicial
system, the encouragement of local self-government and
democratic political parties, freedom of speech, freedom of
the press, freedom of religion and freedom of trade unions.

These are imposing and noteworthy objectives. But in
retrospect they appear to stress too heavily what had already
been done and too lightly what needed to be done. For instance the German people knew they had lost the war in
1945. There was very little the victorious Powers could do
which would deepen their conviction. But even the three
most powerful nations in the world could not prevent the
passing of time and the eventual change in German attitude
toward the defeat. Today the Germans still realize they lost
the war. But four years of introspection have provided them
with excuses and an array of "ifs" and "might-have-beens."

The statesmen at Potsdam would have been wiser had they
provided for some means of teaching the Germans that war
in itself is wrong. This, however, would not have been in
accord with the Russian belief, since the Soviets, despite pro-
testations of their love of peace, are the most militarist nation
in the world, and the Big Three confined themselves to showing the Germans not that war is wrong but that losing a war
is a costly business.

Similarly the provision for the destruction of the Nazi
Party seems superfluous. The National Socialists had been
destroyed by their own defeat. No one in the West had any
intention of permitting a revival. Here the danger lay in

substituting a new kind of authoritarianism for discredited National Socialism. The Russians promptly did so in the eastern zone. In the west, where democratic elements, in the Western sense, have had a chance to develop under German sponsorship, the process has been much slower.

At the time in the American and British zones there was a great deal of talk about "introducing democracy" in Germany. The framers of the Potsdam Agreement were less intrepid. All they desired was to "prepare" for the eventual reconstruction of German political life on a democratic basis. There was not talk of immediate introduction. Perhaps in the light of the basic political conviction of thousands of educated and intelligent Germans, the statesmen were wiser than the eager young men in the zones. For in the American Zone of Occupation, at least, it has been a fundamental misconception that all Germans of this class accept Western parliamentary democracy as the highest type of governmental organization. They do not. To them the authoritarian state where the educated few govern the submissive many, where the interests of the state rather than the interests of the individual are paramount, is the highest form of political structure.

The specific provisions of the political section of the Potsdam Agreement certainly provide the means of eliminating many of the bases on which the authoritarian system in Germany had been built. But these were preparations rather than accomplished facts. Today, four years later, these earnest attempts appear to have been in vain, for authoritarianism is returning to Germany, east and west.

Later in this book we will try to find out the reason for this depressing development. Here it is wise only to re-emphasize the point made above: the Germans who might conceivably have led the mass of the people toward a new conception of government in Germany never accepted democracy as the ideal solution of the problems of government. These men, the teachers, civil servants, clergymen and successful businessmen, naturally gave lip service to American "democracy" when it was introduced in the United States Zone, but it is highly doubtful whether it made a deep impression.

"For you with your big country, your limitless resources it probably is good enough," a student at Erlangen University, north of Nürnberg, said early in the occupation. "But for us here in Germany it would mean anarchy; our minds do not respond to these teachings. We want order and a settled society in which everyone knows his place and his prospects in life. The German is too unstable for your democracy."

It will be noted that this explanation is similar in some respects to the apologias made for the Russian tyranny. I have heard Americans and Englishmen favorably disposed to the Soviet regime argue that the Russians "need" the highly centralized, bureaucratic despotism which rules them because as a people they are wild and emotional. Similar arguments could be made for authoritarianism and against any people.

Let us look at the specific provisions of the political section of the Potsdam Agreement, then and now.

The abolition of military and quasi-military organizations had been accomplished on the field of battle. Few armies have ever been defeated so completely as the Wehrmacht. Even the "Werewolves," the underground organization which the Nazis organized to operate in occupied Germany, functioned only in the imagination of the Nazi chieftains caught in burning Berlin. In northwest Germany the British and Americans discovered and confiscated small stores of arms gathered for the Werewolves. One or two excited youths strung wire across lonely roads or sniped at Allied troops and paid for these actions. On the whole, however, the underground failed to materialize. The reason is easy to discern. In Norway, in France, in the Netherlands, wherever an underground which was active and forceful existed, hope also existed. For the Germans the defeat was complete. There was no great Power or combination of Powers arming to rescue them from subjugation. When the last shot was fired it was all over, for another twenty years at least.

Potsdam called for the disarmament of Germany. As far as the Wehrmacht was concerned this was accomplished. The war machine which rolled to victory after victory in 1940 and 1941 was wrecked and useless by 1945. More than that, it was outmoded. What arms were left were small in number. There were, I recollect, only about one hundred German tanks still in working order on the whole western front.

Denazification, as I have pointed out, was accomplished by victory, not by Potsdam. Four years later the Nazis are still in eclipse and probably will remain so. Too much time is wasted by excited liberals in New York and London worrying about "big Nazis" in Germany, and not enough concern is felt for the bases of authoritarianism or totalitarianism which exist in the Social Democratic Party or the Christian Socialist Party or the Bavarian Party.

The judgment of war criminals and its effect on the Germans deserve an entire volume. It was one of the few quadripartite projects which worked although, even before the first trial before the International Military Tribunal was finished, men wondered if justice in the Western sense was adequately served by a bench which included a Soviet general. German churchmen, then and now, were quick to make this point.

The Germans themselves never appeared to be greatly affected by the trial of Goering, Ribbentrop and the others at Nürnberg. I have always felt that these Nazi leaders had convicted themselves in the eyes of fanatical patriots when they lost the war, and that when the trials were held (1945-1947) the bulk of the Germans were too occupied with the daily struggle for food and shelter to worry about the men whom they had heiled so enthusiastically a few years before. If admiration was felt for any of the principal defendants in the first trial it was for Goering, that Gargantuan caricature of what the Germans consider their more amiable characteristics who, by suicide, cheated the death the Allies had prepared.

Although at the time the war-crimes trials had little effect on the Germans, their long-term effect is considerable. This is because many Germans feel that the defendants were unjustly punished for doing in time of war what the Americans, British and French might do and what the Russians certainly would do. Furthermore, Germans claim that the trials continued far too long and that the first great trial at Nürnberg bred countless others both in Germany and abroad in which revenge, not justice, was served. The easy reply to such criticism is that the Germans were never overly fond of justice when they had power, and it is a reply which has been used in the United States and Britain to justify many of the less pleasant aspects of war-crimes trials. However, in Germany, where Military Government was trying to impress on the Germans that the law should be above men, the reply was less easy to make.

(The control of education was another of the magnificent conceptions of the Potsdam Conference which has never been successful in practice.) Here we encounter the tremendous differences between the Eastern and Western understandings of how agreed statements are implemented.

What did control of education mean to the West? Mainly that the Fascist, totalitarian teachings that had dominated German education during the Hitler years should be eliminated and that German students be given a chance to learn about Western parliamentary democracy. This was the fundamental aim in the West although it was planned, of course, to eliminate National Socialist teachers and instructors.

In the eastern zone control of education meant something else. It meant not only the elimination of National Socialist teachings in the schools but the substitution of Communist teachings and the exclusion of all others.

Tear down the pictures of Hitler in the primary schools and replace them with portraits of Stalin. In the high schools substitute classes on the delights of the Communist system for explanation of Germany's great role in Europe's New Order. Burn *Mein Kampf* and print thousands of volumes of Marx and Lenin and Stalin. Here as elsewhere in the East-West tug of war for Germany the West found itself at a temporary disadvantage; it sought to train Germans to accept a system about which, since it is made up of free men with freedom of thought, it had its doubts and questions. The East had no such doubts and no such questions. It had a system ready. Off with the old, on with the new.

Similar differences of implementation rose in two other objectives of the Potsdam Agreeement.

Today the encouragement of local self-government and democratic political parties in eastern Germany means the encouragement of local government to follow the party line. "Democratic political parties" mean the Socialist Unity Party and the splinter groups of the established political parties which have been allowed to continue to function in eastern Germany because they give the aspect of political unity to the Communist-dominated Socialist Unity Party.

This is a good example of the duality of the German problem. The political development of the Soviet Zone toward Communism which is a part of the general Russian design to win political and economic domination of Germany, is one section of the problem. Western success or failure to woo the Germans away from authoritarianism to democracy, in the Western sense, is another part of the problem. Frequently the two questions have become confused and too many Americans believe it is enough if the western Germans are anti-Communist.

It has taken four years of effort, but in western Germany there are some signs of responsibility of local self-government arising. This may appear a minor repayment for the amount of work that has been lavished on the people by hard-working officials, but the officials themselves do not think so.

"When you consider how these people have been kept under the thumb of authority like the landlords' for centuries, I think we've done pretty well," a Military Government officer in Bavaria said recently. "Now and again at village meetings, some farmer gets up and says what he thinks. Sometimes he protests the action of the village council. Sometimes he prods them to do something. But at least he gets up on his feet and talks. When I see it happen, I feel we may have done some good after all."

I asked him how long this feeling would last after the occupation ended.

His face fell. "I'd like to think that what we've taught would remain," he said. "But I'm afraid it won't. You see, we may have convinced Anton and Alois, the farmer and the carpenter, that they should have a share in the way their village and their county and their country are run, but I'm damned if I think we've made much headway with the big boys."

I asked him what he meant.

"The bishops and the civil servants and the landowners. While we're here, they don't want to offend us. But don't believe for a minute that they like all this talk of democracy. No. They want Anton and Alois to live just as they always have, doing the bidding of better educated and richer men, who 'know what's good for the peasants.'"

"And 'what's good for the peasants' isn't good for democracy."

The encouragement of "democratic" political parties has been no problem in eastern Germany, but it has been one in the west. In the Soviet Zone there is only one truly "democratic" party, the Socialist Unity Party. In the west there are several major parties, all of them tainted to some degree with authoritarianism but all of them also containing some elements of true democracy.

It can be argued for instance that the Social Democrats of western Germany with their tightly controlled and thoroughly organized party structure and the almost dictatorial leadership of the aging, able Kurt Schumacher represent a blueprint for future German authoritarianism. On the other hand the Social Democrats are the foremost fighters against some of the hang-overs of National Socialism and the neo-Fascism of some of the smaller political parties.

Certainly the Potsdam Conference did not envisage the rise in Western Germany of a party like the Bavarian Party. Here is a group which seeks the virtual autonomy of Bavaria, over 60 per cent of whose members and about half of whose leaders are convinced monarchists and which, drawing support from the Church and the big landowners in Bavaria, is obviously the enemy of those democratic stirrings which Military Government has tried to inculcate in the Bavarian *bauer*.

Yet since the Bavarian Party does not seek overtly to lower the prestige of the Occupation Forces, since it is violently anti-Communist, although, it should be noted, it also was opposed to helping pay part of the cost of the Berlin Airlift, and since it eschews the outward signs of neo-Fascism, it exists.

Finally we come to the last specific provisions of the Potsdam Agreement's political section: those calling for freedom of speech, of the press, of religion and trade unions.

To Americans these freedoms are so familiar they are often unused or abused. To Germans in 1945 they were as alien as the drawling G.I.'s from Texas or the cockneys from Peckham. Today, although they have existed, with certain limitations, in western Germany for four years and more they show no great signs of becoming understood bases for a future German democracy.

2

The Potsdam Agreement also established certain economic principles for Germany. These were preceded by provisions for the demilitarization and decentralization of Germany, both obvious necessities. The principles themselves have been the subject of bitter international controversy but today they appear as the last real chance for establishing a united German economy and therefore laying the basis for a united Germany.

"During the period of occupation, Germany shall be treated as a single economic unity," the agreement states.

To this end, the Potsdam Agreement directed the establishment of common policies in regard to mining; agriculture; wages, prices and rationing; imports and exports; currency and banking and taxation; reparation and removal of industrial war potential; transport and communications.

The agreement further provided that controls be imposed upon the German economy only insofar as they were necessary to accomplish four principal aims.

The first of these was to carry out the programs of industrial disarmament and demilitarization, of reparations and of approved trade and exports.

The second was to assure the production of goods and the maintenance of services required to meet the needs of the Occupying Forces and Displaced Persons in Germany and essential to keep German living standards on the level of surrounding European countries, excluding the Soviet Union and the United Kingdom.

The third objective was to ensure the equitable distribution of essential commodities among the several zones so as to produce a balanced economy throughout Germany and reduce the need for imports.

Finally the controls were to affect German industry and all economic and financial transactions in the international field, including exports and imports, with the aim of preventing Germany from developing a war potential.

These controls were to be enforced by German administrative agencies and it was planned that the German authorities "proclaim and assume administration" of these controls.

No one reviewing the economic chaos of Germany from 1947 onward can doubt that these economic provisions of the Potsdam Agreement constitute a wise and statesmanlike attempt to retain a unified German economy capable of supporting itself in time and lessening the heavy drain on Western pocketbooks.

Had Germany's economic unity been established soon after Potsdam and had there been a constant interchange of goods between western and eastern Germany, the people of the eastern zone might have been able to resist the steady destruction of their own political parties by the Communists and, buoyed by the support of the western sections of their parties, maintained their independence.

This would have been a political reverse for the Soviet Union. Yet in the months after Potsdam it was not the Russians who blocked the establishment of the central German economic agencies but France.

France had not been a party to the Potsdam Agreement. But when the French became members of the Control Council they persistently blocked implementation of this most important section of the agreement. They made it clear that an Allied decision must be taken on the future of the Saar, the Ruhr and the Rhineland before their consent to economic unity would be forthcoming and even then consent would be given only if the decision was favorable to France.

Here we encounter for the first time the important role which France has played in shaping the postwar policy of the

Western Allies in Germany. To many France's influence seemed disproportionate to the share she had contributed to the final overthrow of the Third Reich. To others, especially in the United States, France's geographical position in Europe next to Germany seemed to endow her with certain rights and privileges and even to give the French a mystical insight into the best manner in which Germany could be handled.

General Clay is authority for the statement that in the winter of 1945-1946 and even later, when the Control Council was seeking to establish German central administrative agencies as the first step toward treating Germany as a single economic unit, the French persistently opposed this policy.

Subsequently the French have been eager to point out that French policy at the time "saved" the United States and Britain from the consequences of Potsdam. Yet it is an open question whether if the four Powers had been able to follow the Potsdam Agreement, the general situation in Germany might not now be better than it is. Certainly it could hardly be worse.

What lay behind French stubbornness on this point? Since the end of the war various French governments have pursued a single aim in Germany: to keep Germany weak.

This is understandable. The French have suffered more than any other power save Russia from the two world wars. The French feel, as a result of their experiences in the period 1924-1939, that they cannot rely on other powers to help them halt the revival of a powerful German state. Hence their policy aimed at making Germany so weak in the immediate postwar years that the development of such a state would be indefinitely postponed.

The French miscalculated twice. They underestimated

the damage done to Germany by the second World War. They overestimated western Europe's power to recover from that war without the presence in Europe of Germany as a going economic concern.

So in the period 1945-1949 France's position on Germany always took the line that a weak Germany, politically and economically, was the best Germany. And although the fear which France and Frenchmen feel over German recovery certainly is an important motivation in the making of this policy, one wonders how much of the French desire to keep German exports off the world market contributes to the thinking of the policy makers.

Later we will see how the French policy triumphed to a considerable degree with Germany partitioned and the Ruhr under international control. The question France must ask itself in the future is whether the penalties exacted of Germany now may not prove the motivation in the future for a new revival of German nationalism and the establishment of yet another predatory state. At the moment the French appear no more capable of handling a Fourth Reich than they were the Third.

But the Potsdam Agreement contained an even more important cause for international squabbling than the central German administrative agencies. This was the clause on reparations which eventually led to a decisive split between the Soviet Union on one hand and the United States, the United Kingdom and France on the other at the London session of the Council of Foreign Ministers late in 1947.

The clause itself says:

Payment of reparations should leave enough resources to enable the German people to subsist without external assistance. In working out the economic balance of Germany, the necessary means must be provided to pay for imports approved by the Control Council in Germany. The proceeds of exports from current production and stocks shall be available in the first place for payment of such exports.

To the Western Powers, the United States and the United Kingdom, this was understood as saying that reparations from current production, to which there is no direct reference in the Potsdam Agreement, could be exacted only after payment had been made for essential imports. It was, however, expressly stated that this clause did not refer to industrial capital equipment which was dealt with in a separate section of the agreement.

This section, entitled "Reparations from Germany," provided that the reparations claims of the Soviet Union, which agreed to settle Polish claims from its own share, should be met by removals from the Soviet Zone of Germany and from German external assets in Bulgaria, Finland, Hungary, Romania and eastern Austria. The reparation claims of the United States, the United Kingdom and other countries entitled to reparations should be met from the western Zones of Occupation and from German external assets in countries other than those listed above.

However, the Soviet harvest was not yet complete. In addition the U.S.S.R. was to receive from the western zones 25 per cent of the industrial capital removed. This was described as follows:

(a) 15 per cent of such usable and complete industrial capital equipment, in the first place from the metallurgical, chemical and machine manufacturing industries, as is unnecessary for the German peace economy should be removed from the western zones of Germany, in exchange for an equivalent value of food, coal, potash, zinc, timber, clay products, petroleum products, and such other commodities as may be agreed upon.

(b) 10 per cent of such industrial capital equipment as is unnecessary for the German peace economy should be removed from the western zones, to be transferred to the Soviet Government on reparations account without payment or exchange in any kind in return.

The agreement also provided that the amount of this equipment to be removed from the western zones was to be determined within six months and removals were to be completed within two years of the date of determination. The determination of the amount and character of the industrial capital equipment unnecessary for the German peace economy and therefore available for reparations was to be made "by the Control Council under policies fixed by the Allied Commission on Reparations, with the participation of France, subject to the final approval of the Zone Commander in the zone from which the equipment is to be removed."

The average man would say from the above that the Russians got plenty. And so they did. Even the Russians believed it, for Molotov did not begin his bleatings about a return to Yalta and the payment of ten billion dollars in reparations from current production until the Moscow meeting of the Council of Foreign Ministers in March of 1947.

It must be assumed that at this period the Russians were confident they would be able to overcome the technical difficulties inherent in the transfer of industrial capital equipment across Europe from Germany to the Soviet Union and its assembly in some half-developed industrial area, perhaps in Soviet Central Asia.

During 1941 and 1942 the Russians had had considerable success in the transfer of plants from European Russia eastward to the Urals out of the range of tanks and Stukas. Undoubtedly this success emboldened them to believe they could repeat the process with German plants.

From my own observations in the Soviet Union in 1946 and 1947 I would say that the transfer of entire plants was not a success. In the Donets Basin, one of the Soviet Union's most important industrial areas, I saw plenty of German equipment in 1946, but no entire factories. The Soviet engineers hadn't seen any then either. Some of the factories, they thought, might have gone farther east.

Travelers coming to Moscow during this period recounted stories of huge heaps of industrial equipment they had seen along the railroad lines leading from Warsaw to the Soviet capital. I asked a Russian engineer in Minsk if this was part of the reparations bill from Germany.

He shrugged his shoulders. "If we were getting all we should get from Germany, we would not have to depend so much on UNRRA supplies" was his answer.

The conclusion one must draw is that although the Russians did very well at Potsdam, the results of their success were disappointing. Knowing the terrible devastation of Byelorussia and the Ukraine in the years immediately after the war, I am sure that everything was done to move reparations from the Soviet and other zones of Germany into these areas. But in the Soviet Union promise and performance are two very different things.

The political and economic sections of the Potsdam Agreement did not end Russian successes at Potsdam. Mr. Molotov proposed and won American and British acceptance to to the inclusion of Königsberg and the northern third of East

Prussia in the Soviet Union. American and British support was given on the understanding that the final transfer would be decided at the peace settlement subject to expert examination of the actual frontier.

Such a settlement is far more distant today than in 1945. Meanwhile the name of Königsberg has been changed to Kaliningrad, and the city and the area around it, the Kaliningrad Oblast, or district, has earned the reputation in Russia of a "little Siberia" recovering very slowly from the terrible effect of war.

The Russian Army had been in Königsberg since the end of the war. The West, faced by a *fait accompli,* agreed to its inclusion in the Soviet Union. This got to be a habit. For Mr. Truman and Mr. Attlee agreed to another cession of territory which has had a far greater effect on the German problem and, more than any other territorial alteration in the postwar period, will affect the course of German history in the future.

The agreement stated: "The three Heads of Government reaffirm their opinion that the final delimitation of the western frontier of Poland should await the peace settlement."

Having covered themselves with this provision, which even then should have seemed a remote contingency, the American President and the British Prime Minister agreed with Mr. Stalin that, pending this determination, the former German territories east of the Oder and western Neisse rivers, including that portion of East Prussia not placed under the administration of the U.S.S.R., should be "under the administration of the Polish State and for such purposes should not be considered part of the Soviet Zone of Occupation in Germany."

The Polish people, the first to draw the sword against Hitler, were thus rewarded. No person of good will but hopes that this reward compensates them, to some degree, for the agonies and the bravery displayed by them on European battlefields, not the least of which were their own homes. But an objective study of the German problem must also take into account what this cession means not only to the Poles but to the Germans as well.

One potential danger of this settlement is that unless the Soviet Union succeeds in winning political domination over all of Germany, which is its objective, the Oder-Neisse lands will be a target for German demagogues now and in the future. German nationalism always is responsive to appeals for the return of "lost" territories. As early as 1947 grumbling about Germany's dissolution stressed the loss of these rich lands which Germans said deprived the country of any chance for a balanced economy in the future.

There is another danger. The Oder-Neisse lands, although Polish, are like everything else in the new Russian Empire, at the disposal of the Kremlin. As such they are the biggest bribe the Soviet Union could use in its dealings with an independent Germany in the future. No one familiar with the past history of Soviet diplomacy can believe that, if it seemed expedient to use the territory in this way, the political strategists would be moved by any considerations of loyalty to Poland.

Here again, it should be noted, the West was agreeing to an accomplished fact. Polish Communists had followed the Red Army into the territories and set up their administration long before the Heads of State met at Potsdam.

The conference also agreed on the necessity for the transfer to Germany of German populations remaining in Poland,

Czechoslovakia and Hungary and asked the Allied Control Council to report estimates of the time and the rate at which further transfers could be carried out and proposals for the equitable distribution of these Germans among the Occupation Zones.

Agreement on the transfers was reached by the Control Council in Berlin on November 20, 1945. The estimated numbers of Germans to be moved were as follows: from Poland, three and one half million persons of whom two million were to go to the Soviet Zone and one and one half million to the British Zone; from Czechoslovakia, two and one half million persons of whom one and three-quarter million were to go to the United States Zone and three quarters of a million to the Soviet Zone; from Hungary, one-half million persons all of whom were to go to the United States Zone, and from Austria one hundred and fifty thousand to go to the French Zone.

The figures as agreed on were excessively optimistic, even for what was an optimistic period in international politics. Today (1949) there are not less than ten million refugees in the three western Zones of Occupation, and some German authorities put the number as high as thirteen million. Yet the Control Council estimated the total at 6,650,000.

The difference is accounted for in part by the huge numbers of Germans who have fled Soviet rule in the Russian Zone of Occupation leaving their homes in preference to life in the "Zone of Silence." Moreover, hundreds of thousands of Germans, moved into the Soviet Zone from Poland and Czechoslovakia, after a brief taste of life under the new dispensation have continued their migration westward away from the Russians.

These refugees constitute one of western Germany's major

political and economic problems. Because they have lost their homes, their livelihood and, in many cases, members of their families, they form a "protest" group which any German demagogue of the future will find eager to listen to claims for a return of Germany's "lost" territories. To a country already suffering from overpopulation they have added ten millions more, depressing living standards and increasing unemployment. They are one of the grimmest legacies of the Potsdam Agreement.

Politically the Russians got what they wanted at Potsdam. Economically they agreed to the unity of Germany, which, if it had been carried out in the months immediately after Potsdam, would have weakened their political grip on the Germans of the eastern zone by bringing its people into constant contact with the people and products of the western zones, immeasurably freer and better off even in 1945. The Russians were saved from such a result by the intransigence of the French in the Control Council. Later when Russian policy changed, or rather appeared on the surface to change, hope of economic unity had been lost, and although the question was raised at the Moscow and London meetings of the Council of Foreign Ministers, by that time "unity" was purchasable only at the Russian price. This the West was not prepared to pay.

The economic unity of Germany still remains the ideal, not only for Germany but for a Europe which needs a healthy German economy. My own feeling is that had the United States, the United Kingdom and Russia been allowed to carry out that policy in 1945, many of our current problems in Germany could have been avoided and the Soviet grip on eastern Germany loosened.

CHAPTER FOUR

THE RUSSIANS KNEW WHAT THEY wanted. Of all the advantages enjoyed by the Soviet Union in the struggle for Germany, this is the simplest and most explanatory. The Russians want Germany, not as conquered territory, although they would certainly not disdain force if it could be used without interference by the United States, but as a political and economic vassal of the new Russian Empire. They want all Germany, not merely the 46,600 square miles of the Soviet Zone of Occupation or its seventeen and a half million people. This is a fundamental of the foreign policy of the Soviet Union.

In examining Russian policy in Germany since 1945 we must beware of the error made by so many anti-Communists as well as fellow travelers. This is the attribution to the Kremlin and its field workers of devilish cunning, superhuman ingenuity, monolithic unity and unwavering resolution. This, of course, is balderdash. The Russians are men and women. They make errors of judgment. They miscalculate. Greed, envy, ambition and hypocrisy are as endemic to Moscow as to Calcutta or Sioux City. They pull their pants on one leg at a time.

The Russian pose that they are extraordinary fellows who have escaped the foibles and weaknesses of the remainder of the human race has impressed both their friends and enemies. The friends looking for an anchor in a rootless world are

71

impressed, poor dupes, by this government that never makes any mistakes in contrast to our own bumbling progress. The enemies are impressed and frightened by the same thing. One of the sources of the war scare in the United States in 1947-1949, which surely is one of the least admirable reflections of national character in our times, was the belief, widely held, that we must take the Russians at their own valuation as a nation of industrial miracle men. This, of course, was whooped along by the generals and admirals who, seeking a slice of the budget for their services, pictured the Russian progress in industry on a scale to terrify Jules Verne.

The Russians in the Kremlin, being professional revolutionaries outside the Soviet Union, naturally were better prepared in 1945 than the United States or Great Britain for dealing with Germany. The sacred writings of Marx, Lenin and Stalin were filled with suggestions of what to do about Germany. That country, Lenin had written, is the principal link in the chain of revolutions, and the founder of the Communist state in the Soviet Union had also written, "He who has Germany has Europe," a succinct statement which, like the words of many other Communist oracles, turns out to be something which numerous other land grabbers from Charlemagne on down have also realized.

Since the time of Peter the Great a number of other Russians, including the more ambitious Czars and Dostoevski, have expounded the glories of a Russian-German union. When in the spring of 1945 the Russian Army felt German resistance crumbling, the Russians knew what they had to do. Then they made their first major miscalculation on Germany.

This was that the Soviet Army would move faster and farther into Germany than the American, British, Canadian and French armies under the command of General Eisenhower. The reverse happened. The troops under the command of SHAEF not only captured the Ruhr (which the Russians should have expected, although my conversations with a few Soviet Army officers just after the war indicated they did not) but also overran Thuringia, Saxony and parts of Mecklenburg.

The Russians then had to bargain with the West for the withdrawal of the Western armies from a large part of the Russian Zone of Occupation as it had been determined by the Powers and announced in June of 1945. The Russians entered these areas not as conquerors but as late-comers. It is significant, I think, that the major areas of sabotage within the Soviet Zone of Occupation have been those occupied in the early days of the occupation by American and British troops.

Before we progress farther in our examination of Russian policy in Germany, account must be taken of one event which affected the Soviet policy in Germany, the entire German problem and, indeed, the entire civilized world. This was the decision taken sometime in 1945 by the Political Bureau of the Communist Party, the supreme policy-making group in the Soviet Union, to press and emphasize the revolutionary and destructive elements in Marxism and Leninism as they apply to the capitalist and enemy world.

This meant the end of collaboration between the Soviet Union and the Western Allies and the start of that worldwide political friction which we call the cold war. It meant the end of the United Nations as an effective instrument.

I do not believe there can be much doubt that this decision was taken by the Political Bureau. Two Russians, once of world stature, who had a better knowledge of the Western world than anyone in the Political Bureau, save perhaps Anastas Mikoyan, apparently were consulted during the period in which the pros and cons of the decision were being argued in the Political Bureau. Their views were listened to but they were not followed.

In deciding in favor of a renewal of the world struggle between Communism and Capitalism the Political Bureau reverted to what the convinced Communist accepts as orthodox strategy. The wartime co-operation and collaboration with the West was unorthodox, forced upon the Soviet State by the terrible exigencies of the German invasion. There might be, indeed there was, a great fund of good feeling toward the United States among the Russian people in 1944 and 1945, but to the true Communist, America was as much the enemy the day the invading forces wet the Normandy sands with their blood as it is today. A continuation of the wartime co-operation and collaboration would have been possible only if the West had been willing to make continued concessions in the international field to the Russians. Even then we would still have been enemies.

It is probable that this decision, one of the most fateful of current history, was based upon another great miscalculation. This was that the world situation was so favorable to the Russians and the Communist cause that a renewal of the Communist-Capitalist struggle would produce the victory of the Communist parties throughout western Europe.

To many an observer on the continent during the spring and summer of 1945 the tide appeared to be flowing that way. Chaos and despair reigned. Millions of men were returning to broken homes sick of the political systems which had produced two world wars and a world depression in their lifetime. The frame of Western civilization had been broken, by bombs, by guns, by deportation, by cruelty, lust and greed. Save for the British, who had chosen to try a new method of ordering man's political and economic affairs, western Europe seemed without plan or hope.

The reports flowing back to the Kremlin from the faithful in France, in Italy, in Holland, in Germany and even in Norway must have made convincing reading. Profiteering and black marketing on a huge scale. Ruined factories and unemployment. Devastated farmlands and little food. Political quarrels and class hatred. To the directors of the one well-organized, internationally controlled political party it must have looked easy. "A piece of cake" was the R.A.F.'s term for an easy mission. All western Europe must have appeared a piece of cake to the Political Bureau.

Moreover the armed power of the United States, the largest and most powerful of the Western forces, was disintegrating rapidly. Hundreds of thousands of its most effective troops had been shipped home to the United States. The bombers and fighters of the United States Army Air Force, which a few months before had darkened the skies, sat motionless on their airfields. Politically, the United States seemed to believe that the United Nations provided a fairly reliable medium for the settlement of international problems and the atomic bomb a miraculous and invincible deterrent to war. To the Kremlin the United States must have appeared totally unprepared psychologically or physically, for the new type of political warfare which the Communist parties of the world were preparing to wage. The Russians did not then expect that the outcome of their policy might be armed conflict. Indeed it was not until the spring of 1947 that any real anxiety was aroused among the Russians. This came when the West at last ponderously began the preliminaries of rearmament.

Before we leave the Political Bureau decision, to inspect its implementation in Germany, one other aspect should be considered. This was that at the moment the decision was taken, the Soviet Union itself was in a terrible condition. The areas through which the Germans had retreated and which they had occupied had been destroyed as effectively as high explosives and skilled engineers could do the job. The great dam across the Dnieper River had been smashed and torn with 550 tons of high explosive. The coal mines of the Donets Basin were flooded. Great steel factories at Stalino were in ruins. The tractor plants in Kharkov and Rostov were smashed.

No one will know for some time, if ever, why under these conditions the Russians chose political war rather than further collaboration with the West. It may be that the Political Bureau expected an easy victory for Communism in western Europe and through it a supply of the machines and technicians which the Soviet Union needed terribly to repair the damage. It may be that Stalin and his henchmen believed that the sluggish, lethargic Russians of the great plains and the broken industrial areas could never be driven to achieve the grandiose plans for reconstruction in the first postwar Five Year Plan unless the danger of capitalist attack was raised to drive them on. It may be that the victory of 1945 had gone to the heads of the Political Bureau, that at that moment of Russia's history its members found nothing impossible to Communism and the Soviet power.

Since the West was the enemy, the struggle in Germany for Germany took on a fiercer note than elsewhere, for there the Americans, the British and the French were opposing actively the Russian policy. The first task in Germany was to organize the Communist Party, strengthen it with Germans who had spent the war years in Moscow and, through it, achieve the political domination of the country.

After eleven years underground the Communist Party in Germany hardly existed. A few members had withdrawn from politics entirely but had kept their hopes alive. A great many more had joined the National Socialists in 1934 and 1935. The leaders of pre-Hitler days had either fled to the Soviet Union or to western Europe or had been placed in concentration camps.

The first task then was to restore the party's cadres throughout Germany. This was done in 1945 and 1946 chiefly by sending to Germany those Communists who had studied in Moscow, the holy city of their faith, before and during the war and who had been used by the Russians to convert new followers from among the millions of German prisoners of war. The first effect of their return was not good. In many cases they were bitterly resented by the Communists who had remained in Germany.

"What do they know about the people here and what they are thinking?" an indignant Communist leader asked me in Frankfort in 1945. "They have no common background and too much ideology. People don't want that now. They want jobs and houses."

These criticisms of the newly returned brethren undoubtedly were sharpened by the fact that in most cases they received the best jobs in the party heirarchy.

Accompanying the drive for new recruits to the party was a large-scale propaganda campaign based on the Soviet Union's benignant interest in the "real needs" of the German people and the ability of the German Communists to supply these needs if given power. This campaign which began in 1946 sought not recruits for the party but votes. Meanwhile party officials let it be known that the Communists were ready to work with other like-minded "democratic" parties.

This phase of Soviet policy in Germany was neither successful nor long-lived. The Communist Party, although initially it gained a large number of recruits in the Soviet Zone of Occupation, never became a major party on a national scale, although in the western zones its nuisance value was considerable to the Russians.

The reasons for this failure, in a country which many considered to be ripe for Communism in 1945, lie primarily in fields other than the political. The Communist Party was identified with Russia. In Germany in 1945 and 1946 the Russians were identified with their army and that army with rape, looting, murder and arson on a scale equaled, in all probability, only by the German Army in the Soviet Union.

Moreover there were many Germans, not affected by the misdeeds of the Red Army, who were leaning toward Communism but who were repelled by their first look at the human products of the socialist state. They, like millions before them, had swallowed the Russian propaganda. They expected highly mechanized armies, clean, intelligent soldiery with a penchant for ideological discussion. What they got was a mass of ill-controlled troops, unkempt and even ragged, ill-educated and boorish. The welcoming German fellow travelers never quite recovered from the shock even when Soviet officers of another stripe began to open cultural exhibits, sponsor lectures and distribute propaganda dealing with the glories of the workers' paradise.

The Russians did make some impression on German "intellectuals" of the eastern zone. Artists and writers, who showed a proper sympathy for the Soviet objectives in Germany, were generously treated. Actors and musicians of the same persuasion got good wages and rations. On the whole, however, such recruits as the Communist Party gained from these classes did not give it the numerical strength which it sought either in its cadres or in the number of votes.

Finally the Russians encountered in their own Zone of Occupation and in the western zones the Social Democratic Party which, having quickly reorganized immediately after the end of the war, had emerged as a "workers' party," appealing strongly not only to the mass of German labor but to members of the former middle class who had moved down into the laboring class as a result of the war. It, too, professed to be a Marxist party, but not a Leninist or Stalinist one. In the first tests of voting strength within the Soviet Zone it showed remarkable strength not only in minor political elections but in union voting in factories on which the Communists place great importance as indicating the political climate among the proletariat.

By the end of 1945 the Russians must have realized that their efforts to build up a large party organization for the Communists in the eastern zone were unlikely to meet with a resounding success. This presented them with an unexpected dilemma, the solution of which was necessary to the continuation of Soviet policy both in eastern and western Germany. For there is a duality of implementation of the foreign policy of the U.S.S.R. It is carried out by both the Communist parties abroad and by the Ministry of Foreign Affairs in Moscow through its embassies, consulates and missions and at international conference tables. For full effectiveness both agencies must work together and the local party organizations must be strong enough to provide loud "popular" acclaim to the actions of the Ministry.

In Germany with two contrasting ideologies facing each other across the Elbe, the Russians could not allow the party of the Communist fatherland to linger in the doldrums. There had to be a large, vigorous party either Communist in name or Communist in tone to compete with the free parties of western Germany which in 1945, although plagued by the political apathy of the masses, already were showing signs of renewed life.

Germans in the eastern zone commonly ascribe to the Socialists the idea of a merger of the Sozialdemokratische Partei Deutschlands or Social Democratic Party and the Communist Party. If this is so the Russians must have viewed the idea as a lifesaver for their own puny party. Otto Grotewohl, the Socialist leader who first broached the idea to the Communists, was enthusiastically received and the merger went forward. Out of it came the Sozialistische Einheitspartei Deutschlands, the Socialist Unity Party of Germany. Since May 1, 1946, when it was formally proclaimed, it has been the strongest German political party in the Soviet Zone by virtue of its close association with the Soviet Military Administration and has been the servant and toady of the S.M.A. in the political struggles since then.

The opportunity was a shining one for the Soviets. They saw a chance to weaken the Socialists, which has been done, and to boost the strength of their own party. When on April 21, 1946, the final details of the merger were worked out, the new party was to have approximately 1,121,000 members. Of these 511,000 were Communists of the Soviet Zone and 60,000 Communists of the Soviet Sector of Berlin. The remainder of the party was composed of 530,000 Socialists of the zone and 20,000 Socialists of the sector. The best commentary on the success of the Russian drive to build a strong Communist Party in eastern Germany and eastern Berlin is the fact that after a year of effort in which bribes, strong-arm methods and cultural inducements were used, the Communists numbered only 21,000 more than the Socialists.

There was no evidence that the party merger was carried out on the impulse of the bulk of the membership of the Socialist Party. There was a party referendum in Berlin on March 31, 1946, when the membership in the western sectors of the city voted seven to one against the merger. Good judges of the political temper of the Soviet Zone and Sector at that time believe that a free election in the party in both areas would have resulted in a vote of at least four to one against the merger.

In addition to masking the lack of appeal of their own brand of political party, the Russians had scored another important victory in the merger, for it was a long step forward along the path to a single state party. Such a party is indispensable to the workings of Communism in the satellite states and of course in the Soviet Union itself.

The merger has repaid the Soviet optimism in many respects. The SED has been the faithful mouthpiece of Russian policy in Germany and the sounding board for Moscow's propaganda. It represents to the German of Hesse or Lower Saxony in the west, bemused and confused by the tangles of party politics, a species of that type of internal order so dear to his heart. His compatriots in Dresden or Leipzig or the Soviet Sector of Berlin could tell him a different story, but they are unlikely to do so.

Perhaps the most important function of the SED has been to support in Germany, through a variety of methods, the objectives of Soviet policy there as laid down by Moscow. To the American in Germany this support appears transparent and submissive. However, it has a certain influence on left-wing opinion in the western Zones of Occupation and it is used extensively outside Germany by Russian propagandists to demonstrate how closely the Germans of the Soviet Zone follow the line of peace and plenty in opposition to the supposed war-mongering of the United States.

One of the principal Soviet objectives in Germany has been the unity of the country, although this unity is to be achieved at the Russian price, *i.e.,* political domination. When in 1948 the United States, Great Britain, France and the Benelux Powers decided in London to push the establishment of a state in western Germany, the SED was turned loose to campaign for German unity. One of the methods employed was a plebiscite held in the Soviet Zone and the Soviet Sector of Berlin. Since in the police state, and these areas come under that heading, it is not difficult to induce people to sign their names to any government-sponsored document, millions signed. Some of course were impelled by the natural German urge to see their country reunited. Others signed to be safe. At any rate the Soviet Military Administration was presented with a huge testimonial which its spokesmen said "proved" the will of the Germans for unity against the "split-ting" tactics of the West. Thus the SED earns the high salaries and the extra rations its members receive.

The SED has been fertile in producing other pressure groups within the zone. Leagues for German Mothers, German Farmers and, perhaps, even German Chimney Sweeps have been and will be evolved to beat the drum for the Russian policy. Mr. Molotov in his debates with the West over the green baize table of the Council of Foreign Ministers often cited these groups as representative "democratic" organizations to which his colleagues should listen. Wisely they declined.

The pre-eminent position of the SED, like that of any political party in a police state, is internally unassailable since it does not have to submit to free elections. However, it has other weaknesses from the Russian standpoint which from time to time evoke purges and loud declarations of good resolutions for the future. These have not yet eliminated the weaknesses.

Although the Socialist content in the original merger was a little smaller than the Communist, former Socialists continued in the first years of the party's existence to supply a great deal of its efficiency. The Communist members were in many cases sorry fellows who had joined the Communist Party for better food or higher wages or the chance to engage in the black market under the aegis of the Soviet Military Administration. Very few of them resembled the young, intense zealots, selfless and sacrificing, whom the party likes to picture as its recruits and who, to give the devil his due, form a considerable percentage of its neophytes in the Soviet Union and abroad.

Thus although party policy flowed from Moscow via Wil-

helm Pieck, the aging boss of German Communism, the organization of the party was run in a large measure by former
members of the Social Democratic Party. They were men
and women of better and more independent mind than the
Communists in the SED and thus they interpreted the ukases
from Moscow as they saw fit and not as laid down in the
sacred writings. This was a cardinal sin and as early as the
winter of 1946-1947 produced small-scale purges in the party.

As the Soviet propaganda campaign against the West became more virulent, the Russians and the German Communists encountered another difficulty with the former Socialists.
The latter were intellectually incapable of swallowing the
monstrous lies with which the Russians embellished their anti-
American and anti-British propaganda. They remained convinced that Socialism was Germany's salvation, but they were
not willing to admit that the Americans and British were
preparing for a new war in the western Zones of Occupation.
This, too, produced anguished cries of "spies and saboteurs."
Actually there were plenty of spies and saboteurs at work but
not along these lines.

Almost since its establishment the SED has been the cover
for active agents and saboteurs in eastern Germany. Some
are former Social Democrats who have soured on the merger.
Others are German Communists who entered the party soon
after the war and are now, because their own rewards were
not great enough, for sale. These and a few thousand other
Germans whose only object is to get rid of the Russians and
the SED form what is often referred to as the "underground"
in the Soviet Zone.

This is an underground in the sense that subversive activities are carried out against the Occupation Power, the SED

and the German *Land* governments. But these activities are those to which any underground is forced in a strictly policed state: the writing of pamphlets, the transmission of scraps of information westward, "go-slow" tactics in important industrial plants, the theft of important pieces of machinery, the maintenance of an underground railroad passing refugees westward across the heavily guarded zonal frontier.

Since the cold war reached its maximum intensity in Germany in the summer of 1948 there have been a few, a very few, examples of acts of violence by the underground. In the summer of 1948 a number of SED functionaries were murdered, a party headquarters burned and two party meetings broken up when someone thoughtfully tossed a grenade into their midst. Each act was punished rigorously with arrests and deportation to forced labor in the uranium mines of southeastern Saxony.

Another failing of the party has been its inability to maintain the level of industrial production desired by the Soviet Military Administration. This was true even before the United States, France and Great Britain clamped the counter-blockade on the eastern zone depriving it of the bulk of its industrial raw materials from July 1948 to May 1949. The reason was the same as that which holds the industry of all the Communist-dominated states in thrall: in a system which prizes ideological purity above technical ability production is bound to lag behind that of a free society.

The purges of Socialists from the party organization were accompanied by an equally severe purge in the industrial organization of the Russian Zone.

This removed for ideological reasons many of the ablest plant managers and industrial engineers of the eastern zone.

At the same time a considerable number of other technicians, concerned lest they follow unlucky colleagues eastward to the industrial areas of the Soviet Union, left the eastern zone. Thus when the counterblockade was imposed, the zone's industrial force was qualitatively weak, so much so that it could not successfully handle the new problems which resulted from the shutting off of the normal sources of raw materials and the necessity for substitution and improvisation.

The SED is also plagued, like other Communist or Communist-front parties of eastern Europe, with Titoism. Time after time the Moscow-schooled stalwarts of the party have arisen at meetings to curse the besetting sin of "narrow nationalism" and urged the members to accept the Soviet Union as a great friend and ally.

"The German Communists," a friend in the eastern sector of Berlin once told me, "contain a great many people who are strongly opposed to Stalinism. They joined the party years ago, well before the war. Much of what now happens in Moscow disgusts and annoys them because they feel the direction of the party is away from Marxism and Leninism. But they remain in the party because they believe that someday, perhaps when Stalin dies, that direction will change and Communism again become the hope of the world."

Other German Communists, newly converted, are too bound up with the old German nationalism of Hitler days to be satisfactory politically in the eyes of the party bosses. Here Pieck, Walter Ulbricht and the others are encountering conditions which are of primary importance to the political conflict for Germany.

Unlike the Poles or the Bulgars the Germans cannot be sold Communism on racial grounds. They are not Slavs. Indeed they regard the Slavs as inferior beings. Again they were not liberated by Russian Communism; they were conquered by it and the conquest left scars which will take years to heal. Finally almost all Germans, including the new members of the German Communist Party, have a strong feeling of national pride. They cannot consider Germany, which they hold to be the world's leader in technique, in science, in art, a vassal of the Soviet Union. All these factors increase the resistance to the missionary work carried out by the Russians in the Socialist Unity Party, just as they helped prevent the rise of a genuine, popularly based Communist Party in the eastern zone in 1945.

Thus, although the SED presents a picture of strength and unity to the world, it is beset by difficulties and weaknesses. In the summer of 1948 a shrewd German lawyer, escaping from Dresden via Berlin, estimated that in a free election in the Soviet Zone the SED would get no more than 30 per cent of the votes.

"But there will be no free elections," he said, "no more free anything. So I am going."

During 1947 and 1948 the Russians, obviously conscious of the weakened position of the SED, began to allow the recruitment of a large number of former National Socialists in the party. Today former Nazis hold many of its most important posts. Paul Markgraf is chief of police in Communist Berlin. Luitpold Steidle is on the German Economics Commission. Bernhard Bechler is Minister of the Interior in Brandenburg.

Behind these leaders stand tens of thousands of other unrepentant Nazis who see in the SED and in Russian militarism their chance to free themselves and Germany from their current woes. Denazification in the eastern zone was ended on February 27, 1948, in Marshal Sokolovsky's Order No. 35, and since then an increasing number of former Nazis have been introduced into the government organizations, especially the police, industrial plants and the party apparatus. The Russians are conscious of the appeal which such slogans as "A strong and united Germany" make to such men. They also know that the former Nazis, precisely because they have been Nazis, will slavishly follow every Russian directive lest they be arrested on the easy charge of "Fascism" and put away.

The Russians also have made use of the National Democratic Party as a means of rallying former Nazis to their cause. And they have used the reinforced police of the eastern zone as an inducement to lure former Wehrmacht officers back into service.

From the standpoint of such men as bald, affable General Serge Tulpanov, the representative in Germany of the potent Agitation and Propaganda Committee of the Central Committee of the Communist Party of the Soviet Union, the SED must be accounted a failure. Primarily this is because the party, with all the backing the Russians could give it, has failed to excite enthusiasm for either Communism or the Russian ally in eastern Germany. It is significant that the strongest spontaneous moves toward the resumption of friendly ties with the Soviet Union have come not from the paid politicians of the eastern zone, who are content to mouth meaningless propaganda, but from men like Professor Dr. Ulrich Noack, head of the Nauheimer Kreis, a small organization of intellectuals, which sees Germany's salvation in a return to the spirit of Rapallo where, after the first World

War, the new Soviet State and Germany patched up their differences.

Even when Soviet support of the SED was at its maximum in the summer and autumn of 1948, the Russians had little confidence in its leaders' ability to conduct successful political campaigns. In November of that year a German Communist intellectual confided to me at a cocktail party that the SED did not have "leaders of a high caliber" and that the most effective Communist leaders in Germany were men like Max Reimann and Willi Agatz in the western Zones of Occupation.

By early 1949 the leaders of the SED were calling for the establishment of "a party of a new type" in Germany. The Russians are slow to give up the forms of established political media but quick to change the methods and personnel of such media if they fail to meet requirements. By then it seemed they were ready to remake the SED into a more successful vehicle of Russian policy as carried out by a foreign Communist Party. This development coincided with a marked shift in the overt policy of the Soviet Union as carried out by the Ministry of Foreign Affairs.

CHAPTER
FIVE

IN CONTRAST WITH THE MANEUVERS
of the SED, the approach made by the Ministry of Foreign
Affairs of the Soviet Union toward the problem of Germany
was carried out in the open. Yet granted the deviousness
with which the international Communist parties disguise
their eventual objectives, there is a marked similarity. In the
initial phase of postwar Russian policy toward Germany,
both the Ministry and the Communist Party in Germany
failed. The approaches differed but the result was the same.

The chief protagonist of Soviet foreign policy as expressed
by the Russian Government from 1945 to 1948 was Vyacheslav Molotov. How much of the stubbornness, the boorish-
ness and the bad faith which characterized Soviet foreign
policy in its contact with the West was the product of his
own personality no one will ever know. One thing is clear:
Molotov did not act on his own. As the member of the Political Bureau with the greatest seniority, save for Stalin, Molotov participated in the policy-making meetings of that body.
He did not make policy, he participated in the making of
policy. He was not a "messenger boy" of the Political Bureau. He expressed views in which he believed and which he
had helped formulate.

And, it should be remembered, he and his fellows on the
Political Bureau were not jailers for Joseph Stalin. Stalin was
the dominant figure of the meetings of that body. The idea

that Stalin is the "prisoner" of the Political Bureau is ludicrous. However, it has been widely proclaimed that this is
so because in the past Stalin has been the only Russian who
has made concessions of any kind to the West. This is interpreted as a sign that "Uncle Joe" is really a nice old fellow
who likes the West and would go farther if the Political Bureau allowed it. Hogwash. Stalin is the boss. And as boss
he is the only man in the Soviet Union who can make concessions.

It is evident that the official, diplomatic approach of the
Soviet Union toward the West in the period 1945-1948 was
conditioned by the personality of Molotov. Here is a man to
study as the perfect example of the machine representative
of the machine state.

Long ago Lenin called Molotov the best file clerk in the
Soviet Union. This description has frequently moved Western diplomats to an underestimate of the man. But when
Lenin said it, the description was high praise. Even today
the lack of system in the Soviet Government is appalling. I
recall asking an official of the Ministry of Posts and Tele-
graphs if he could guarantee to send 125,000 words out of
Moscow each twenty-four-hour period if the Council of Foreign Ministers met there. He replied with the greatest good
will he was sure he could but he would have to find the paper
on the Ministry's capacity. It took him four days to find the
paper.

Molotov is not a leader of men, but he is immensely effective as a "second man" in the Soviet organization; a Castle-
reagh rather than a Pitt, a Hopkins, not a Roosevelt. He is
stiff, wary and, I think, a little shy. One night at a reception
in Moscow I saw him standing talking with Vishinsky, then

his deputy, now his successor. They were completely alone at one end of a long room. Molotov was as suspicious as though he had been talking to an imperialist warmonger. Vishinsky was smiling, eager and at ease.

A small man with a bullet head, cold blue eyes and stiff, awkward movements. Like many of the top Communist bosses he is "dedicated." But whereas some like Stalin and Kalinin and Mikoyan retain some semblance of warmth and gregariousness, Molotov lost his somewhere along the way. When Stalin rises to propose a toast at a banquet, even a toast to President Truman, he gives the appearance of sincerity. Molotov proposes a toast as though he were reading a report on fertilizer production in Minsk.

In tracing the development of Soviet foreign policy in the postwar years Molotov cannot be excused of one disastrous error. It took him from the brief New York conference of the Council of Foreign Ministers in 1946 until the longer meeting of the same body in London in the early winter of 1947 to realize that the game was up, that there were no more easy diplomatic victories like Potsdam to be picked up by the Soviet Union.

Two meetings of the Council of Foreign Ministers in Moscow and London contributed to the great break on Germany. This division of opinion was of the maximum importance to the future of Germany. It is doubtful if its effects will be erased in our lifetime. It is probable that it set back the Russian cause in Germany for many years.

Soviet foreign policy as it developed in the last half of 1946 and the first two months of 1947 sought three objectives in Germany, all of which were components of the principal objective: the domination of Germany by Soviet foreign policy through Germany's submission to a Communist or Communist-dominated party in Germany. These objectives were, first, the establishment in Germany of a central government which could be taken over by the Communist Party or by a "front" movement in which the Communists were the driving force; second, the payment by Germany to the Soviet Union of reparations out of current production amounting to ten billion dollars; and, third, acquisition by the Soviet Union of a dominant voice in the administration of the industrial area of the Ruhr.

When one reads the description of the proceedings of the two meetings of the Council of Foreign Ministers in Moscow and London, one is struck by the dominance of these themes in Soviet policy as expressed by Molotov and occasionally by Vishinsky. Other subjects arose: the question of Germany's frontiers, the integration of the Saar Basin into the French economy, the United States proposal for a disarmament treaty concerning Germany. But these three points were those on which the Foreign Ministers fell out. No matter what concessions the Russians may make in the future, they will remain the basis of Russian policy. For only by securing them can the Russians reach the ultimate goal of dominating the German State.

Let us review the bidding, if possible with the orginal inflections, by which the Soviet Union sought these aims at the fateful conferences in Moscow and London.

It was not until the sixth session of the Council on March 15 in Moscow that the Russians made their bid for a central German state.

Thereafter, the subject was always in the air.

It was Vishinsky, his face red and his white hair tumbled,

who began the attack. The springboard was the economic union of the American and British Zones of Occupation. This, Vishinsky said, prejudiced the future political situation in Germany in favor of federalization rather than centralization. Two days later Molotov asked annulment of economic fusion of the two zones as an infringement of the Potsdam Agreement.

On March 22 Molotov put forward the first official Soviet suggestion for a government of Germany when he called for the immediate creation of a provisional German government. This state, he declared, should be centralized and strong, based on the constitution of the Weimar Republic. That document has always had a peculiar attraction for the Russians, principally because it provides for voting by proportional representation on every elective level. Proportional representation means the "list system" whereby so many Communist candidates have won power in free elections.

The provisional government, Molotov declared, must have a two-chamber legislature. The President of the Republic would be elected by this legislature. To beguile his listeners, Secretary of State Marshall, Foreign Secretary Bevin and Foreign Minister Bidault, he announced Russia's desire that the proposed state guarantee freedom of speech, worship, press and assembly. Nothing was said about freedom of the individual or that individual's immunity from arbitrary arrest.

Finally Molotov asked that the Central Administrative Agencies, provided for in the Potsdam Agreement, be set up without delay and that the Allied Control Council in Berlin, composed of the four military governors, be empowered to draw up a provisional "democratic" constitution based on the constitution of the Weimar Republic.

Having thus set out his objectives, which, although open to opposition by the other Powers, had an important effect on public opinion in Germany, Molotov began to prepare the way for Communist domination of the sort of government he proposed.

On April 2 he advocated the inclusion of the various Communist-front organizations in Germany in the provisional German government. At the same time he urged that the provisional government be organized and govern Germany under the Allied Control Council while the constitution of the state was being drafted. This government, he insisted, must include "democratic" and "anti-Nazi" organizations such as the Free German Women's League, the Farmers' Aid Society and the League of Culture.

Then the Soviet delegation presented a formal plan for the form of the German government. This plan demonstrates so clearly not only what the Russians wanted, and still want, in Germany it is worth outlining.

First, said Molotov, there must be a political structure entirely "democratic" based on "democratic" elections and "analogous to that envisaged by the Weimar constitution."

The Soviet Foreign Minister proposed, however, that the duties of the President of the German Republic be restricted to those of the head of a constitutional state with no independent executive powers.

As a first step toward organizing this state the Central Administrative Agencies for finance, industry, transportation, communications and foreign trade must be established under the Allied Control Council.

It is noteworthy that at this point the difference between Soviet and Western ideas on the organization of a unified German state were not as far apart as they later became. For, the same day, the Council of Foreign Ministers agreed to a British proposal on the four stages by which such a government would be established. These were:

(1) The setting up of the Central Administrative Agencies.

(2) The nomination "at an early date" of a representative German body which would advise the Allied Control Council on the general aspects of the work of the Central Administrative Agencies and on the number and size of the various *Länder* or states within the German State. This body would also work out, within the framework of principles agreed on by the Allied Control Council, the details of a provisional constitution.

(3) The provisional constitution and other recommendations of this advisory body were to be submitted to the Allied Control Council for approval and, in accordance with the provisional constitution as approved by the Allied Control Council, elections were to be held and a provisional government formed to operate the provisional constitution.

(4) When a thorough trial had been conducted of the provisional constitution, it was to be amended after taking into account the recommendations of the provisional government ratified by the German people and approved by the Allied Control Council. At this stage a new government was to be duly elected.

Now it can be argued, as it was argued at Moscow, that the Russian willingness to accept this British plan was attributable to the fact that no agreement had yet been reached by the Foreign Ministers on the all-important question of Germany's economic unity. But it was my impression then, and it is now, that had economic unity been agreed on at that meeting, the Russians would still have gone along with this plan. Then and now they wanted their political opportunity in all of Germany. Since then events have revealed the weakness of the Russian case and the bankruptcy of the Communist Party anywhere in Germany including the Soviet Zone. But Americans must never forget that the Soviet Union plays a farsighted game. It is looking not toward next month or next year but a decade into the future. The mistakes of the Political Bureau, and I believe they are many, appear as the results of a recurrent tendency to move too swiftly toward distant objectives, developing antagonisms that might never have emerged if the Ministry of Foreign Affairs or the Communist Party concerned had been willing to play a long, slow game.

Throughout the remainder of the Moscow conference, Molotov continued to seek the establishment of the German provisional government. Interspersing his demands with vigorous attacks on Bizonia, the economic fusion of the British and American Zones of Occupation, he urged the establishment of the Central Administrative Agencies as a first step toward a German government. On April 5 he asked that three months after their establishment a "German advisory council" be formed.

Finally, with the agreement of the other Foreign Ministers, a four-point plan for the organization of the Central Administrative Agencies for Germany was sent to the Allied Control Council in Berlin for "examination."

Throughout the period in which he strove for the speedy establishment of an all-German government, Molotov never relaxed his efforts to gain what he described as "adequate" representation for those Communist-front organizations which he declared were not represented by trade unions in Germany.

Day after day in the bare assembly hall of the House of the Aviation Industry on the outskirts of Moscow, Molotov returned to his appeals for the organization of a German state in which the "main responsibility" of the governing power was to rest with the federal government. It was clear from his interpretation of the word "federal" that by this word he meant a unified, highly centralized government. To win approval of his plan he made one important Soviet concession. He withdrew "state security," the power of the state to maintain a secret police, from the list of powers of the central government which he had placed before the Council.

Once, on April 7, he proposed that the German people decide by plebiscite whether they wanted a centralized government in their future state. The proposal was rejected flatly by the United States, Britain and France.

The basis for the Western objection to this and other suggestions by Molotov on the establishment of a central German government lay in the fear that such a government in time would be dominated by the Communist Party. To this must be added the French dislike of the idea of any central government in Germany, or indeed of any regional government in Germany which might provide the starting point for German recovery.

The discussions by the four ministers on the form of the future German government from the outset lacked reality. For, as early as March 17, Molotov had prepared the ground for new demands that the Soviet Union receive ten billion dollars in reparations from Germany as "guaranteed at Yalta." This was the Russian condition for the economic unity of Germany. Without such unity the formation of a government was obviously impossible.

The Yalta "agreement" to which Molotov referred was the important passage quoted in an earlier chapter in the secret protocol of that international meeting in which it was agreed that the Moscow Reparations Commission "should take in its initial studies as a basis for discussion the suggestion that the total sum of the reparation . . . should be twenty billion dollars and that 50 per cent of it should go to the Union of Soviet Socialist Republics."

Throughout the Moscow conference the Russians argued long and hotly that this meant that the Soviet Union was to get its ten billion. Secretary of State Marshall rejected the Russian demand on the grounds that the reparations provisions in the Yalta Agreement had been superseded by those in the Potsdam Agreement in which no over-all reparations figure was set. Furthermore he pointed out that at Yalta, President Roosevelt had agreed to use the figure only as a basis for discussion and had not regarded it as a final commitment to the Soviet Union.

This did not satisfy Molotov. By the end of the month he had made reparations of ten billion dollars largely from current production the price of that German economic unity which Secretary Marshall sought. "No solution can be reached on the larger problems of Germany that does not include a solution of the reparations problem in accord with Soviet desires," Molotov declared.

He insisted that reparations deliveries would not lower the standard of living in Germany to the minimum level, as Secretary Marshall had declared, and claimed it would be "no hardship" for the Germans to pay the Soviet Union the ten billions over a twenty-year period. The American argument, a telling one, that the Potsdam Agreement on the economic unity of Germany was not conditioned by the acceptance by the four Powers of reparations from current production, was avoided by Molotov.

There will always be a suspicion in my mind that the Soviet Foreign Minister was guilty of bad timing in making this stand on reparations from current production at the Moscow conference. I got the impression during the conference that if, six months before, the Soviet Union had put forward a proposal that the emphasis in the reparations program for the Soviet Union be shifted from capital removals to current production some headway could have been made. But when reparations from current production were introduced "crudely," to use a favorite Russian word, as a condition for something already agreed on, the Soviet spokesmen got nowhere.

But this was a time when the Russians still counted on bulling their way through any problem to a successful conclusion. So when Secretary Marshall, on April 3, circulated a plan which would provide limited reparations from current production in an effort to end the deadlock it was rejected by the Soviet delegation at the next day's meeting. The Russians wanted their ten billion or nothing.

The compromise solution which the United States delegation advanced was based on the proposed general increase in the level of industrial production in Germany. Once this level was raised, so ran American reasoning, there would be fewer plants available for capital removal. The United States was willing to have experts study the possibility of permitting the extraction of reparations from current production in those plants originally scheduled for removal as reparations.

At the time when this plan first was circulated the United States was not irrevocably committed to it. But the American delegation wanted the plan discussed. This the Russians were unwilling to do. It was all or nothing for Molotov. He got nothing.

At a subsequent secret session the compromise plan was again put forward. Secretary Marshall said the United States would be willing to assign to the plants concerned their full value as of the day they were first put into operation, not their removal value. This would have meant a substantial increase in the amount of reparations in current production taken from each plant left in Germany. Again the Soviet delegation refused to budge.

The blunt refusal of the Russians even to discuss a compromise solution was symbolic of the attitude adopted by Molotov throughout the conference. But although he was adamant on the objectives of Soviet policy, he consistently attacked Western aims in Germany.

By that time the aims of the three Western Powers, although generally diverse and indistinct, had begun to develop two courses of action. Some sort of international organization would have to be created to administer the Ruhr, Germany's industrial citadel, and, for economy and efficiency, the United States and British zones would have to continue as a single economic unit.

The merger of the two zones had taken place the year before. The initiative came from the United States which in default of four-Power agreement on economic unity declared before the Allied Control Council on July 20, 1946, that it was ready to administer the United States Zone in conjunction with one or more of the other zones as an economic unit.

Nine days later it was announced in the House of Commons that the British Government had decided to accept the offer. The French, on August 10, rejected the offer but called for the establishment of economic agencies for all four zones, excluding the Saar.

Later we will see the enormous influence which this fusion had on American policy in Germany. At the moment, consider it as one of the two focal points of Soviet attacks before the Council of Foreign Ministers. Here for the first time was the beginning of a structure in Germany in which the Russians could not directly intervene; an economic organization which might be the basis for future political partition. And partition violated the fundamental Soviet objective of a united and easily dominated Germany.

"The tendency towards federalization in western Germany amounts to prejudicing the future political status of Germany in favor of federalization rather than unification," Andrei Vishinsky shouted to the Council on March 15. Two days later Molotov formally demanded the annulment of economic fusion of the two zones, as "an infringement of Potsdam." Day in and day out Molotov returned to the attack. When in the second half of April the meeting drew to a close, Molotov and Vishinsky still were assailing the merger with undiminished fervor.

The Soviet delegates coupled their attacks on Bizonia with demands for a "share" in the control of the Ruhr.

This vital area "must" be placed under the joint control of the Soviet Union, the United States, the United Kingdom and France, ran the Russian argument. Only thus could the peace of Europe be assured and Germany prevented from becoming the breeding ground of new wars. The campaign of vilification and abuse against British administration in the Ruhr with the supposed introduction of "foreign monopolist capital"—by a British Labor government—grew so heavy that there were some who feared Foreign Secretary Bevin might break off negotiations on the spot or succumb to apoplexy. The consequence of the campaign was a strengthened British opposition to allowing the Russians a foothold in the Ruhr.

Soviet policy in this meeting was full of sound and fury, yet today, two years later, it appears curiously inept and "signifying nothing." Granted that the unification of Germany, which means a foothold in the Ruhr and the end of Bizonia, was the over-all Soviet objective, Molotov and Vishinsky chose curious methods to obtain it. By raising the reparations issue they blocked economic unity on which eventual political unity would be based, kept Russia out of the Ruhr and guaranteed the continuation of the bizonal fusion.

What is the answer to this contradiction? It lies, I believe, in the psychological state of the Political Bureau and the Soviet Foreign Ministry at the time. Having gained a comparatively easy victory at Potsdam, the Russians believed that the same conditions prevailed at Moscow nearly two years later. They refused to accept that Soviet policy in the intervening period had aroused the West's fears of the new Russian imperialism, that Communism, although still strong in France and Germany, was not so great a threat as it had been during the Potsdam conference and thus was not able to provide a telling chorus of approval for the demands of Molotov and Vishinsky. The tide of Soviet power and influence in western Europe had begun to ebb. The fall was very slight, it is true, but the tide had changed. The Russians, sometimes considered the "great realists" of modern diplomacy, failed to see this.

The curious interrelation between Soviet foreign policy as expressed by Molotov, Vishinsky and the Ministry of Foreign Affairs and the furthering of that policy by Communist parties abroad is underlined in one of the supreme miscalculations made by the Russians at Moscow.

On April 11, Molotov four times rejected the pleas of French Foreign Minister Bidault that the Saar be integrated into the French economy. From that moment, the French delegation moved closer in thought to the American and British delegations and away from the Russians. The French people and subsequent French governments have not forgotten Soviet intransigence over the Saar. A number of American public figures have claimed credit for the fact that since 1947 French foreign policy on Germany has moved, slowly it is true, into alignment with that of the United States. This credit should go to Molotov. Other factors, of course, influenced the development. But if we are to take a starting point for the realignment of French policy on Germany, April 11, 1947, is the date.

Why did the Russians with their supposed political sagacity refuse the French requests? I believe it was because they hoped that eventually they could trade their approval of the integration of the Saar into the French economy for French agreement to an arrangement by which the Soviet Union through the Soviet Military Administration would be granted a share in the control of the Ruhr. This trade was never made. The United States and Great Britain agreed to the integration of the Saar into the French economy and the Russians through their own intransigence shut themselves out of the Ruhr.

2

All the main points of Russian policy, made at the Moscow meeting, were remade with greater sharpness and accompanied by even more abusive language at the London meeting of the Council of Foreign Ministers which opened November 25, 1947.

As a result the Soviet Union forced the three Western Powers to conclude that agreement on any of the basic questions dealing with German economics and politics was impossible and that they were merely wasting time and giving Molotov and Vishinsky an opportunity for spreading propaganda by remaining in session. There was "no room for brokerage" and the conference broke up: one of the critical errors of Soviet foreign policy since the war. Before we examine the chain of developments which resulted directly or indirectly from the failure at London, let us see what happened there. The London meeting was the last Soviet attempt to bulldoze the West into agreement over Germany. All the bad manners of the Russians in international debate which had grown tiresome at Paris, New York and Moscow in other international discussions here reached their climax.

The five-point agenda of the conference included the following basic points on Germany:

(1) The preparation of a German peace treaty;

(2) Economic principles including reparations;

(3) The form and scope of the provisional (governmental) organization of Germany;

(4) The implementation of the decisions on demilitarization taken at the Moscow session of the Council of Foreign Ministers;

(5) The United States draft for a disarmament and demili-

tarization treaty on Germany (the Byrnes forty-year security pact).

If agreement had been reached on even one of these, or if agreement had even been approached, the settlement of the German problem might have been worked on throughout 1948. But it was soon apparent that no agreement was possible.

Molotov opened the meeting with a long assault upon the policies of the Western Powers and their desires for "an imperialist peace." Secretary Marshall rebuked him for "alleging evil motives which are figments of propaganda" and asked the Council to try to reach agreement for the benefit of "the entire world." Between such conflicting viewpoints, that world is caught.

The first Soviet bid for a central German government at this conference was made by Molotov on November 29. He based his argument on the futility of trying to complete a German peace treaty without a German government to assist in its preparation or to sign it at its completion. Bizonia had grown stronger since the Moscow meeting and the Soviet Foreign Minister evidently was moved by fears that, if the Council meeting failed to produce agreement, the Western Powers would make their own arrangements for a bizonal or trizonal government and sign a peace treaty with it.

"No ersatz government for Bizonia will be an adequate substitute for the Soviet proposal of a central German government," he declared.

Events proved him half right. After the failure of the London conference the Western Powers did begin the organization of a German Federal Republic, including geographically the French Zone of Occupation as well as the American and

British zones. However, a peace treaty was not discussed.

It is strange that Molotov, aware of this danger to Soviet Russia's aims of dominating all Germany and not merely a quarter of it, should have persisted in a course which made the breakdown of the meeting inevitable. His error once again may be traced to the fundamental Soviet misconception apparent at both Moscow and London; that the Western Powers under Soviet pressure would make concessions to the Russians in order to continue the conferences and get some agreement on Germany. Neither Molotov nor, apparently, the members of the Political Bureau yet realized that the United States and Britain finally had made up their mind that there could be no further retreat.

There "must be a German government," Molotov declared, "because unless there is someone to sign it [the peace treaty] there will be no one to carry it out.

"The formation of a German government is no less urgent than the preparation of a peace treaty," he concluded.

The Potsdam Agreement, to which the Russians are so fond of referring in order to find substantiation for their arguments, did not help Molotov in this case. For the agreement says "the Council of Foreign Ministers shall prepare a peace treaty to be accepted when a German government is set up adequate for the purpose."

"Facts are stubborn things," as Molotov is fond of saying. In this case the facts are that the Foreign Ministers are empowered to prepare a peace treaty which can be accepted later by a German government.

Early in December the second essential point on the agenda, economic principles, was raised. Here the division between West and East was as great as, if not greater than, it had been at Moscow. In addition, this time Molotov was not even discussing the matter before the Council. He continued to speak in broad generalities appealing directly to the German people.

At this point Secretary Marshall put forward what he called "common principles" on which economic and political unity could be based. These included "basic freedoms for the individual, the abolition of zonal boundaries except as the delimitation of occupation areas with no hindrance to the free flow of persons, ideas and goods throughout the whole of Germany and a clear determination of the economic burdens the German people are to bear."

Finally the Secretary of State, already wearied by the continuous barrage of propaganda which flowed from Molotov's mouth day in and day out, asked, "Are the members of this Council prepared to create the conditions under which German political and economic unity can become a reality?"

The Soviet answer came two days later on December 7 when Molotov submitted three proposals to the Council. They were:

(1) With the institution of German Central Administrative Agencies and the laying down of procedure for the fulfillment by Germany of her reparations obligations and other main obligations, interzonal economic barriers shall be abolished and the conditions necessary for the free flow of goods throughout Germany shall be established.

All zonal German economic agencies embracing one or more zones shall be abolished.

(2) The level of industry shall be raised to approximate an annual steel production of ten to twelve million tons.

The German Central Administrative Agencies shall plan

the rehabilitation of Germany within the above limits and subject to Germany's duty "to fulfill without reservations the reparations obligations and other main obligations imposed upon her."

(3) The Allied Control Council is to be authorized to institute as quickly as possible the German Central Administrative Agencies as agreed upon at Potsdam.

The various zonal commanders shall exercise supervision over these agencies in their respective zones.

This is the sort of Soviet proposal which bristles with "hooks" and "jokers." It was sometimes alleged by observers at meetings of the Council of Foreign Ministers that members of the American and British delegations spent too much time looking for the hidden meanings and clauses capable of a double interpretation in Soviet proposals and not enough time on the principles the Russians were enunciating. The answer is that during the "twilight sleep" period of Russo-American relations not enough time was spent considering the actual wording of Soviet state papers and too much on extolling the virtues of the Russian people. These are many; but they do not justify blindness on our part.

In the proposal put forward by Molotov there was a "hook" in the first paragraph. The Soviet Foreign Minister advocated the organization of the Central Administrative Agencies but only after agreement had been reached on how Germany is to fulfill her reparations obligations. These obligations it should be recalled were to include the Soviet Union's ten billion dollars. Moreover the lifting of interzonal economic barriers and the free flow of goods—Molotov did not mention freedom of ideas and persons as Secretary Marshall had—were also dependent on Russia getting her reparations.

The proposal called for the abolition of Bizonia, a natural step if economic unity could be achieved, but here tied to the reparations question. Finally Molotov, always repetitive, made his point again. The economy of Germany would be rehabilitated under the new level of industry, he declared, only if Germany paid her reparations.

It is worth noting that when this proposal was published in the Soviet licensed newspapers in Germany much was made of the "magnanimity" of Molotov's proposals for establishing the Central Agencies, lifting the zonal barriers and raising the level of production. Very little was said about the reparations demands.

The Soviet Foreign Minister also stipulated that the various zonal commanders supervise the Central Administrative Agencies. The supposition was that although these groups were to have the maximum freedom possible at that stage in Germany's postwar development in the three western Zones of Occupation, the Soviet Zone command would retain the same checks on these Agencies as it did on all other German bodies.

But Molotov's demands were not over yet. It was a cold and foggy period in England. Day after day in the big, high-ceilinged room at Lancaster House the long Russian sentences droned on, "the making of a new place of arms from which the Soviet Union is to be attacked . . . the protection of Nazis and other war criminals by the military governors of the imperialist Powers. . . ." The members of other delegations fidgeted and scratched. Tempers grew short. Still the voice droned on.

On December 8, Molotov returned to another principal objective of Soviet policy, the Ruhr. Wrapped up in a long

rambling speech were a demand for four-Power control of
the Ruhr in which the Soviet Union would have a veto, the
abolition of Bizonia and ten billion dollars in reparations in
twenty years. All this was adorned by the sort of diplomatic
double talk to which the other delegations had been exposed
at Moscow.

"The Soviet delegation does not believe the question of
reparations is a preliminary condition for the solution of
economic unity," Molotov proclaimed. "The Soviet delegation has believed and continues to believe that the two questions should be considered simultaneously."

Molotov demanded that the immense amount of reparations be made up of removals of complete industrial equipment in working order, annual deliveries of goods from
current production, German assets abroad and various services. His speech that day must be considered, from the purely
German standpoint, one of the most unfortunate ever made
by a foreign diplomat, for it broke up the London meeting
of the Council of Foreign Ministers and made the partition
of Germany for a considerable period inevitable.

The next day Secretary Marshall flatly refused to consider
the Soviet reparations claims.

The reparations issue had been "decided at Potsdam," the
Secretary of State added, and henceforth the Soviet Union
was to receive only the deliveries of individual plants found
to be in excess of the needs of the German economy. A day
later, Secretary Marshall, weary and angered by repeated
Russian attacks on the "looting" of Germany carried on by
the United States, announced that, according to United States
estimates, the Russians were removing German assets from
the Soviet Zone at the rate of $500,000,000 annually. He asked

the Council of Foreign Ministers to agree that after January 1, 1948, there would be no more removals. This was comparable to asking the James boys to go straight just after they had knocked off the richest bank in the territory. There was no answer from Molotov. One wonders whether Marshall expected one.

Ernest Bevin later estimated that since the beginning of the occupation, the Soviet authorities had taken seven billion dollars' worth of assets out of Germany. As the West continued to return the Russian fire, the atmosphere of the meeting steadily declined. It was amusing and perhaps a little terrifying, when one considered what was at stake, to hear ordinarily thoughtful American diplomats exult, "Wait till you read this speech; the Old Man [Marshall] really gave it to 'the Hammer' [Molotov] today."

On December 12, Molotov returned to the attack, wildly remaking all the charges against the Western Powers which they had already heard and attempted to refute. "Such a method of procedure makes it rather difficult to inspire respect for the Soviet Government," Marshall declared. Three days later the Council of Foreign Ministers adjourned indefinitely.

"The United States," Secretary Marshall declared in his final statement, "has consistently pressed for certain fundamental decisions by the Occupying Powers. . . . The Soviet Union alone refused to agree."

3

As the oratory of the conference died away it became apparent to thoughtful observers in the capitals of Europe that the Soviet Union had blundered.

The three Western Powers had had their differences over Germany. But these diminished in the months just after the London conference, and under the compelling belief that no agreement on Germany with the Russians was possible, the United States, Britain and France began to plan the construction of a federal republic in the three western Zones of Occupation.

From the American and British standpoint, this was the time to improve the existing bizonal arrangements and lay the foundations for eventual German self-government. In this they were joined, reluctantly it is true and with many doubts and misgivings, by the French. But it is doubtful if either the West, or the Germans to whom the Western Powers ultimately had to turn for support, would have gone as far toward establishment of the Western German State had it not been for another Russian action.

This was the coup engineered by the Communist Party of Czechoslovakia under the direction of the officials of the Soviet Foreign Ministry and the parent party in the Soviet Union. The event put the fear of Stalin into the German politicians as nothing before had done. General Clay believes it was the principal motive, stronger than economic recovery or the revival of nationalism, behind the German efforts in late 1948 and the first half of 1949 to establish a federal republic in western Germany.

The net result of the London conference was to find the three Western Powers fairly well agreed on policy in western Germany with that policy centered around the construction of a West German State which would be anti-Communist in politics and which would have a strong economic base. The Soviet Union would be shut out of the Ruhr.

Those who believe that the foreign policy of the Soviet

Union is a successful one should study these results. There can be little doubt of the ultimate Russian objective in Germany: the domination of the country. The Soviet policy, advanced at Moscow and London, both in its proposals and its implementation, instead of bringing the Soviet Union closer to that ultimate objective, retarded progress and even raised new barriers to its accomplishment.

Since their intransigence at London had effectively cut them off from further diplomatic contact with the Western Powers, the rulers of the Soviet Union were forced to cast about for new means other than diplomatic agreement by which they could attain their ends in Germany. Despite the dangers that hung heavy over Germany and particularly Berlin during the first seventeen months after the failure of the London meeting of the Council of Foreign Ministers, dangers which were the potential of the Russian policy in the country, the methods which the Soviet Military Administration employed show a curious ineptitude. This was true not only of Russian dealings with men like General Clay, General Sir Brian Robertson, the British Military Governor, and Brigadier General Frank L. Howley, the United States commandant in Berlin, but in their dealings with the Germans both east and west.

The Russians now were thrown back on the mobilization of their own Zone of Occupation as a base for their political campaign to win Germany. When we consider the motives which led the Soviet Union to impose the complete land blockade of Berlin on June 19, 1948, this development must be accounted an important factor. If the zone were to be an effective political base, then the Americans, British and French, with their propaganda, their political agents and the hopes that they represented for millions of Germans in the outer darkness of the Soviet Zone of Occupation, must be driven out of Berlin. So the Russians must have reasoned.

But this was not the only factor. The three Western Powers, along with the Netherlands, Belgium and Luxembourg, met in London in the spring of 1948. Out of that meeting, early in June, came an agreement on the formation of a West German State. Here was something the Russians most emphatically did not want. The Berlin blockade was clamped around the city in the hope that it would force the West into another meeting of the Council of Foreign Ministers at which the Soviet delegation could again bid for control of all of Germany.

Under those conditions, the Russians argued, the organization of the eastern zone could be given a secondary place. Indeed, it was not until it became apparent that the Western Powers had decided to hold fast in Berlin that the Soviet Military Administration gave its full attention to the mobilization of the Soviet Zone.

This took the form of preparing an East German State. The action was not pure imitation of the efforts of the United States, Britain and France in the west, however. For this was ostensibly an "all German" state, one which could be considered as such by the Russians and those Germans, deluded enough by national passion, who would be willing to accept it.

The Soviet task was difficult. The prestige and influence of the Socialist Unity (Communist) Party had declined steadily in the winter of 1947-1948. It dropped still farther shortly after the blockade was imposed on Berlin. In the Soviet Zone of Occupation, its leaders, Wilhelm Pieck, Otto Grotewohl and Walter Ulbricht noted signs of rising anti-Communist and anti-Russian feeling. As early as May 1948, Pieck called the executive committee of the party together and told them in a blunt, fierce speech into which the old, sickly leader of German Communism poured all the energy he has left, "We are losing position after position to the reactionaries," that is, to the German anti-Communists and indirectly to the United States, Britain and France and all they stood for in Germany.

In western Germany the bankruptcy of the Communist Party was equally evident. In the elections of November 1948, the Communist members were swept out of the executive board of the Ruhr miners union. I asked Willi Agatz, one of the most energetic, intelligent and resourceful of German Communists, how this had happened.

"The capitalists organized a campaign around the so-called blockade of Berlin," he said, "and lied to the workers about the improvement in western Germany."

This was as near as a Communist leader will come to admitting the party has made a mistake.

Nevertheless the Russians have persevered in their attempts to organize an East German State. Curiously, they have been hampered by their own propaganda. Granted their total power in eastern Germany, they could have organized this state, or a reasonable facsimile, at any time since the end of the London conference. But Soviet propaganda in Germany for three years has pictured the Western Powers and the non-Communist politicians of western Germany as the "splitters" of Germany. Thus when the time came for the Russians to organize their own state in east Germany, they had to prepare it at a pace just a little slower than that set by the Parliamentary Council at Bonn which was writing a constitution for a West German State. This was very slow.

The instruments developed by the Soviet Military Administration and the Socialist Unity Party as the basis for the East German State are worth examination as examples of how Communist totalitarianism is disguised under a mannerly show of parliamentary democracy.

The Volkskongress or People's Congress is the larger, more representative and less important of the two. It has 1,500 members of whom 1,000 are elected in the Soviet Zone and 500 in the three western Zones of Occupation. The Communist claim that theirs is an "all German state" rests on this contingent of 500 from the western zones. These delegates are elected in the sense that their names are approved by vote, usually unanimous, in internal elections of Communist Party groups in the three western zones.

The Congress exists to approve the actions of its superior body, the People's Council. This organization of indeterminate membership is made up of the leaders of the Socialist Unity Party from all over the eastern zone, the most satisfactory, that is pliant, representatives of the eastern zone "splinter" parties of the major German political groupings like the Free Democratic Party and the Christian Democratic Union, and representatives of various Communist-front organizations from all over the zone.

As the meetings of the Council and Congress show, the average delegate has very little to do or say. When in the autumn of 1948 the constitution for the proposed state was being discussed, one delegate of the eastern zone C.D.U. had the temerity to protest the rather cloudy phrasing of the article on religious liberty. He was silenced in the meeting

by a screaming, almost hysterical Communist who gave the
usual type of answer: the constitution was the product of the
SED, hence religious freedom was guaranteed.

The tone of such meetings irresistibly recalls the hysteria
of National Socialism. Here is all the bigotry, the hypocrisy
and the mad, brutal force that characterized the Nürnburg
rallies before the war. Here are the countrymen of Goethe
and Heine and Beethoven raving drunk with political passion, shrieking their promises and their plans. The difference
between these assemblies and those great evocations of national hysteria staged by the Nazis is that the response of the
body of the group, whether it is the People's Congress or the
People's Council, is not so unanimous or so frenzied as it was
during the National Socialist regime.

Partly this seems due to the fact that a large percentage of
the Socialist Unity Party, including most former members of
the Social Democratic Party, are only lukewarm to the aims
of the People's Council and Congress. They are nationalistic
and they want not an eastern state or even a faked "all German" state but complete German unity.

But there is another cause for the lethargy that steals over
these meetings unless they are extremely well organized.
This is the lack of vigor, intellectual and physical, which one
encounters in most eastern-zone Germans.

A British intelligence officer thinks this is due to a psychological conflict arising from the fact that the followers of
Russian policy in the eastern zone believe inwardly that they
are siding with the principal enemies of their nation although
outwardly they mouth slogans like "Toward a free, united
Germany."

Whatever the cause, the fact remains that during the

months of crisis in Berlin from June 1948 to May 1949, it was not the Socialist Unity Party which staged the most convincing demonstrations of resolution and sacrifice for their cause but the hitherto divided Germans of the non-Communist parties.

I have seen demonstrations in many countries from the vast outpourings of the proletariat in Moscow to celebrate the deification of Stalin to the orderly processions that wind through London's quiet streets on a Sunday afternoon on their way to demonstrate in Hyde Park. Never have I seen less convincing demonstrations than those staged by the Socialist Unity Party in Berlin.

The demonstrators, arbitrarily selected from the factories of Berlin and the Soviet Zone, go through the motions with a lack of interest which must be downright embarrassing to the Russian officers who, with the help of the leaders of the SED, stage-manage the show. Fat, tired Wilhelm Pieck reiterates all the old slogans. There are dutiful cheers. The "demonstrators" march past the reviewing stand carrying the same old banners with the same old slogans and then, once out of sight of the police, roll up the banners and hurry homeward. The German proletariat is through for the day.

Never has the failure of the campaign to impose Communism on Berlin and the eastern zone of Germany been illustrated more emphatically than in the contrast between the mass demonstrations of Communist and anti-Communist forces in Berlin in the summer of 1948.

On September 9, 1948, after the Communists with the help of the Soviet Military Administration had broken the city-wide power of the elected city government of Berlin, there was an anti-Communist demonstration in the Place of the

Republic, hard by the Brandenburg Gate. It was a warm, sunny afternoon and for hours the men and women of Berlin, thousands of them from the Soviet Sector, tramped the hot streets toward the meeting place until in the great concourse facing the ruined Reichstag there were approximately 300,000 people.

This was no regimented demonstration. Here was a genuine evocation of anti-Communist feeling. It was a tremendous and terrifying experience.

"If there were no Russian soldiers just beyond that gate," a British military police officer said, "these types would go into the eastern sector and tear the Bolshies limb from limb."

When the demonstration was over a youth climbed the Brandenburg Gate and tore down the red flag that hung at its top. As he did, there came a scatter of shots from the Soviet-Sector police and then, with slowly increasing power, a great, rumbling roar of approval from the hundreds of thousands crowding the Place of the Republic. It was the nadir of Communism in Berlin.

The events in Berlin and the Soviet Zone of Occupation during 1948 gave a false picture of Russian strength in eastern Germany. I believe that at the very moment when the Soviet Military Administration appeared to hold all the cards and when the Socialist Unity Party was speaking with the greatest show of authority, the Russian campaign to win control of Germany was suffering its most severe setbacks since the beginning of the occupation.

We have seen how the overt arm of Soviet foreign policy, the Ministry of Foreign Affairs, failed at Moscow and London to achieve its goals. The story in Germany since the end of the London conference has also been one of failure. In eastern Germany the Socialist Unity Party has not been able to create a true basis for a Communist government of a "people's republic" in the Soviet Zone of Occupation. Competent United States and British intelligence officers, who know the strength and weaknesses of the Communist and Communist-front parties throughout the satellite lands of eastern Europe, assert that the Socialist Unity Party is the weakest of all.

"Our task of course is made difficult by the unreasoning hatred of a number of Germans," a German Communist once explained to me. "It must be admitted that the Russians do not always make it easy for us. We get advice and encouragement at the topmost level, of course. But just when we have established a firm basis for the party in a city, then there is a crime of violence in which Russian soldiers are involved. When that happens the people turn against us."

Another factor of immense importance contributed to the loss of prestige of the Socialist Unity Party and the Soviet Military Administration in Germany. This was the defeat of the Russian-imposed blockade of Berlin by the spectacular method of flying supplies into the city in American and British transport planes, the Airlift. Ultimately this also was a defeat for over-all Soviet foreign policy everywhere, but its greatest effect was in Germany.

When the blockade was imposed in June of 1948, the Russian policy makers at Potsdam summoned the leaders of the Socialist Unity Party to Supreme Soviet Headquarters at Potsdam and there informed them that by autumn the Westerners would be out of Berlin and the great city fully incorporated into the Soviet Zone.

The Germans went home and talked, for their prestige, never high, needed the assistance of such grandiose declarations. The provincial papers of the Soviet Zone discussed what should be done, when the Western Powers withdrew from Berlin, with such "traitors" as Ernst Reuter and Luise Schroeder who had worked with those Powers. Plans for a great propaganda campaign designed to convince the foolish inhabitants of the western sectors of the error of their ways in supporting the West also were laid. I think it may be taken for granted that lists of those political and civic leaders who would have to be "removed," once the Western Powers departed, were drawn up and studied. It was a great opportunity for the German Communists to flex their muscles and they made the most of it.

When at one minute past midnight on the morning of May 12, the blockade was lifted the German Communists and their Soviet masters suffered a drop in prestige throughout the Soviet Zone from which they may never recover.

The propaganda machine made violent efforts to present the lifting of the blockade as a Soviet victory, on the theory that Russia had always wished to supply the whole city's fuel and food but had been frustrated by the counterblockade of the Soviet Zone imposed by the three Western Powers. This specious argument got nowhere. The Germans knew who had won and who had lost. And in the western sectors of Berlin they rightly assumed a good share of the credit for themselves.

"So Ivan is beaten, eh? Well, the air bridge (the Anglo-American Airlift) did part of it, but we did a lot too." Thus a German workman just before the lifting of the blockade. "Don't forget if we hadn't held fast last winter and refused to go over to him, and if our wives hadn't been willing to go without heat and electricity, the Airlift wouldn't have beaten him. We've shown him he may be able to bully the Czechs and the Poles and those others, but not Germans."

Ivan was beaten in Berlin on the blockade issue. But he is not, most emphatically not, beaten in Germany. Always before him are the words of Lenin. And always in the mind of Molotov or Vishinsky or Gromyko, or whomever else the West must deal with over Germany, is the belief that the West is an enemy. To lie to this enemy, to make agreements which can be broken when it suits Soviet foreign policy, to agree to one interpretation of free elections over a conference table and to implement another, more ominous interpretation in Halle or Dresden are part of the political war with the Western enemy. The Russian diplomat is a soldier in the class war and he will use a *ruse de guerre* as swiftly as the Communist organizer in an American union.

We will see in subsequent chapters how much United States policy in Germany has been influenced by the cold war with Russia. But Soviet policy has been affected by this same factor and in a similar manner. Too much attention has been paid to driving the Western "enemies" out of Germany and not enough to establishing a firm base for Communism in Germany.

As a result, not only in the eastern zone, but all over Germany the Russians have presented Communism, expressed either by the Communist Party of Germany in the three western zones or the Socialist Unity Party in the Soviet Zone, not as a party working for the German people's good but as an ally of the Soviet Military Administration. The German Communist Party in pre-Hitler days, although it was subservient to Moscow, was a vigorous, outspoken organization which posed as the friend of the proletariat. The post-Hitler party has been the ally of a ruthless occupation force intent on subjecting the proletariat to its demands and, in many cases, to destroying its means of livelihood.

What courses are open to German Communism and Soviet foreign policy in pursuit of their long-term objectives? If Germany is to be won for the East, then there must be a thorough change in the orientation of the Communist Party. It must become again the friend of the worker rather than his oppressor and the ally of his national enemy. And Soviet foreign policy must drop the repressive elements of its policy in Germany, reparations and removals first of all, and emerge as the ally on equal terms of a reviving Germany.

THE STORY OF AMERICAN POLICY
in Germany from the Potsdam Conference onward cannot be
separated from the cold war with the Soviet Union. For
Germany is both the most important battleground of that
war and its greatest prize. Yet, oddly, there was a period at
the end of 1945 when, had it not been for an unforeseen cir-
cumstance, the United States and the Soviet Union might
have agreed on the first steps toward the creation of a united
Germany.

According to General Clay, at that time Deputy Military
Governor, the Russians in the months immediately after Potsdam were willing to proceed with the establishment of the
Central Administrative Agencies provided for at that conference. But, Clay added, the efforts of the Americans, British
and Russians, the three Powers represented at Potsdam, were
blocked by the French whose policy seemed to be to approve
everything in the Potsdam Agreement which agreed with
French policy for Germany and oppose everything else.

This was, Clay believes, our "last chance" for a joint policy
in Germany. The refusal of the French to accept certain basic
provisions of the Potsdam Conference, at which they had not
been represented, may well prove, for weal or woe, to have
been a turning point in the postwar history of Germany.

Since then French Military Government officials in Germany often have preened themselves on their success in "sav-

ing" the United States and the United Kingdom from the "errors" of Potsdam. This is a harmless bit of national vanity, but it does not absolve the French from sabotaging the effort to begin the economic unification of Germany to which the three great Powers had agreed at Potsdam.

As it became apparent that the French would block any steps toward the establishment of the Central Administrative Agencies, the tempo of the cold war increased and agreement on other basic questions dealing with Germany's economic unity became increasingly remote. As a result of these conditions, the beginnings of a new American policy in Germany became apparent.

It is easier to enumerate the negative aspects of this policy as it developed for the next three years than to explain its fundamental objectives and their relationship with over-all American foreign policy. For this at its inception was not a policy carefully worked out by high-powered State Department planners in Washington; it was, in the main, a policy developed out of the exigencies of the situation in Germany and of the reaction of the Departments of Army and State to day-to-day happenings there.

The policy did not aim at a soft peace with Germany. It never contemplated the rebuilding of German military strength for use against the Russians or for any other purpose. It was not the result of pressure in Germany by what left-wing writers describe as "big Nazis" and "powerful Ruhr industrialists." The policy had many faults but these were not among them.

Any examination of American policy in Germany in the post-Potsdam period shows that this policy developed as the result not only of Russo-American difficulties but of the situa-

tions which arose and were dealt with in Germany. The be-
lated realization of the Soviet Union's true aims in Germany
had a noteworthy effect on policy making but so, in their
time, did such important but unrelated developments as the
rise of the black market, the terrible winter of 1946-1947 and
the political apathy of the German people.

And since policy is made by men, the personalities of the
principal American officials in Germany played a part, a very
important part, in shaping that policy.

Of these officials the most important was Lucius DuBignon
Clay, who, for four years, first as Deputy Military Governor
and then as Military Governor, exercised a profound influence not only on the making and implementation of United
States policy in Germany but also on the whole conduct by
the West of the cold war in that country. Clay's influence
extended far beyond the confines of the United States Office
of Military Government in Berlin; it was felt in the foreign
offices of the other Western Occupation Powers and even, it
is probable, in the sessions of the Political Bureau in the
Kremlin. At two meetings of the Council of Foreign Ministers in Moscow and London, Clay was a trusted adviser of
Secretary of State Marshall. By the end of his office in Germany, the name of Clay rightly or wrongly had become
synonymous with United States policy on Germany.

The personality of General Clay explains a great deal of
American policy. He was by training a soldier, an officer of
the Corps of Engineers, which traditionally draws the best
brains of each West Point graduating class. Yet his early environment, including a father who was a United States sena-
tor, had a strong political tone. Clay was not one of those
generals who simply could not understand what the politi-

cians were talking about. And he was able to grasp the significance to Germany of events outside that country, notably the Labor success in the British General Election of 1945.

I remember a curious contrast in the attitudes of General Eisenhower and General Clay toward that event. Eisenhower, naturally, was surprised and sorry that Churchill, "that grand old man" as he called him, had been repudiated by the British electorate. Clay, on the other hand, was considering what effect this change in government would have on British policy in Germany.

The American politicians who objected to Clay's dominance over American policy in Germany on the grounds that he was a soldier missed the truth.

They could have handled a soldier of the common or garden variety easily enough. Clay with his politico-military background, his long service in Washington, his standing in Congress was something else again, a man who combined soldierly resolution with an adroit and subtle mind and a command of the art of public explanation.

During the last year of his office in Germany, I suppose I talked to General Clay on the average of three times a week. Our conversations naturally centered on Germany but they also touched on such varied questions as the development of recoilless artillery, the making of the American constitution, American policy in China and the personality of Charles de Gaulle.

The mind thus revealed was not only unusual in a soldier but unusual for anyone. It was at once reflective and decisive. During the hectic summer of 1948, General Clay made a large number of decisions with great speed. Often these were attacked as "snap decisions" made without thought. This just is not true. Clay had foreseen since December of 1947 the possibility that Berlin would be blockaded by the Russians. In his own mind and in council he had developed the ideas which lay behind many of his decisions long before the need for any action arose. Some of the decisions were wrong; a great many were right. But none was the result of the in-stinctive desire of the ordinary military man to give an order, any order, in a tight situation.

General Clay's political outlook has a curious strain of the old Southern liberalism of the first years of this century. The at-times old-fashioned attitude which he adopted toward the politics of Europe in this decade might have been laughable had it not expressed a certain moral rectitude and sobriety which seem to have vanished from the American political scene.

What did Clay believe in for Germany? Private enter-prise, the old but not antiquated viewpoint that the starting point for democracy is the town meeting, the desirability of making Germany pay her own way and contribute to Eur-ope's rehabilitation, the folly of turning the first industrial power of central Europe into a rural nation, the dangers in-herent in the reconstruction of a united Germany balanced between West and East.

One of Clay's most admirable and least recognized quali-ties was his insistence from 1945 through 1949 that in Ger-many the law must be placed above men. He was unmoved by the storm of abuse which broke about his head when he agreed to the reduction of the sentence imposed earlier on Ilse Koch, the notorious Bitch of Buchenwald. There was ample evidence, he pointed out, to show that Koch was im-moral, that she was a thoroughly bad character. But, he added, her morals were not in question. There just was not enough evidence of her alleged atrocities, he said, to warrant life imprisonment.

When this decision became the target for a nation-wide campaign of protest, the general was somewhat surprised because he had believed that Americans must realize that justice in the United States or in Germany must be above politics and policies. He felt that if the United States ever descended to the point where nation-wide pressure campaigns could alter legal decisions, it would be moving onto the same level with the prewar totalitarian nations of Italy and Germany and the postwar totalitarianism of the Soviet Union.

In this entire affair General Clay exhibited the sort of moral courage and respect for ancient verities of the law of which Americans boast so much and which they practice so infrequently.

One of General Clay's blind spots, in my estimation, was his inability to comprehend the importance of the appeal which the Social Democratic Party makes in Germany to the working classes. Granted his background and training, Clay could not be expected to endorse either the Socialists or their leaders, but it seemed to me he persistently underestimated their strength and misinterpreted their policies. When in March and April of 1949 Dr. Kurt Schumacher and the other leaders of the party appeared ready to prevent the completion of a constitution for a West German State unless their party's wishes on the degree of centralization were met, Clay, who looked on the constitution and the state as the culmination of his work in Germany, was exceedingly angry. This was natural. But his anger was so great that for a time he seemed to lack his usual calm judgment of the political forces in western Germany and exaggerated the amount of authoritarianism and nationalism among the Social Democrats.

As Russian intransigence of German unity developed at the meetings of the Council of Foreign Ministers and of the Allied Control Council in Berlin, American policy for dealing with western Germany also developed. As early as May of 1946 Clay suggested in a report to the War Department, as it then was, that plans for the ultimate establishment of a West German State be considered and that since recent Russian actions in the Allied Control Council appeared to rule out economic unity on any but Soviet terms, some sort of economic union for the American and British Zones of Occupation be planned for the near future.

There was no direct answer by Washington to these suggestions. But in July of 1946 General Joseph T. McNarney, then the United States Military Governor, announced at an Allied Control Council meeting that the United States and the United Kingdom would proceed toward the economic unification of their Zones of Occupation and made an offer to the Soviet and French Military Governors to take similar steps toward the economic unity of Germany.

Philip Noel-Baker, Minister of State, speaking in the House of Commons on Britain's acceptance of the American offer, made it clear that the Foreign Office hoped that eventually all four zones would merge.

These announcements produced roars of disapproval from the Russian propagandists although the immediate reaction of Marshal Vassily Sokolovsky, the Soviet Commander in Chief in Germany and Military Governor, was remarkably mild; he termed the merger plan "unwise." The Soviet political strategists, however, ordered the organization of a noisy propaganda campaign attacking the United States and Britain as the "splitters" of Germany and accusing them of preparing western Germany, especially the Ruhr, for "new militarist adventures" against the Soviet Union. We have seen how this propaganda ran through Molotov's speeches at the Moscow and London conferences, contributing to the incredible boredom with which the Soviet "case" was received.

The maximum importance must be conceded to the merger of the two largest western zones. The economic importance of the move, despite the fact that this was paramount in the minds of the planners, was not so great as the political significance. For the merger was the first offensive action taken by the Western Powers in Germany, an action which was planned and carried out, on the American side, by Secretary of State Byrnes and General Clay.

Clay's report on the advisability of establishing some sort of a western zonal union, if Soviet refusal to accept a general German economic union continued, was unanswered but not unnoticed in Washington.

Secretary of State Byrnes, who knew, liked and respected General Clay as a result of the latter's wartime work in Washington, saw in the general's suggestion for the merger of the American and British zones, first a method of forcing the Soviet Union to realize the West would not wait forever for German unity and would do something to speed unity in the west at least and second a path to greater economic productivity for the two zones and an eventual reduction of the expense of occupation.

Meanwhile in Germany General Clay and General Sir Brian Robertson, the British Deputy Military Governor, had discussed what could be done toward zonal fusion in the west, if it proved impossible at the Allied Control Council meetings to secure four-Power agreement. But it should be emphasized that even then the Americans and the British were hopeful that some agreement could be worked out for the establishment of the Central Administrative Agencies.

In May Clay began the preparation of a program which worked out, in detail, the organizational plans for the Central Administrative Agencies. This was rejected by the Russians and the French, but parts of it became the basis for the economic fusion of the American and British zones.

In the period between May of 1946 and the opening of the Council of Foreign Ministers in Moscow in March of 1947, the economic fusion of the two zones developed slowly. This was due in part to the fact that both the American and British governments still hoped that some measure of complete unification of Germany might be achieved, in part to the terrible winter of 1946-1947 which presented both Occupation Powers with urgent problems on a day-to-day basis, and in part to the fact that economic recovery in the two zones had not yet approached the point where the benefits expected from fusion would be clearly visible.

Moreover the implementation of fusion was affected to a considerable degree by the economic jolt suffered by Britain during the winter. It soon became obvious that in the economic development of the two zones, the United States would have to bear the bulk of the costs.

The American position, when the Moscow conference opened, was complicated by several factors which, although they were not matters of position on Germany, nevertheless influenced policy.

The first of these was the personality of the new Secretary

of State, General of the Army George C. Marshall. Here was a revered and distinguished figure, belaureled by the outcome of the war, a man of Olympian calm and a profound and commanding view of world affairs. We Americans are sometimes disposed to confuse sport with government or diplomacy and the exuberant young diplomat who remarked to me in Moscow that "we've got an All American on this team now" symbolized the general rejoicing.

"When I saw this calm, dignified figure with the rugged, really American face, I felt that at last you had a spokesman of a stature commensurate with the power and prestige in Europe of the United States," a British friend declared.

In retrospect, it might have been better if there had been a shade less confidence in Secretary of State Marshall's manner and rather less of his Olympian calm. For the soldier-turned-statesman was now face to face with problems not open to arbitrary and incisive decision and with men who regarded him simply as the temporary spokesman for a system they detested.

Throughout the Moscow meeting the American delegation was prone to circulate long, beautifully worded statements on economic unity, government organization and democracy. These were greeted rapturously by the press and, in public, by the diplomats of the other Western countries. Rereading them today gives one a feeling that the United States delegation was living in a Never-Never land in which the Russians could be convinced of our righteousness by high-sounding declarations. It was all very wonderful, but it was not negotiation or diplomacy.

It has been suggested that the impression made by American policy on the Russians at Moscow was slight because General Marshall as chief of the delegation was a man accustomed by a lifetime of soldiering to orders, not negotiations. Undoubtedly there is some truth in this. No man, however great, can slough off the habits of a lifetime, but it must be remembered that the last years of Marshall's military life had been spent in negotiation with the chiefs of the other fighting services and with the British political leaders and Chiefs of Staff. In these negotiations there was always behind him the tremendous power and prestige of the United States position as the industrial arsenal of the Western Allies. This factor was evident to the British, for instance, in all negotiations with General Marshall.

It was not present at Moscow. There was no way of forcing the Russians to do as General Marshall and the American delegation desired. However, there was the tried and true diplomatic method of making minor concessions in order to induce your opponent to leave his prepared position and move nearer your position.

When East and West became deadlocked over the question of Russian reparations from Germany, Marshall tried this method with the concession, made at a secret meeting, of assigning the output of factories which were to be left in Germany as a result of the rise of the level of industry, to the Soviet Union as reparations from current production. This production was to equal only the value of the plants, hence it would not continue over a long period, but the Secretary of State and the United States delegation were willing to value these plants at considerably higher figures than previous estimates.

To the Secretary of State and his advisers this seemed a generous and practical concession. But Molotov, as we have seen, refused to budge. His stubbornness at this point convinced many members of the United States delegation that it was no use trying to negotiate with the Russians on the critical question of reparations. This attitude continued over into the London conference that winter and played its part in building the wall of mistrust between the Russians and the Western Powers which was never scaled in the years 1947 and 1948. Indeed, so deep was the suspicion that prevailed in the United States camp about whatever the Russians said or did, I am convinced that no Soviet concessions short of complete surrender to American views would have contributed to progress.

The intransigence shown by both sides during these two conferences was the negation of diplomacy. It was the product of Soviet bad faith and stubbornness on other issues, but the United States delegations at Moscow and London appeared too prone to let Russian ill manners excuse their own poverty of diplomatic approach.

Whenever he was in a particularly sunny mood, which meant he was displaying the geniality of a trapped tiger, Molotov sought to enliven his tirades to the other ministers with homely Russian proverbs. At the Moscow conference he might have used an American saying to the effect that too many cooks spoil the broth. The United States delegation would have caught his meaning.

Secretary Marshall entered the international arena accompanied by a large number of seconds, towel flappers, strategists and water boys. In addition to John Foster Dulles, the Republican adviser on the delegation, there were Ben Cohen and Charles E. "Chip" Bohlen of the State Department, General Clay and Ambassador Murphy from Berlin and a host of minor experts on the German question summoned from both Berlin and Washington.

In addition there was the resident ambassador, Lieutenant General Walter Bedell Smith. General Smith had been secretary of the General Staff in Washington and General Marshall had known and liked him there. During the Moscow conference and in the subsequent London conference General Smith played a prominent and often influential role in the deliberations of the American delegation.

The coming together of so many able, experienced and ambitious men in an advisory capacity insured that the new Secretary of State would be the recipient of a vast amount of advice and that, in view of the novelty of his post, it would be difficult for even his notable intelligence to weigh the utility of this advice in the making of policy. There were times therefore when the very weight of brain power coupled with the diversity of ambition and experience slowed rather than accelerated the preparation of the American case.

A salient example of this was the manufacture of the famous United States statement on democracy. This was a striking declaration of the American viewpoint on the interpretation of a word which the Communists now have seized as their own, although, in my view, it added very little to the strength of the American position. Whatever its merits, it took five hours for the American delegation to prepare the statement.

Two members of the United States delegation have told me since that Secretary Marshall was not "at home" in the diplomatic atmosphere during the Moscow conference. He was angered at the obvious Russian unwillingness to grasp his main concession over reparations and at the whole tone of the Soviet case. It was a disappointing introduction to international diplomacy.

The failure at Moscow was not as pronounced as at London, but the conference did end with very little progress toward the economic or political unity of Germany. Meanwhile in that unhappy country the dollar costs were mounting; Britain, the partner in bizonal fusion, was broke or nearly so; production still lagged far beyond plan, necessitating a great flood of imports paid for by the United States; and the German people, sunk in political apathy, showed few signs of the psychological recovery which would help themselves and western Europe.

The American delegation at Moscow reasoned they had done their best to win a united Germany in the Council of Foreign Ministers. The United States had tried to pursue the policy laid down at Potsdam. Obviously a united Germany was far in the future. The next best, or it may even have appeared the best course to the more rabid Russian haters, was to complete the German economic union in the west. After the Moscow conference General Clay was ordered to accelerate the establishment of a German administration for the bizonal area. An economic commission, chosen by the various *Landtags,* or state legislatures, was already in being, but it was not popular. Scattered in cities and towns throughout the British and American zones were the skeletons of other German organizations which could be given additional personnel and put to work to give Bizonia a real German administration.

There was no intention then of establishing a political state. As far as political control by Germans was concerned it rested with the *Landtags* on a territorial basis. There was no higher authority then nor was one contemplated. The idea of a West German State was in the minds of many American and British officials of Military Government, notably Generals Clay and Robertson, but there was a genuine hope that it would not be necessary to go that far. But faced with worsening economic conditions throughout the two zones, the two Western Powers, with the United States taking the lead, were convinced that everything possible must be done to improve production and the German standard of living.

Those who cavil at the economic improvement in western Germany as a "danger" to Europe should consider the danger to Europe of a continuation of the situation prevailing in Germany in 1946 and 1947.

Ernest Bevin, who has a knack of going to the heart of the matter, told a Foreign Office official, "They say it will be dangerous to peace if we go ahead and create the conditions for a Western German State. I say it will be more dangerous to peace if we leave western Germany an economic cesspool. I've worked all my life for peace; it's not likely I would allow a military state to develop."

Certainly neither the economic fusion of the American and British zones, nor the economic recovery it was supposed to facilitate moved as fast in the period between the end of the Moscow conference and the start of the London conference as the State Department and Foreign Office had hoped. There was a great outcry in the Communist press of Europe against the alleged reconstruction of German war potential and this found its echo among those in the United States who cannot or will not understand that Germany is not a single problem, that it is part of the world problem and that if Germany, in the heart of Europe, is ill nourished, impoverished and discontented, Europe and the world will suffer.

During this period the French Republic stood aloof from the Anglo-American plans to improve the situation in western Germany. For a different reason, fear of Germany, the French echoed the Russian protests over the supposed revival of German industrial strength. This was during a period when the American and British authorities in the Ruhr spent their time devising various "incentive schemes" to bring the per capita output of the Ruhr coal miners up to a figure which would satisfy French requirements. However, it is the habit of French politicians to warn of Germany's might when that country's impotency is evident and to do nothing about Germany when she is a power in Europe.

Germany, as Mr. Bevin has pointed out, was a greater danger to peace in 1946 and 1947 than she was in 1948, although in the latter year she was certainly a more important threat to British and French commercial interests on the continent.

The Moscow conference, or rather the failure of the Moscow conference, speeded the organization of the Bizone. But it was the failure of the London conference which gave the final impetus to the Western plans for the establishment of a Western German State. Once again the proposals and suggestions of the American delegation, seconded by the delegations of the United Kingdom and France, were rejected. Once again the Soviet Union refused to make any concessions or to consider those few, and they were very few, made by the West.

Secretaries of State, ambassadors and generals are human. They suffer from heartburn and frustration. A few diplomats of the old school survive, men who can sit for hours blandly listening to outrageous attacks upon their veracity and honesty and then are able to return with icy politeness to the point. But the stock is almost exhausted in the Western Powers and the anger, long simmering, felt for Molotov by Secretary of State Marshall and his principal lieutenants at London boiled over at the close of that meeting of the Council of Foreign Ministers.

How much of the decisiveness of the steps which followed that failure are due to these very human feelings, no one can estimate. But they played their part in turning, temporarily at least, American policy from its primary objective of seeking Germany's unity through negotiation with the Soviet Union toward the establishment of a government in western Germany which in time might become so strong it would provide the basis for the reunification of Germany along lines acceptable to the United States.

The adoption of the west German scheme meant that the United States in fact, if not in theory, would be halting for the present its efforts to bring the Soviet Zone of Occupation into a united Germany and would be turning over the Germans of that zone to Soviet rule unaffected by Western offers for establishing a free flow of goods, information and persons between eastern and western Germany.

It also meant that the West would give up the long-term objective of gaining enough influence in eastern Germany to affect the course of events in Czechoslovakia and Poland. Since 1945 General Clay had felt that by winning entry into eastern Germany, the United States might be able to sustain the libertarian forces in those countries. The establishment of the Central Administrative Agencies, which he pushed with such fervor in 1945 and 1946 in the Allied Co-ordinating Committee meetings, was, he felt, one method by which Western influence could have been spread to the borders of Czechoslovakia and Poland and the growth of Communist power in those countries checked.

However, months of frustration in this Committee, in later meetings of the Allied Control Council and in two meetings of the Council of Foreign Ministers convinced him that the Russians would never agree to economic unification or even the free organization of the Central Administrative Agencies which was a prerequisite of that unification. He turned, and American policy turned simultaneously, toward the establishment of the West German State.

Although the London meeting ended with many statements by Western politicians on the advisability of constructing this state out of the three western Zones of Occupation, the making of Trizonia proved more difficult than had been imagined. Many good judges, for instance, believe that the entrance of the French Republic delayed the completion of a constitution for a West German State formed of the American and British zones by at least six months.

Although the concept of a federal republic in the west had been in the minds of American and British planners since 1946, it was a new development to the French, and to some of them an ominous one. Thus when early in 1948 representatives of the United States, the United Kingdom, France, Belgium, the Netherlands and Luxembourg met in London to salvage some political and economic organization out of a partitioned Germany, the French were disposed to tread warily on the path toward a German federal republic.

This was a perfectly natural attitude on the part of the

French representatives. Every Frenchman bears in his heart, rather than his mind, the long history of German aggression against France. This is not something which can be put down on paper, but it is one of the most important political facts in Europe. In early 1948 the logical French recognized the need for some political and economic reconstruction in western Germany, if the industrial resources of that rich area were to be used for the benefit of Europe. Such recognition was of the mind. But Frenchmen everywhere saw another side to the revival of the Ruhr. They saw not coal for French forges, but coal for great new steel plants. They saw not steel for new railroads, but steel for new tanks. In a reconstructed Ruhr they envisaged not a great industrial area laboring for the good of Europe, but an area powerful enough to dominate Europe. And these sentiments were of the heart.

At the six-Power talks in London, therefore, the French demanded certain assurances of security against the renascent Germany they and their Allies were contemplating. Such assurances were all the more necessary from the point of view of the French Government because of the insistent attacks made on the programs and policies under discussion at London by the French Communist Party and General Charles de Gaulle and his Rally of the French People. Fortunately the power of both the Communists and of De Gaulle's followers had declined during the winter. The French delegation were able to proceed, albeit warily, with the Americans and British toward a West German State.

It is not my intention to follow these negotiations in London, since they contributed little to the making of United States policy on Germany. The broad policy, the construction of a federal state out of the three western zones of Germany, had been decided when it was discovered at the Moscow and confirmed at the London meeting of the Council of Foreign Ministers that the price asked by the Russians for unity was much too high.

But the agreement reached in London was of the utmost importance for it marked the precise formulation of that policy, modified by the wishes of the British, French, Dutch, Belgians and Luxembourgers. It seemed to me then, and still does, that given the refusal of the Russians to agree to unity on any terms but their own, the agreement represents the best possible course open to the west.

To begin with, it associated the Benelux countries in policy regarding Germany. Thus three countries which had suffered in various degrees from German aggression were included in policy making. It might have been prudent to invite the Danes, who also have a common frontier with Germany, to the meeting, but this was not done.

The recommendations agreed to in London and submitted to the governments concerned placed the maximum emphasis on the role of the German economy in the European economy. On April 16 the Combined Zone (British and American) and the French Zone had been included in the Organization for European Economic Co-operation, ensuring, it was hoped, close co-ordination between the trizonal area and the economy of western Europe.

Equally important was that the six nations, after years of futile talk, finally did something about the Ruhr. They agreed to recommend the establishment of an international authority for the control of the Ruhr in which the six countries would participate with Germany but which would not involve the political separation of the Ruhr area from Germany.

This last in itself was a considerable victory over the more extreme views of some French circles which had sought, since before the end of the war, the political separation of the Ruhr from the remainder of Germany. It also marked the final disappearance from American policy of the Morgenthau Plan's drastic provisions for the Ruhr.

In the establishment of the international authority, control of the distribution of coal, coke and steel of the Ruhr was contemplated, to prevent the industrial concentration of the area from again becoming an instrument of aggression, and to make certain that the Ruhr would contribute to all the countries participating in the European economic program, including of course Germany itself.

Out of these recommendations came the International Authority for the Ruhr announced in December of 1948.

The political recommendations of the six Powers centered around the construction of a German federal republic. The German people in the different states of the west, it was recommended, "should now be free to establish for themselves the political organization and institutions which will enable them to assume those governmental responsibilities which are compatible with the minimum requirements of occupation and control and which ultimately will enable them to assume full governmental responsibilities."

The Military Governors of the three western zones were instructed to meet with the Ministers-President of the zones and authorize the latter to convene a Constituent Assembly for the preparation of a constitution to be approved by the participating states. The selection of the delegates to this assembly was to be in accordance with the wishes of the *Landtags* in each state.

Finally the West described the sort of state it had in mind for western Germany: "a federal form of government which adequately protects the rights of the respective states, and which at the same time provides for adequate central authority and which guarantees the rights and freedoms of the individual."

A constitution which did not conflict with these general principles was to be approved by the Military Governors and submitted for ratification to the respective *Länder* of western Germany.

This recommendation is the principal fruit of the conference. But the organization of the proposed state was beset by many difficulties. Partly these were the outcome of the differences between the leading German political parties, but partly they were due to the size and intricacy of the task set by the Americans, British and French at London when they agreed to take measures to co-ordinate the economic policies and practices in the Combined Zone and the French Zone.

The long series of meetings on the measures to achieve this co-ordination provided an attractive opportunity for those French who had always been lukewarm toward the construction of the German federal republic to delay its birth. For the emergence of the new state did not depend on the writing of the constitution alone, it depended on the co-ordination of Western occupation policies, on the writing of an Occupation Statute delimiting the powers of the new German government and of the occupation authorities and finally on the establishment of certain control agencies. In the formulation of these the French negotiators, who included many loyal De Gaullists like General Pierre Koenig, the French Military Governor, moved so slowly that at times progress was not discernible.

Their basic dislike of a West German State and their loyalty to De Gaulle were sharpened by another factor: the economic recovery of western Germany. This began soon after the introduction of a new and more valuable currency in western Germany on June 21, 1948. Coal production, the basis of industrial recovery, began to rise almost immediately. By the end of 1948 it has bettered 300,000 tons a day in the Bizone alone. This represented a rise of 100,000 tons over the figures of two years before.

Steel production increased, although not quite so fast. The coming of the new money brought farmers into the markets with agricultural produce hitherto hoarded. Goods which had been obtainable only on the black market began to appear. The index of industrial production rose to over 80 per cent of that in 1936.

The French, discerning beyond the frontier the smoke of the industrial Ruhr, naturally were concerned. As each day produced new feats of production, new indications that the old German genius for industrial organization still lived, they became less and less enthusiastic about the establishment of a West German State which would unite, in any form, the restless energy of the Germans. In the period between June of 1948 and March of 1949 when the recovery of the Ruhr was the most important economic fact in Europe, their thoughts turned more and more to the security measures of the London agreement.

The deep-seated apprehension of the French overlooked one important factor in assessing the Ruhr recovery. The currency reform certainly had accelerated this recovery, but it was still a supported economy, maintained by American dollars. In 1948 the United States, for instance, contributed $1,150,000,000 to the German economy.

The security provisions which gripped the attention of the French had been prefaced by the declaration that the American, British and French governments were not ready to put in motion any general withdrawal of occupation forces from Germany "until the peace of Europe is secured." This was and is a fundamental of American policy. The presence of American troops in Germany would involve the United States in a war with the Soviet Union should the Red Army move across Germany to attack France. This reassured some Frenchmen, those who saw the Soviet Union rather than Germany as a potential aggressor. Despite the profound antagonism in France toward the Germans this group is increasing. And of course the declaration also soothed those Frenchmen whose greatest fear is German aggression.

The security measures went much farther, however. To guarantee the maintenance of disarmament and demilitarization, the three Military Governors were instructed to organize a military security board in the western zones of Germany. This board was empowered to make the proper inspections and necessary recommendations to the Military Governors.

The board was established for the period in which the Occupying Powers retain supreme authority in Germany.

It was also agreed that prior to any general withdrawal of the forces of occupation a new agreement was to be negotiated with respect to the necessary measures of demilitarization, disarmament, control of industry and the occupation of key areas. It was also recommended that a system of inspection be instituted to guarantee the maintenance of agreements on Germany's disarmament and demilitarization.

To me, this is the weakest section of the London agreements. It is usually not difficult to reach agreement at international conferences on the broad objectives to be followed.

What is difficult is the working out of the details. And when such details affect the curbing of the Power which twice in our lifetime has overrun Europe and plunged it into a long period of chaos, the omission to work out the details now is a scandalous lack of foresight.

Although the Military Security Board has been organized for the period of occupation—that is, as long as the Western Powers retain the supreme authority—nothing has been done to speed the detailed planning of security after the troops march west.

The final words of the London recommendations took the form of a gesture to the Soviet Union. The recommendations were described as facilitating, rather than precluding, four-Power agreement on the German problem. This statement appears to be based on the reasoning that the Russians would be willing to accept German unity at the Western price, although Russian delegations had spent two meetings of the Council of Foreign Ministers asserting that such unity could come only if the Western Powers knuckled under and accepted the Russian price.

The London recommendations provided the basis for the efforts in the fateful summer and winter of 1948 to establish both the Allied framework for a West German State and the constitution for that state. In them American policy is unquestionably dominant. Let us see how that policy progressed when it encountered the rebirth of German nationalism and the German political parties.

For the last half of 1948 and the first half of 1949 introduced a new factor into western Germany. The increase in industrial production, the rise in living standards and the prospect of once again attaining some form of independent government plus the realization that Germany had a part, and an important one, to play in the East-West struggle compounded to produce a renaissance of German nationalism. Since it occurred at the same time as the revival of industrial output in the Ruhr, it raised grave fears throughout western Europe and in the United States, based on the idea that the new nationalism would use industrial production, as it had been used before, as a weapon of German aggression.

Later we can examine the sources of this nationalism. At the moment it is perhaps prudent to distinguish between the millions of Germans who have a patriotic wish to see Germany prosperous and united again and the intensely nationalist Germans who from the end of 1947 onward saw in the power struggle between the United States and the Soviet Union an opportunity to reassert German sovereignty in Europe and seize the leadership, if not the control, of the western continental countries.

The latter group drew a great deal of attention. People in the United States, who should have known better, wanted to know why so many "big Nazis" were allowed to return to power. Others, egged on by the Communists in the United States and the western European countries, asserted that western Germany was ready or soon would be ready for a war of revenge for the defeat of 1945. In time, it was believed that all Germans with any aspirations for the return of Germany's sovereignty and unity were new Bismarcks and Hitlers planning some fresh aggression.

So great was the outcry that for a considerable period in the winter of 1948-1949 it was feared that sentiment in the United States would interfere with the construction of the West German State. In the uproar the benefits were completely overlooked which the right kind of German nationalism—one British general said it would be called "patriotism in France or

Britain or America"—would bring to a revived Germany. Few Americans in Germany missed the dangers inherent in a revival of the old Hitlerian nationalism; that has always been evident. But men like Generals Clay and Robertson and Ambassador Murphy knew that Germany could not continue without political hope and that the Germans who looked forward to the day when their country would be prosperous and united again were a form of insurance against such a revival.

When this nationalism was expressed by political parties, however, it became, in the eyes of the chiefs of American and British Military Government, a real danger to the construction of the Western German State. This paradoxical attitude came about because in the formulation of the constitution at Bonn, the Social Democrats, the best organized and most united of the west German political parties, consistently advocated the construction of a fairly strong, centralized republic instead of the federal organization to which the Americans, British and French had agreed on at London.

General Clay, as I have shown, was bitterly antagonistic to the Socialists' formulas for the new Germany. He believed that the tendencies of Dr. Kurt Schumacher, the leader of the Social Democratic Party, were authoritarian and feared that they might block the formation of the Western German State; he felt sure that neither France nor the United States would ever consent to the sort of constitution that Schumacher sought for western Germany.

Thus in the spring of 1949 United States advisers favored the Christian Democratic Union and the Christian Socialist Union and what was termed the "moderate" wing of the Social Democratic Party at Bonn.

The Berlin blockade had an important bearing on the

plans for the West German State. The Minister Presidents of the west German *Länder,* who were at first lukewarm and, in some cases, even hostile, to the construction of that state as long as any opportunity existed for the reunification of Germany, were convinced by the blockade that the Soviet Union would never agree to unification save on terms that meant their own dismissal and the defeat of their policies. Hence from the middle of June 1948 onward they were far more receptive to the idea of the West German State than they were when the recommendations of the London meeting first were announced.

The struggle for Berlin which reached its peak after the imposition of the Berlin blockade has been represented as contributing heavily to the revival of German nationalism. This is true as far as Berlin itself is concerned. There the workers and the housewives who sturdily refused to consider the beguiling Soviet offers of huge but ectoplasmic supplies of bread, potatoes and meat during the long, dreary, but not severe winter of 1948-1949, who put up with shortages of electricity and gas, who arose in the town halls of western Berlin to assail the Russians, with plenty of Communist stool pigeons marking them in the audience, all felt they had reasserted themselves as Germans.

Although in the first months of the blockade their actions were greeted approvingly in western Germany—and undoubtedly in eastern Germany—by the spring of 1949 the blockade had become an expensive bore to large sections of the population in the west.

"It's not our fight," I heard a Bavarian crowd shout in April of that year. "Let the Russians and the Americans worry about it."

Whereas in Berlin the interdependence of Americans, British and French on the one hand and Germans on the other was well understood, in the western zones the extreme nationalists saw in the continued presence of occupation forces only a bridle to their own ambitions.

The new nationalism in its extreme form, grossly exaggerated by some publicists, exerted a delaying effect on Western policy after the publication of the London recommendations. On the other hand the more moderate forms of nationalism helped convince Germans that the path opened by the London meeting afforded them the best chance for the eventual recovery of sovereignty and independence.

In situations such as this there are almost no absolutes. Thus there were extreme nationalists who pushed the construction of a West German State and moderates who clung to the idea of a *modus vivendi* with the Soviet Union which would lead to a united Germany. Nationalism did not bring about a change in United States policy but it affected it strongly. And it taught one lesson: from the spring of 1949 onward after four years of occupation the Germans were again a power in their own land—a confused, divided power, to be sure, but still one capable of moving toward national action in the reassertion of their national identity.

American policy in Germany has come a long way since 1944 when the Morgenthau Plan was something new in international politics. It has been altered by the changing situation in Europe, notably the political struggle between the United States and the Soviet Union. A great number of men from Morgenthau to Clay have affected its growth and mutations.

As this is written the implementation of United States

policy for Germany has reached a punctuation point. The era of punitive military policy is over. The generals and the colonels are departing although, because of Germany's peculiar strategic situation, the armed services will for a long time retain an important voice in the making of future policy for that country. The civilians are coming in to meet the new problems arising from the approach toward sovereignty.

Although it is difficult to present a detailed prediction of how United States policy will develop in the future in Germany it is safe to observe that, as long as the Soviet Union seeks Germany for the furtherance of its ideological and economic plans, United States policy must avoid the creation of a Germany which can be kidnaped into the Communist camp. This means avoiding the establishment of a highly centralized Germany which could be seized by a strong minority group. Equally it means the avoidance of a reactionary Germany, even a decentralized one, which could be beguiled by Soviet promises of unity and strength into throwing its weight to the East.

CHAPTER
SEVEN

OF THE FOUR GOVERNMENTS
which in the summer of 1945 began to grapple with the problems of the German occupation, none was in a more advantageous political position to deal with them than the newly elected Labor Government of Great Britain. In the division of Germany into spheres of occupation, Britain had been given the country's industrial heart. But the great industrial area of North Rhine-Westphalia had another significance. It was also the stronghold in western Germany of the Social Democratic Party of Germany, an organization which ideologically was much closer to the triumphant Socialists in Britain than it was to the Communists of the Soviet Union, the Democrats of the United States or any of the parties which struggled for power in France.

In pre-Hitler days liaison between the British Labor Party and the Social Democrats had been close; there had been an intermingling of the great personages of German and British labor and the trade-union movements. Before and during the war Britain gave asylum to German Social Democrats who had escaped the Hitler regime. A number of them, including Waldemar Von Knoerrigen, the present Social Democratic leader in Bavaria, even worked for the British Government on propaganda directed toward Germany during the war.

In Britain, the new government was pledged to a program of nationalization of industry which was not far different in principle from that suggested in pre-Hitler days by leading German Social Democrats. Many of its leaders, men like Ernest Bevin, were, they boasted, "old trade-union men," who would be expected to appeal personally to the German Social Democrats. In Germany itself, British Military Government at the outset boasted a much better-prepared personnel than that of the other powers. In the American organization for instance there were experts galore on the upper levels, but when one dug deeper into the Military-Government structure one found a great deal of confusion, not only about American plans and policies but about the society to be governed. In the first summer after the war, traveling through the British Zone, I was impressed by the large number of experienced and able men who knew exactly why they had been sent to Germany, exactly what the local problems were and precisely how and where their particular task fitted into the whole job of Military Government.

Britain, it seemed in the summer of 1945, was the best equipped of the Occupation Powers to influence the future political structure of Germany and the only Power which possessed an important ideological alliance with a powerful German political party. The German Communists at this date, although vocal, did not equal the Social Democrats in importance or prestige in either eastern or western Germany.

However, in the ensuing four years, Britain's influence dwindled in Germany as that of the United States rose. There were many reasons for this, but perhaps the most important was the near collapse of the British economy in the winter of 1946-1947. In the economic storm, the Labor Government had all it could do to keep the economy of the home islands going. It could not assume the financial responsibilities involved in the economic revival of the Bizone. Hence although British Military Government officials shared in the administration of the area, the dominant voice in economic policy was that of the United States which was putting up the money.

At the same time, the United States, the most powerful of the three Western Occupation Powers, emerged as their spokesman. At the last three meetings of the Council of Foreign Ministers, the American delegations, in a very real way, led the West.

Such leadership was not obtained, however, by bullying. Since 1946 the British and the United States have been closer on a general policy for Germany than any two of the Occupation Powers. In the beginning of the occupation British policy was judged more lenient to the Germans and the revival of the German economy than that of the United States. The Morgenthau Plan had its adherents in London but they were not members of the Cabinet. In the past three years there have been differences between London and Washington and between Generals Clay and Robertson in Berlin on the implementation of policy but on the whole the two countries have worked amicably together toward the achievement of that policy.

One important difference should be noted. In Germany, British officials have in many cases been far more willing to give the Soviet Union the benefit of the doubt.

There was no less conviction among them that Germany was the key to the East-West struggle for Europe. But, it seems to me, there was always present a willingness to negotiate with the Russians, to listen to the Soviet point of view. This may result from the absence among most British Military Government officials of the almost pathological fear of the Soviet Union, communism and its plans which has animated many American officials both at home and in Germany. It may spring from the great treasure of gratitude which Russia amassed in Britain in 1941 when it sustained the shock of the German onslaught and diverted the Luftwaffe from British to Russian cities. The British, it must be remembered, were the allies of the Soviet Union for a longer time and during conditions of much greater stress than were the Americans.

At the height of the Berlin crisis in the summer of 1948, the British, by far the weaker power, were much less concerned with war and threats of war than the Americans. On the other hand, they appeared willing to negotiate over the Berlin position, a tendency which appeared to General Clay and other Americans sheer madness.

"There is no sense in negotiating the fact that we remain in Berlin," I recall Clay saying. "We are here by right, and right is not subject to negotiation."

British willingness to accelerate the economic recovery of Germany was emphatically stated as long ago as the autumn of 1946. On October 22 of that year Foreign Secretary Bevin, in a review of foreign affairs before the House of Commons, made a series of statements which give an admirable view of British policy for Germany in the period between Potsdam and the breakdown of the London meeting of the Council of Foreign Ministers.

The general British principles enunciated by Bevin included:

(1) The establishment of political conditions which would secure the world against any German reversion to dictatorship or an aggressive policy.

(2) The establishment of economic conditions which would enable the Germans and the outside world to benefit in conditions of peace from German industry and resources.

(3) The establishment of constitutional machinery in Germany for these ends which will be acceptable to the German people and thus likely to be permanent.

"We contemplate a German constitution which would avoid the two extremes of a loose confederation of autonomous states and a military centralized state," Mr. Bevin said. "Certain questions would be exclusively reserved to the center; the regional units would be exclusively competent in all the remaining powers. Allowance would thus be made for local differences in tradition, religion and economic circumstances."

The British had been first to espouse an increase in the level of industrial production in Germany, and the first quadripartite agreement on this subject, reached in Berlin in January of 1946, represented a compromise between the British figure and the Russian figure. The level of industry is anchored to the level of steel production. In Berlin, the British sought an annual production of 10,500,000 ingot tons of steel a year while the Russians wished production limited to 3,000,000 tons. A compromise figure of 5,800,000 tons, put forward by General Clay and Ambassador Robert D. Murphy, finally was accepted.

At the Paris meeting of the Council of Foreign Ministers early in 1946 the British delegation, led by Mr. Bevin, proposed that annual steel production be raised to 11,000,000 tons.

"We met with strenuous opposition," the Foreign Secretary later told the House of Commons, "and the figure was left at 7,500,000 tons.

"However, the facts have proved that our estimate was right if the devastation in Germany is to be dealt with."

Furthermore Bevin told the House that Germany must become self-supporting as quickly as possible, more coal must be produced and kept in Germany and German industry should be free to expand subject to a measure of international control. But, he added, "active" support should be given to the German plans for the socialization of the country's basic industries.

On the whole, this was a much bolder attitude toward German recovery than any taken in public by American statesmen up to that time. The necessity for German economic recovery was clear enough to men like General Clay and Ambassador Murphy, but a public proposal to this end appeared to be political dynamite.

Almost from the end of the war the British have been deeply concerned with the prospect that Germany might form what Mr. Bevin once called "a depressed area in the center of Europe."

"If we allow this to happen," he said shortly before the Moscow conference, "and there is not a reasonable standard of life, it may drag down all the standards of other countries, and what is worse, may well prevent the recovery of many. On the other hand, we have to provide for the security of Europe, and I am not yet sure whether, even after two wars and two defeats, the Germans really recognize the effects of defeat and the stupidity of war as an object of policy. . . .

"While there is a lot of talk about Eastern and Western Powers, I am obsessed, above all else, by the possibility of those major Powers having differences which might result in the resurgence of Germany."

The above does a good deal to illuminate British policy for Germany. Today as then, Britain does not want a poor Germany which would be a drag on the economic standards of Europe. But it does not want a Germany so strong that it can again threaten the security of Europe, which in this air age includes Britain. Above all Britain does not want a Germany which can benefit from the division between East and West.

The British Foreign Office never went so far as the Morgenthau Plan or the Germanophobes of the Quai d'Orsay in considering the territorial dismemberment of Germany. The view of the Labor Government has been that the best way to get a democratic and peaceful Germany is to form a decentralized state with a minimum of power vested in the central government and with the bulk of the powers held by the states.

Mr. Bevin himself has always been a strong opponent of the idea that a more centralized government in Germany would be easier to control. His opposition springs from his own journeyings to Germany after the first World War.

From the outset the Labor Cabinet devoted a great deal of consideration to the problem of the Ruhr. It opposed the view put forward by the French when first they were admitted to the councils of the Occupying Powers that the Ruhr be separated permanently from the remainder of Germany in order to win security from future aggression. In 1946 Bevin's view was that the "creation of a separate province under international control, to be fitted ultimately into a federal Germany" might be a better safeguard. Here again we find the British, at this period (October 1946) at any rate, thinking ahead of the Americans. At that time, although General Clay and a number of his subordinates already were opposed to any separation of the Ruhr from the remainder of Germany, it was obvious that State Department thinking had not yet hardened on the subject.

British policy always has emphasized the necessity of creating economic unity in Germany. Russian refusal to agree to the measures necessary for such unity has been the basic cause for the British, as opposed to the American, division with the Soviet Union over Germany. As I have pointed out, the British, both in Whitehall and Berlin, never were as concerned over Russian domination of Germany as the Americans because they did not think the German Communists were strong enough to achieve it even if political unity was attained. But they were concerned in their difficult economic position with the failure to achieve economic unity, and time and again Mr. Bevin charged the Russians with breaking their pledge in the Potsdam Agreement.

The provision for economic unity in Potsdam is "unqualified, unconditional and unambiguous," said a British note sent to the United States, the Soviet Union and France in August of 1946.

"It is a fundamental principle of the Potsdam Agreement that during the occupation Germany shall be treated as an economic whole. The Agreement states that common policies shall be established in regard to import and export programmes for Germany *as a whole,* and that one of the purposes for which Allied controls shall be imposed upon the German economy is in order to ensure the equitable distribution of essential commodities between the several zones so as to produce a balanced economy throughout Germany and reduce the need for imports."

In this same statement, the British flatly rejected the Soviet reparations claims, a rejection which Mr. Bevin's rumbling baritone was to echo across the green baize tables of three subsequent meetings of the Council of Foreign Ministers.

"His Majesty's Government have never accepted the Soviet claim to ten billion dollars' worth of reparations from Germany," the statement said. "They refused at the Yalta Conference to consider this claim as a basis for discussion, and in any case the Reparations Agreement reached at Potsdam supersedes all previous agreements and discussions about reparations."

Up until the winter of 1946-1947, the British policy in Germany appeared the clearest and most popular with the Germans of the four. The British advocated the restoration of the German economy earlier than the United States. They opposed the Soviet reparations grab from the start, which was at Yalta. Although they sought a decentralized Germany they did not seek, as the French did, to separate the Ruhr permanently. In general, Military Government in the British Zone was competent and sagacious.

In that period Britain was in every way a full partner with the United States in the western occupation zones. When the British Government accepted the United States offer for the economic fusion of their zones in July of 1946, it did so as an equal partner. Even then, however, the budgetary expenditure in Germany was causing some concern. In that year it was around £80,000,000.

The original agreement for the fusion signed in New York by Mr. Bevin and Secretary of State Byrnes provided that from January 1, 1947, the two zones should be treated as a single area for all economic purposes. German administrative agencies for this end should be set up under joint U. S.-U. K. control. A Joint Export-Import Agency was to be organized to take initial responsibility for foreign trade. And the American and British governments should become responsible on an equal basis for costs of approved exports brought into Germany after December 31, 1946, insofar as they could not be paid for from other sources.

A supplementary agreement establishing the machinery for the closer economic integration of the two zones was signed in Berlin on May 29, 1947. This provided for the establishment of a German Economic Council composed of members nominated by the states of the two zones on the basis of population and proportionate to the party strength. This council was established to formulate proposals on general economic policy for the approval of a Bipartite Board composed of members of the two Military Governments, American and British. The Germans also were asked to form an executive committee representing the *Länder* and assuming day-to-day responsibility for the co-ordination and supervision of the work of the bizonal economic agencies.

For the first two years of the occupation we saw Britain bearing an equal share with the United States both in the making of policy and the costs of the occupation. But from late 1947 onward, Britain began to yield some of its influence on political and economic policy making in Germany. In September of that year the British Government notified the United States that the dollar shortage would make it impossible for Britain to continue the 1946 agreement sharing costs in western Germany. After negotiation, the two countries on December 17, 1947, signed a new agreement under which the United States undertook to finance virtually the entire cost of the British-American bizonal area and thus assumed an additional liability of about $400,000,000 a year.

In return, the United States gained the dominant voice over exports and imports in Bizonia. A State Department statement at the time declared that the agreement "provides with respect to two of the principal bipartite agencies responsible for economic affairs, for United States control commensurate with the larger financial undertaking of the United States."

The two agencies are the Joint Export-Import Agency, which handles the external economic affairs of the two zones, and the Joint Foreign Exchange Agency which deals with foreign accounts and the finances of the various economic agencies.

The agreement did not mean the end of British expenditure in Bizonia. It stipulated that Britain contribute $70,000,000 worth of goods and services obtained from sterling-area sources in 1948, and a further commitment of $17,000,000 in sterling for additional supplies if they were available from sterling-area sources was included.

Britain also was required to contribute about $18,000,000 in goods and services and about $16,000,000 in sterling toward the financing of bizonal operations in 1947. The total cost per annum of the bizonal operations was estimated then— this was before economic recovery had begun in western Germany—at close to one billion dollars.

The economic recovery in western Germany which set in after the currency reform of June 1948 was accompanied by a real measure of economic recovery in Britain. The British, although they welcomed the American assumption of the dollar burden in 1947, had never been wholly pleased with the dominant-voice formula which the United States had gained in return.

Hence, when in March of 1949 the American, British and

French began belatedly to try to complete a Trizonal Fusion Agreement, one of the prerequisites of the West German State, it was found that strong opposition was developing in the Foreign Office to American retention of control of the Joint Export-Import Agency and the Joint Foreign Exchange Agency.

At talks in London, the British delegation presented a complicated new plan under which United States control would be drastically reduced. This was rejected by the American delegation which argued that as long as the United States provides the bulk of the funds it must continue to exercise its control of these agencies even when the bizonal organization gives way to a trizonal organization.

The British, however, argued that the powers of the United States Military Governor now are limited to those powers reserved to all three Western Military Governors under the London Agreement of June 1948. This document says the Military Governor has the right only to "exercise minimum control over German foreign trade, over internal policies and measures which would adversely affect foreign trade, necessary to ensure respect by the German authorities for the obligations entered into by the Occupation Powers in regard to Germany and the proper use of funds made available in Germany."

The British also argue against any measures which will give the trizonal Military Government organizations, American, British and French, any right to intervene at the state level or lower in the British Zone of Occupation.

In these talks the British also indicated they intend to protect the continuation of their present Military Government organization, numerically the largest of the three maintained by the Western Powers.

I have examined this part of the British picture in Germany in detail because, to me, it reflects a reassertion of British independent policy in Germany. As long as the United States continues to pay the bill for western Germany, it will be difficult for the British to achieve any large measure of economic control. But Britain may be able to make a greater financial contribution and this, and probably this alone, would affect the dominant-voice formula.

Moreover, the British showed in these talks that they intend to maintain their apparatus of Military Government in the British Zone, a development which certainly will not simplify the problems of either the Allied Trizonal Administration or the government of the proposed German Federal Republic. But it will maintain British influence over Germany's economic heart long after American and French influence in the economically less important American and French zones has dwindled. It is altogether possible then that in the West German State, the ubiquitous British will sustain and even increase their influence over their zone even though that influence has not been accompanied since 1947 by any real financial control of the zone's foreign trade.

As I have indicated, the British position at the Moscow and London meetings of the Council of Foreign Ministers was overshadowed by the Americans. This was true, although perhaps to a lesser extent, at the meeting in Paris in the late spring of 1949. But it should not be regarded as a constant condition. As Britain's economic position revives, so will her international influence revive. And in five years it may be Britain, not the United States, which will wield the greatest political power in Germany.

A great deal will depend on the outcome of the next British General Election. Since early in 1949, the Labor Government has been paying close attention to the Social Democratic Party in western Germany.

Herbert Morrison, Lord President of the Council and one of the ablest brains in the Labor Party, made the long pilgrimage to Hannover in the spring of 1949 to talk to Dr. Kurt Schumacher, the head of the German party. Since Mr. Morrison's visit coincided with the most heated period of the party squabble between the Social Democrats and the Christian Democrats over the constitution for the West German State, it was believed by many Americans that the two Socialists were acting together to forward the interests of their ideology. Actually nothing of the kind happened at the meeting. Mr. Morrison, who is a pretty fair talker himself, hardly got a word in edgewise but sat and listened to a long harangue by Dr. Schumacher on almost every facet of the German question.

A constant stream of minor officials of the British Labor Party, Labor Members of Parliament and authors and writers flows from London to western Germany. If, as some believe, the Social Democrats become the dominant party in the proposed German Federal Republic, their ties with the Labor Party in Britain will be extremely strong.

Parallel to this development, however, is the undoubted affinity between many of the leading industrialists of the British Zone of Occupation and some of the British officers in Military Government there. It is not only from American officers that one will hear high praise of the ability, industry and political innocence of the German managerial class.

The British, it would seem, are preparing for either a Social Democratic or a Christian Democratic victory in the German Federal Republic.

The American visiting the British Zone carries away one strong impression. The British there do not feel, as so many Americans do, that their country is in a permanent decline. This is true not only of the many members of the Labor Party who have found jobs in Germany but of Liberal and Conservative Military Government officials as well.

"Sixty years ago when we had the money and sea power, we didn't worry much about ideas," a young transport expert told me in the Ruhr. "Now we have neither money nor power, but we've got ideas. And ideas will win this battle in Germany, not money or power. Of course I'm a Socialist, but even if I were not, I think I'd have come to the conclusion that the only idea that will beat Communism here is Socialism. Suppose it goes the other way, suppose the same sort of people that ran Germany in the prewar years get back. What political idea do you have then? And you have to have a political idea to beat the Communists. The 'mixture as before' won't do."

This is the sort of argument one hears often in the British Zone. It is important in that it reveals why the British are confident politically and why they foresee a renaissance of their influence in Germany.

2

When in 1945 the French hoisted the tricolor to the top of the Sieges Säule, which proclaims the German victory of 1870, on the Charlottenberger Chausee in Berlin, they were proclaiming not only France's part in the victory over the ancient enemy but France's intention to play an important part in the making of policy for Germany. In the years since then, France indeed has played an important role, although in doing so she has antagonized many American and British Military Government officials in Germany and, perhaps equally important, produced fear and contempt among the Germans.

At the moment, the French concern for what the Germans think and feel is at a minimum. For four years, the French have been determined that what happened in 1870, in 1914 and in 1939 will never happen again.

In the gloomy winter of 1940-1941 in London, the British used to speculate what they would do with Germany when the war was over. (It is symptomatic of the spirit of the times that no one ever was interested in discussing what the Germans would do with Britain.) All sorts of theories were advanced and gravely discussed by the newspapers and over the air.

A French officer whom I knew was always infuriated by these discussions.

"For these English it is still an intellectual discussion," he said. "Even with London burning. For us, for the French, the future of Germany is a matter of life and death."

His words, I think, may be taken as the guiding principle for French policy toward Germany in 1945, 1946, 1947, 1948 and the first months of 1949. In the spring of 1949 a slight softening of French policy toward Germany was evident. Whether this is permanent or only a transitory phase it is difficult to say. At any rate it does not eliminate from the minds of the French the basic premise that Germany is the enemy.

This belief naturally put the French policy makers and Military Government officials at odds with the Americans and British after 1946, when the military and political menace of the Soviet Union emerged. The French do accept Russia as a danger. But in contemplating that danger, they do not wish to overlook the, to them, greater danger of Germany.

During the Paris meeting of the Council of Foreign Ministers in the late spring of 1949, a Frenchman expressed this attitude admirably.

"I am a bourgeois of the bourgeoisie," he said. "I hate the Germans and I hate the Russians. But I am old enough to remember that after the first World War the politicians said 'beware of the Bolsheviks' and talked about the Red terror and when we woke up it was German and not Russian armies that marched into Paris.

"You Americans are right in being concerned with the Russians. But do not let your concern blind you to what the Germans will do if you let them. If Germany is united again, that is the time to reinforce your army."

The strength of the French fear of Germany is demonstrated by the fact that even after the partition of Germany enforced by the failure of the London meeting of the Council of Foreign Ministers, this fear was as vivid as ever. French opposition to a centralized West German State was as great as if that state would comprise all Germany. For to France forty-five or fifty million Germans in a West German State are almost as big a menace as sixty or seventy million in a united Germany.

The menace is not only military and political, it is economic as well. No nation in Europe regarded the economic revival of western Germany in the summer of 1948 with greater distaste than the French. For although France was

obtaining a healthy share of the Ruhr's coal output and had
won economic control of the Saar and that area's economic
integration into the French economy, the French saw in the
German revival a real threat to their own economic position.

When it was suggested that the German revival was in the
interest of France and all western Europe, the French answer
was that this was only a temporary interest and that the long-
term effect of the revival even in a partitioned Germany
would be to enable that country once more to achieve the
economic domination of western Europe and, once political
unity is achieved, political domination as well.

The effect of this French attitude on popular opinion in
western Germany has been to produce both fear and contempt. Save in Bavaria, there is a strong feeling that France
will do everything it can to repress German revival, economic
and political, and that the objective of French policy is to
maintain Germany on a colonial status, a belief which the
Communists do their best to foster.

"Look what the French have done already," said a German
in Bochum. "They've got the Saar. They get a lot of Ruhr
coal which could heat German homes. My brother says
they've stripped their zone almost as badly as the Russians
have stripped the east zone. And if they ever get control of
the Ruhr, they'll ruin it."

At the same time this man and many other miners and
steelworkers with whom I talked during the winter of 1948-
1949 exhibited a healthy contempt for the French.

"Here we are, living in ruins with years of work before we
can even clear away the debris," said one miner, "and the
French keep telling the Americans and the British to beware
of us. If they're frightened of us, why don't they make France
strong?

"Anyhow, they're confusing people like us with the Nazis and the rest. My God, we don't want any more war! And we don't want any more Hitlers. Maybe there are Germans who do. But when we workers get control we'll finish them."

What does France want in Germany and for Germany? What is the French policy which has developed out of the national desire to settle once and for all the German question? In the political field, France seeks the slow establishment in Germany of a loose political confederation in which sectional rather than national policies will be developed.

The objective is a divided Germany and a prolonged occupation during which all important powers will be held by the Occupying Nations. And French economic policy for Germany complements this aim. The French were among the most enthusiastic supporters of the Morgenthau Plan. They sought to lop off the Ruhr from the rest of Germany, adding economic to political decentralization. And they have objected almost since the beginning of the occupation to anything which might tend to increase German production.

This French policy at the outset was close in some respects to what American planners in Washington aimed at achieving in Germany. But when the United States and the United Kingdom began to consider the economic revival of western Germany and the establishment of a West German State, they ran into prolonged and tenacious opposition from the French. For theirs was and is a policy that conflicts with the basic French view on Germany and it is this conflict which is at the bottom of the long Franco-American debate on Germany.

In the six-Power conference at London in the spring of 1948 the French gave only grudging consent to the establishment of a West German State. On a number of occasions they delayed the negotiations for a trizonal fusion arrangement, a prerequisite for the establishment of that state, and even after the American, British and French governments had announced, in April of 1949, that they had reached complete agreement on Germany in their talks in Washington, the French sought to limit the powers of the west German government and retain a veto power for themselves in the projected trizonal fusion.

Both American and British intelligence sources in western Germany frequently have assured me they suspect that French influence and perhaps money are behind the various separatist movements. I know that a number of American Military Government officials are convinced that the French support the Bavarian Party, a group which seeks Bavarian separatism. Such separatism if carried to its avowed objective of a semi-independent Bavarian state would suit the French policy for a weakened, divided Germany.

The center of the conflict between French and American policy on Germany is the Ruhr. The Ruhr to the French is not only an industrial arsenal which thrice has armed Germany for attacks on France, it is also—and this is important to a country struggling to recover its economic health—the strongest industrial competitor to France in Europe. The French insistence on Germany's continued industrial inferiority is not compounded entirely of military fears. Like the British, although to a much greater extent, the French fear German competition in world markets and even a future influx into France of cheap German-made consumer goods. Some sort of control of the Ruhr is necessary in the French view not only for France's political security but her economic well-being as well.

"We failed to take over the Ruhr in 1918 and look what

happened," General Ganeval, the French commandant in Berlin once told me. "We had better not fail to win control of the Ruhr this time. It may be our last chance."

Granted these basic French objectives in Germany, it can be seen why the conflict between France and the United States deepened when the French learned of the directive of the United States Government sent to General Clay in the summer of 1947. Clay, incidentally, became the focus of French attacks for the policy which he carried out, so much so that the French gave the impression that the general was making policy as he went along rather than acting on a directive.

This directive of July 15, 1947, naturally aroused the French fears of German recovery.

On the subject of German self-government it said: "You [Clay] will continue to promote the development in Germany of institutions of popular self-government and the assumption of direct responsibility by German governmental agencies, assuring them legislative, judicial and executive powers, consistent with military security and the purposes of the occupation.

"It is the view of your government that the most constructive development of German political life would be in the establishment throughout Germany of Federal German States *(Länder)* and the formation of a Central German Government with carefully defined and limited powers and function. All powers shall be vested in the *Länder* except such as are expressly delegated to the Central Government."

In outlining United States policy toward Germany the directive said: "An orderly and prosperous Europe requires the economic contributions of a stable and productive Germany as well as the necessary restraints to insure that Germany is not allowed to revive its destructive militarism."

Finally in setting forth general economic objectives, the directive said that one of these was "to encourage the German people to rebuild a self-supporting state devoted to peaceful purposes, integrated into the economy of Europe.

"Although the economic rehabilitation of Germany, within the framework of these objectives, is the task and responsibility of the German people, you should provide them with general policy guidance, assist in the development of a balanced foreign trade and ensure that German efforts are consistent with, and contribute to the fulfillment of your government's objectives."

It is safe to say that no Frenchman reading these words would be much concerned with the mention of "necessary restraints" or the provision "there should be no relaxation of effort to complete and effectively to maintain the disarmament and demilitarization of Germany." What would impress and worry him is the references to "economic rehabilitation" and "a stable and productive Germany."

Since the Ruhr is the most important industrial area, the French delaying action against American policy centered around it. The Ruhr presented a dual problem: it had to be controlled but it also had to be productive. Moreover, beyond these pressing, immediate needs loomed the greater problem of the future ownership of the Ruhr's industrial plants and coal fields. This is not entirely a German matter. Stockholders in the great industrial plants of the area include Americans, Britons, Frenchmen, Dutch and Swedes.

As General Clay saw it, the task was to organize the Ruhr in such a way that, although German industrial rearmament would be prevented, the area would produce the coal, coke, iron and steel needed in Germany if the economy were to revive and the heavy load be lifted from the back of the American taxpayer. At the same time, he believed that the foreign investment would have to be safeguarded and some future form of ownership decided.

Such views were in direct contradiction to those held by the French. From the start of the occupation, indeed even before the end of the war, the French sought the complete political separation of the Ruhr from Germany and its control by an international body in which the Germans would have little or no voice.

The principal argument for such a procedure advanced by its advocates in France was that once the Ruhr was separated from Germany that country, having lost Silesia to the Poles, and the Saar to the French, never would be powerful enough to begin another European war. The counterarguments were first that the separation of the Ruhr from Germany would limit production there and create a political situation in which the return of the Ruhr to Germany would be the basis for a strong nationalist movement. Furthermore, it was argued, the Soviet Union in its drive to win domination of Germany would be aided toward that objective if it promised the reintegration of the Ruhr into Germany once a Communist government was established.

During the six-Power negotiations in London in the spring of 1948, the French fought American and British plans for the Ruhr. The conference recommendations accepted the trizonal organization of western Germany and the ultimate establishment of some sort of west German state and a limited revival of Ruhr industry under the control of the six Powers. But the final ownership of the Ruhr was not discussed. This omission raised grave doubts and sharp questioning in the French Assembly where, after heated debate, the London recommendations were passed although the French reserved their position on some questions.

During the summer of 1948, the American and British Military Government economic experts began the preparation of a plan setting up a trusteeship for the Ruhr's industries. This plan was fought skillfully by General Joseph-Pierre Koenig, the French Military Governor, who objected strenuously to the provision that the final ownership of the coal, iron and steel industries should be left to a "representative, freely elected German government" and who demanded that the French be given full participation in the control agencies in the Ruhr.

The main point of the French objections was the future-ownership clause which says in full:

In the first place the Military Governors wish to make it clear that the restoration of a pattern of ownership in these industries which would constitute an excessive concentration of economic power will not be allowed. Nor will the return to positions of ownership and control of those individuals who permitted and encouraged the aggressive designs of the National Socialist party be permitted. Secondly the Board considers the question of socialization to be one that is properly within the competence of a representative, freely elected German government, the sovereignty of which may extend over the whole of Germany or may be confined to Western Germany only. Accordingly the Board will not take any action in regard to the coal and iron and steel industries in the Combined Area which will prejudice a decision by such future German government as to the pattern of ownership to be established for those industries. At such a time as a representative, freely elected government either for Germany as a whole or Western Germany alone is constituted it shall be at liberty to resolve this question within the limitations of military government policy already expressed.

The wording of the clause represented a British proposal. The British Government, as I have pointed out, expects a Socialist government in Germany in the future. Being Socialists themselves, they regard socialization of the Ruhr as a necessary step for Germany and for the peace of the world. They argued successfully that a future German government be allowed to decide the ownership of the Ruhr's industries.

Despite pressure from the French and some uneasiness on the part of the State Department, the British insistence that the wording remain unchanged was accepted.

The French request that its Military Government officials be admitted immediately into the control agencies such as the U. S.-U. K. Coal Control Group in Essen was met by the Anglo-American rejoinder that once the fusion between the French Zone of Occupation and the American and British Zones of Occupation was completed, the French automatically would join the control agencies.

When the trusteeship plan, officially entitled Law No. 75 for "The Reorganization of German Coal and Iron and Steel Industries," was announced, the French made the most energetic protests. These were based on the claim that the French had received no prior notification of the new plan. The fact was that General Koenig had been kept informed by Generals Clay and Robertson throughout and that it was the French Military Governor's objections which had delayed completion of the plan so long.

So great was the French outcry that in the end the State Department gave way. French officials were allowed to join the control agencies in the Ruhr although no pressure was put on the French Military Government to speed the fusion of the French Zone with the Anglo-American Bizone. And French Foreign Minister Schuman in a speech asserted France's intention to insist on a veto power in the trizonal military-governmental organization which must exist in western Germany before the German Federal Republic is established.

Law No. 75 was followed in December by the announcement of a new control, the International Authority for the Ruhr. This Authority seeks to permit German recovery while at the same time assuring that the resources of the area will be used for the good of Germany and Europe and not to enable Germany to become again an aggressor nation.

Basically the Authority represents the maximum that the French policy could obtain in the control of the Ruhr. In many respects, it is more harsh than either the American or British economic experts wished. In any case it is worthy of examination as the primary control instrument in Germany. And just as the Power that controls Germany controls central Europe, so the Power or group of Powers that controls the Ruhr controls Germany.

The agreement establishing this Authority was announced in London on December 28, 1948, after a series of meetings in which representatives of Belgium, France, Luxembourg, the Netherlands, the United Kingdom and the United States had drafted a detailed agreement establishing this Authority in accordance with the provisions made in the London Agreement of June 2, 1948.

It should be emphasized that the Authority, although the most important control agreement of the Western Powers for the reasons outlined above, is not the only such agreement. There are others all aimed at assuring the disarmament of Germany, the furtherance of recovery in Europe, the establishment of a democratic Germany and the promotion of economic co-operation between the countries of western Europe —objectives that the United States, Britain and France all regard as the best basis for a healthy economy, which in turn is the primary defense against Communism.

Among the other arrangements for preventing aggression is the Military Security Board which is designed to co-operate with the Ruhr Authority. This board is to have general responsibility for the maintenance of disarmament and demilitarization in the interests of security. But as regards industrial disarmament, a far more important field than counting the number of soldiers and officers in Germany, the board is to act in accordance with the Western Powers' agreements on prohibitions and limitations on German industry published in April of 1949.

The International Authority for the Ruhr and the Military Security Board thus are intended to provide the safeguards under which a peaceful, democratic Germany may be reintroduced to the European community and play its part in that society as a responsible and independent member. The Ruhr Authority specifically is intended to ensure that the resources of that area are to be used solely in the interests of peace and the promotion of economic recovery. Such are the objectives of this important piece of international planning.

One of the principal functions, perhaps the most important function, of the Ruhr Authority is to make a division of the coke and steel from the Ruhr between German consumption and export. It is hoped that this will provide adequate access to these raw materials for countries of western Europe, notably France, and at the same time give the German economy enough to continue its rehabilitation. In this provision there is a French victory. France has won the right to draw a continued flow of much-needed raw materials from its ancient enemy and thus can be assured that all the Ruhr's resources are not being husbanded for the purpose of German aggression.

The functions of the Ruhr Authority in this field are coordinated with the larger operations of the O.E.E.C. in its work of promoting the economic rehabilitation of the countries participating in the European Recovery Program.

The Ruhr Authority has the right to ensure that the German authorities do not allow artificial or discriminatory transport, trade and price practices, quotas, tariffs and similar governmental measures or commercial arrangements which would distort the movement of Ruhr coal, coke and steel in international trade.

The agreement on the Authority foresaw that although within the period of occupation its decisions will be carried out largely by the occupation authorities—that is, Military Government or its successor—after the occupation period it will have to deal mainly with the German government. Then will come the period, incidentally, when the greatest friction is expected to develop over the Authority; just as similar friction will mount between the Germans and the Western Powers on all other means of control in Germany.

The Authority is charged with responsibility for safeguarding foreign interests in the coal, coke and steel industries of the Ruhr in conformity with international agree-ments.

Supervision over Ruhr industry is the guts of the Ruhr problem. In writing the agreement which established the Authority, special attention was paid to this. The coal and steel authorities previously established by the United States and the United Kingdom for the Bizone had extensive pow-ers over these two industries when the Authority was set up. Their powers extended over production, investment, develop-ment, management and direction. During the negotiations for the establishment of the Authority, French officials were integrated into these control agencies. It was also agreed that those supervisory powers of these agencies which the six Nations considered necessary to achieve their objectives of security and economic well-being in Europe would be trans-ferred to the Ruhr Authority, the Military Security Board or its eventual successor or to some international authority.

The weakness of this provision is that detailed plans have not been made for the form and scope of the successor of the Military Security Board after the period of occupation ends.

The powers now exercised by the steel and coal control agencies are to be transferred to the International Authority for the Ruhr or the Military Security Board or some other international body, if the six Nations consider this necessary for the security and well-being of Europe. These powers would include supervision over production, investment and development but would not be powers of detailed control. The six-Power communiqué on the Ruhr Authority said that detailed control "would unduly interfere with normal and regular responsibilities of management," a statement with which many will disagree. In the view of many Frenchmen, for instance, it was the Allied reluctance after the first World War to interfere with the day-to-day transactions of German industry that enabled it to lay the long-range plans which led to rearmament.

Those powers of supervision to be transferred to the Authority by existing Military Government agencies, notably the coal and steel control groups, are to be adequate to prevent the revival of excessive economic concentration in the coal, coke or steel industries of the Ruhr. Moreover, the six Powers pledged themselves to prevent the old owners of the coal fields and steel plants of the area from acquiring ownership interests or positions of direction and management in those industries. When we take a final look at the Germany of today we will see to what extent this pledge has been kept.

Perhaps the weakest part of the agreement on the Ruhr Authority is the admission, made in a subsequent communiqué, that the agenda of the meeting did not include the question of the final ownership of the industries concerned. This proved unsatisfactory to the German Socialists, who believe that until the Ruhr is socialized Germany and the world will have no security against the rise of new Krupps and Thyssens; unsatisfactory to the French, who feel that any German ownership, national or individual, is a danger to them and strongly oppose the trusteeship idea of Law No. 75; and unsatisfactory to millions of Americans and Britons, who regard the permanent exclusion of the old ruling families of the Ruhr as essential to peace in Europe.

The men who established the International Authority for the Ruhr knew its imperfections and knew that they would be criticized for them. As one of them said, "It's not perfect, nothing ever is, but I think it is a reasonable safeguard.

"Like all such safeguards it depends ultimately on the good will and resolution of those who must carry it out. And by that I do not mean only the Germans."

The communiqué stipulated that "when a German government is established"—by which, presumably, it meant a government for a West German State—it will have the opportunity of acceding to the agreement. In the meanwhile the vote for Germany on the Authority's council will be exercised by the occupation authorities. When a German government has undertaken the full obligations of its membership, it will enjoy full voting rights except in matters of security and default.

The Authority itself consists of a council composed of representatives of the six governments which signed the agreement and, ultimately, of the German Federal Republic, if—and it may be a big if—that state accedes to the agreement.

The voting rights of the members of the Authority on the Council are: the United States, three votes; the United Kingdom, three votes; France, three votes; Germany, three votes; Belgium, Luxembourg and the Netherlands, one vote each.

Eight favorable votes are to be sufficient for every decision of the Authority save in three instances where matters of the maximum importance are under discussion. For instance the Authority may make an allocation of pig iron for export if at any time it decides by twelve affirmative votes that such an allocation is necessary in order to ensure adequate access to supplies for other European nations.

Article 18 of the agreement looks forward to the real question of the future of the Ruhr, the control of that area in the period after the Occupation Forces have been withdrawn and Germany is moving toward something approaching her old position in the world. The Article states:

(a) At the end of the Control Period, or at such earlier time as may be agreed upon by the Occupying Powers, such of the existing powers of the Occupation Authorities as are necessary to ensure:

(i) that there shall not be allowed to develop, or be restored, any pattern of ownership in the Ruhr coal, coke or steel industries, or trade and marketing agreements among such industries, which would constitute excessive concentration of economic power;

(ii) that persons who have been, or may be, found to have furthered the aggressive designs of the National Socialist Party do not hold positions of ownership or control in the Ruhr coal, coke or steel industries or the trade and marketing organizations of such industries; and

(iii) that adequate information is made available for the purposes specified in sub-paragraphs (i) and (ii) above, will be transferred to the Authority or to the Military Security Board or its successor or to some other body created by international agreement and charged with ensuring the achievement of these objectives with respect to these and other industries in Germany. The Authority shall co-operate with any other body to which such powers may be transferred.

The Authority's ability to check German industrial rearmament is bolstered by the provision, in Article 20, of its right to obtain reports on production, distribution and consumption of coal, coke and steel and "to make any investigations, including the examination of witnesses, which it considers necessary to verify the information."

"In the past," said the communiqué issued by the six Powers when the Authority was announced, "the resources of the Ruhr have been used for the purposes of aggression. The six governments are determined that, through the security measures referred to above, any recurrence of such a situation shall be prevented. They are equally aware that the political and economic welfare of Europe requires the full and effective use of the industrial production of the Ruhr and the participation of a democratic Germany in the comity of nations, all enjoying a reasonable standard of prosperity. The establishment of the Ruhr Authority is an innovation in the international economic field. It is not being set up to limit free competition by European industries in the markets of the world. It has a constructive function to fulfill in promoting the general economic well-being of Europe and in re-establishing international confidence. If operated wisely, the Ruhr Authority may be regarded as a further contributory step towards a more intimate economic association among the countries of Europe."

In these last chapters we have been dealing with the expression and formulation of Russian, American, British and French policy in Germany. We have seen how in western Germany the three Atlantic Powers have been diverted from their original problem of planning for the political and economic future of Germany as a whole, to similar planning for the western half of Germany. And we have seen how in the years 1946-1949 the shadow of Russian aggression grew so large that the Americans and British thought more of how the Soviet Union was to be checked in Germany than of the dangers of a possible German economic and political revival with nationalist overtones. And of how the French, with the fear of Germany always uppermost in their hearts, found themselves in conflict with the Americans and British and only "went along" on the plans for western Germany at the price of various controls, such as the International Authority for the Ruhr, to ensure German disarmament.

There are some signs as this is written that an uneasy

equilibrium is being established between East and West in Germany and that the cold war which has been so hot in Germany may reach a touchy truce. If this is so, then the Germans have their great opportunity to take a hand in the struggle for Germany, perhaps to settle the German problem. Already there are stirrings in men's minds in eastern and western Germany. And although a frontier guarded by Russian bayonets and Russian machine guns runs like a jagged scar from the Bay of Lübeck on the Baltic to Hof and Adorf where the frontiers of the Soviet and United States Zones of Occupation and Czechoslovakia meet, Germany is struggling toward the resumption of her national identity.

Let us look at Germany after ten years, five and a half of war and four and a half of occupation.

CHAPTER
EIGHT

The Germany which is emerging today is the product not alone of war and occupation but of the East-West struggle for it. Once the most highly centralized state in Europe, it has been rived by this conflict into two areas and a city, Berlin, which itself is split by East and West. Such great differences mark off the lives and hopes of the average Germans in the areas dominated by East and from those in the Western-controlled zones that it is difficult at the moment, and indeed unwise, to think of them as citizens of the same nation. These differences in material standards, in outlook and in mental and physical abilities will deepen as the partition continues, and one of the real fears of western Germans is that years of life under Soviet rule will so deaden their compatriots in the east that when "Der Tag" comes and Germany is united once more, the easterners will hinder rather than help the development of the state.

The Germans in western Berlin refer to the Soviet Zone of Occupation as the "Zone of Silence." Or sometimes they call it "Russian Germany." Those that travel through it do so in fear of the Russians although without much fear of the German police.

"Why fear them?" a boy I know said after he had returned to Berlin from a vacation at Rügen on the Baltic. "They're Germans caught by the Russians. A cigarette, a little gossip about Berlin and they let you go. They make a great fuss about your papers but even that can be fixed. We are all Germans and we are all feeling sorry for ourselves these days."

Those Germans who live in the Soviet Zone have reason to feel sorry for themselves. For the zone, which includes the *Länder* of Mecklenburg, Brandenburg, Saxony-Anhalt, Thuringia and Saxony, has been methodically reduced to economic beggary by the Russians and its people subjected by the Soviet Military Administration and the Socialist Unity Party to a political regime which is in theory, if not in fact, a police state. I say in theory because the Russians and their German Communist stooges have not yet been able to stamp out the bitter antagonism of 95 per cent of the population, anatagonism which, in the words of one intelligence report, makes the Soviet Zone "the most strongly anti-Communist area in Europe."

Recently I talked with a German industrialist who had bought his way out of Leipzig to the western sectors of Berlin and who was en route to western Germany and, at fifty-eight, the start of a new life. I wanted to know what had happened to the economy of the eastern zone. What for instance was the worst blow?

"The worst began to happen to us in 1945 and we have had nothing else since," he said. "Perhaps, as you say, we brought it on ourselves—one heard stories of the S.S. in the east. But if we did, my God, we are paying now! The young men talk of a new Germany being born of all this suffering in the zone. Born of what? Of empty fields and silent factories?"

The economy of the Soviet Zone received its initial blow at Potsdam when the United States and the United Kingdom agreed that what are commonly referred to as "the Oder-Neisse lands" were to be allowed to remain under Polish occupation. This area, comprising the *Länder* of Silesia and Pomerania, included the Lower Silesian industrial district, of considerable importance to the German economy, and some of the best farmland in Germany. In the ensuing two years the city dwellers of the eastern zone, who in the past had depended to a great extent on the farm produce from this area, got along on the meager imports from western Germany, the agricultural production of the north and the tiny trickle of wheat imported by the Soviet Military Administration as a political gesture.

Thus at the very start of the occupation, the Soviet Zone lost about a third of its area, including a great part of its industry and some of its best agricultural land. This occurred before the Soviet Military Administration had begun the systematic looting of the zone, a looting which followed the more brutal although less systematic job done by the Soviet Army when it first entered Germany. Where Soldier Ivan from Zaporozhe took a watch, a phonograph and a handful of spoons, Comrade Ivan from the Soviet Military Administration took the factories, the railroad equipment and the raw materials.

"Of course we were a rich country," runs a German joke. "The Russians have been looting the east zone for four and a half years and they still find things to steal."

The Soviet Aktien-Gesellschaften or Soviet-owned German industrial plants have proved to be the most efficient method of looting the eastern zone. These plants are owned by the Soviet Military Administration and administered by its officials. Sometimes the managers are Germans and occasionally

Russians work under the Germans. The workers are Germans who because of their position are extremely vulnerable to Soviet political pressure. Whenever the Socialist Unity Party wants to provide "popular" endorsement for one of its policies it is able to produce mass meetings and petitions from such factories where the worker either joins in or loses his job.

No one knows accurately how many S.A.G. plants there are in the east zone. In many cases where the Russians have taken over a plant, they have retained its old name. By the spring of 1949, however, it was believed that Soviet ownership of assets might be as high as one third of the total industrial assets. In some key industries, of course, the figure is much higher. The entire automotive industry, including plants making trucks, busses, cars and motorcycles, is owned by the Russians. They own also between 90 and 100 per cent of the basic chemical industries and 93 per cent of the natural and synthetic fuel industries. Recently they have increased their holdings in the textile industry in Thuringia after first preparing for the move by claiming that widespread sabotage by "imperialist agents" made it necessary.

How much has the Soviet Union taken out of the Soviet Zone? At the close of the London meeting of the Council of Foreign Ministers, Mr. Bevin estimated that the value of removals and current production was about seven billion dollars or only three billion dollars less than the amount the Russians then were demanding as reparations, largely from current production in Germany. At present the entire production of whole industries is being sent out of eastern Germany to the Soviet Union or to satellite states in eastern Europe. In some industries enough production is left in Germany to provide for the Occupation Army, the Soviet officials and the faithful in the Socialist Unity Party.

As in every country behind the iron curtain, the workers of eastern Germany are subjected to ceaseless propaganda to increase production. The Russians have introduced a Two Year Plan with production quotas for individual industries, plants and individual workers and a wage scheme based on a basic salary for the worker's "norm" (and a very low salary it is) plus bonuses for production above the "norm." When a worker or a group of workers consistently exceeds the "norm," it is raised, sometimes without any increase in the basic salary, and as a result the individual works harder than before for the same money and with less prospect of a bonus.

Despite such stratagems and the fact that the plants owned by the Soviet Military Administration receive in normal times a steady flow of raw materials, the general level of industrial production within the Soviet Zone has not been up to Russian expectations. Even before the imposition by the United States, Great Britain and France of a counterblockade in the summer of 1948, production was unsatisfactory in many principal industries. When the counterblockade shut off the flow of coal, iron and steel, machinery and electrical equipment from western to eastern Germany, production dropped still farther. By March of 1949 only the natural and synthetic fuel industry, which is carefully nursed by the Russians, was meeting the quota given it under the Two Year Plan.

As can be seen from the above, the Russians gradually are imposing a planned economy very like their own upon the eastern zone. They also apparently are infusing German industrial production with some of their own inefficiency and lowering its qualitative standards. The goods produced in the Soviet Zone have steadily deteriorated in quality year by year, so much so that buyers at the Leipzig fair from western Germany have grown progressively less interested in purchase.

"Why, this looks just like the stuff you make in Russia," an American told a Soviet officer at the last fair. The Russian took the remark as a compliment.

To boost per capita production the Russians even have introduced the Stakhanovite system to the Soviet Zone. The German Stakhanov was a miner named Adolf Hennecke who daily performed prodigies at the coal face. He was presented to all German workers as an example of a man who was not only assisting in the "reconstruction of the Fatherland" but making a pretty penny to boot.

Production in the eastern zone has not benefited much as a result but the production of jokes has. During the grim winter of 1948-1949 the people of both east and west Berlin related dozens of jokes about Hennecke and his production feats. The Russians, who are sensitive to ridicule, toned down the Hennecke campaign subsequently.

The campaign is interesting in that it shows the peculiar inelasticity of Soviet methods in Germany and the stubbornness of the belief that what worked in the Soviet Union a year, five years or a decade ago will work in Germany. This is as true in economics as in politics. The Russians in the east zone are succumbing to that same regimentation of thought which ultimately will defeat Communism or any totalitarian idea.

This is evident in the course of Soviet political actions in the eastern zone. I have described how when it became apparent that the German Communist Party in the Soviet Zone would never be strong enough to dominate the zone's political thinking, the Russian political strategists contrived the merger of the Communists with the east zone's Social Democratic Party. This produced the Socialist Unity Party, supposedly an unbeatable combination of all left-wing sentiment in eastern Germany. This had been done elsewhere in eastern Europe and had been successful. The Russians assumed, wrongly, that it could not fail in Germany. It did fail.

It is one of the paradoxes of the Soviet rule in Germany that this failure was expressed in terms of a victory. In the middle of May 1949 the Russians decided to make the elections to the Third People's Congress of the Soviet Zone the occasion for a mass endorsement of Russian plans for German unity. To the list of candidates presented to the voter was added a statement that the voter in voting "yes" and approving the list also approved Russian policy for Germany. The Russians expected an overwhelming approval, 90 per cent or more, which would have strengthened the Soviet case at the Paris meeting of the Council of Foreign Ministers. Ceaseless propaganda in the press, over the air and in thousands of factory meetings plus the potential threat of police action seemed to insure such an outcome.

The Russians overlooked the courage of the Germans and their own unpopularity. Despite the police, the propaganda and the threats, 33.9 per cent of the voters rejected the Communist nominees and the Russian policy.

It was a stunning defeat. Germans in the eastern zone reported to Berlin that in many places 50 per cent of the voters had voted against the Russians, and that the night after the voting ended there were anti-Russian and anti-SED demonstrations throughout the zone. Certainly the defeat shook the party.

"You must reorganize the party at once," a Socialist Unity

Party official was told by party headquarters in Berlin. "Party?" he asked. "What party? After today there is no party."

Before assessing what effect the defeat will have on future Soviet policy in eastern Germany, there is the tantalizing question of why the Russians were so inept as to hold the election at all. It may be that in the eastern zone, as elsewhere in the world, they rely too heavily on the estimates of native Communists who generally are less realistic than the Russians. It may be, too, that the Russians still do not understand the depth of feeling against them and their German Communist allies in the east zone.

Even before the elections there were signs of Soviet dissatisfaction with the way the SED was doing its job in eastern Germany. One Soviet estimate claimed that the party "has failed to arouse a real enthusiasm for Marxist-Leninist teachings among the masses" and has been unable "to explain the sincerity of the Soviet Union's friendship for the German people." It also seems clear that Russian troop commanders in the eastern zone had for some time been reporting the unpopularity of the German Communists in the rural areas.

The Russian propaganda organs have spoken of a "party of a new type" or the establishment of a "National German Front." It is too early to say whether these are the same organization described differently or alternate courses which the Russians believe open to them. In any case the present party organization seems insecure.

At present there are in the Soviet Zone, in addition to the Socialist Unity Party, various other political parties which the Russians allow to exist so that the fiction of political freedom may be maintained. These include "splinter" groups of the

Christian Democratic Party and the Liberal Democratic Party of the western zones. Both these groups, from the violence of the attacks made on them after the May elections, played an important part in organizing the protest vote and both would disappear if the Russians proceed with the establishment of a German National Front.

The front would form a catch-all for the political parties of the East and would be dominated by the Communists. Supposedly "national" in character it would profess to speak for all Germany and not simply for the eastern zone. Here again is something the Russians have tried elsewhere.

Encouraging as the decline of the Socialist Unity Party's influence may be, it has been accompanied in the last year by a more sinister development. This is the organization of a strong force of "People's Police" in the Soviet Zone. By the end of 1949 the total police force in the zone is expected to reach a strength of just over 400,000, of which at least 120,000 men will be organized as mobile battalions, armed with rifles, machine guns and mortars, and designated as "People's Police." The police plan also calls for the strengthening and reorganization of the K-9 division of the police, an organization which seems to combine the worst features of Hitler's Gestapo and Stalin's M.V.D.

Here again the contrast between Russian plans and German fulfillment is marked. The men of the mobile battalions chosen mainly from among the German prisoners of war remaining in the Soviet Union have proved "unreliable" according to one Soviet Zone report. Scores deserted as soon as they returned to Germany. Many more, despite the Soviet efforts to keep them away from the ordinary people of Germany, have become infected with the anti-Russian sentiment of the zone. Enough remain, however, to present a convincing show of strength at parades and party rallies.

Much has been made of the appeal which these most military of policemen hold in a Germany which by no means has forgotten the days of triumph a decade ago. Certainly the "People's Police" with their uniforms, their flags and their bands awaken old memories and perhaps old yearnings for military glory. It is difficult, however, to know what percentage of the people of the eastern zone still entertain such feelings. The unreconstructed Nazis, of whom there are many both in the police and the Socialist Unity Party, certainly do. But I feel that the overwhelming antagonism to Communism and the Soviet Union chills the martial enthusiasm many may feel at the sight of the "People's Police" as they march through the forlorn streets of eastern Germany.

The Germans who have come to the top in the east zone since the end of the war are a strange collection. They include "old Communists" like Wilhelm Pieck, the titular head of the Socialist Unity Party, renegade Social Democrats like Otto Grotewohl, former Nazis like Bernhard Bechler, the Minister of the Interior in Brandenburg, and dozens of young, tough veterans of the war who are "on the make" under the Russians. Over this strange coalition is the Soviet Military Administration.

The zone they rule is a sad sight.

"Things are just falling apart," said a German who had journeyed from Dresden to Magdeburg and then escaped to the British Zone last autumn. "There isn't enough to build anything, except houses for the Russians and the SED, so, of course, there are no repairs. I don't mean repair of the bomb damage. I mean repairs of what we have. One day a crack in the pavement and in six months there is a hole a man can fall into. Everything is old—old trolley cars, old railroad cars, old machinery in the factories. Everything that was nearly new in 1945 the Ivans have taken. And every day the newspapers tell us how wonderful things will be when the Two Year Plan is finished. Wonderful for whom? The Russians?"

This is a recurrent theme: everything goes to the Russians. Day after day the trains steam eastward with freight for the insatiable colossus beyond Poland. The Russian hand is everywhere, in the shopkeeper's till, in the farmer's barn, in the factory's warehouse. When one reads the reports of the looting of the zone and of the police tyranny which daily comes closer to omnipotence, it is amazing that any fire remains beyond the Elbe. But the fire is there. The situation has not yet progressed to the point where the Germans found themselves in Norway in the second World War or the French in Spain during the Peninsular War. But the Russians sense already the bitter, brooding enmity that surrounds them and their German toadies.

This enmity has not yet developed into an underground movement comparable to any of those which enlivened the days and nights of the Germans in occupied Europe during the second World War. Perhaps it never will. For the Soviet Zone is garrisoned by over 400,000 Russian troops who are supplemented by the "People's Police" and the ubiquitous agents of the M.V.D. Under such conditions the organization of an underground resistance movement is far more difficult than they were, say, in Yugoslavia during the war.

"But if the Russians ever take their troops out of here," said a German in Leipzig in the spring of 1949, "there will be a rising against the Communists. My God, how they are hated!

We won't ask for rifles from the Americans. Just give us knives."

An anti-Russian cartoon passed stealthily from bench to bench in a workshop; a new joke about Hennecke; the murder of a Communist official (the east zone Germans seldom attack a Russian, knowing full well the penalty that would be exacted); a clandestine newspaper giving the news of the free world—these are the expressions of resistance in the Soviet Zone.

"The blockade of Berlin helped us," said a German from Halle, a refugee in western Berlin. "We had been alone with the Russians and the damned Communists a long time. And then every night and every day there were the American and British planes flying into Berlin. A lot of us had given up. I suppose a lot more will give up. But the news of those planes made me realize again that there was another world and that a German might be welcome in it if he wanted to work and live at peace. All over Halle people said to one another, 'They are still flying, every day more and more.' I tell you it was a tonic."

Personally, I find it hard to forgive the Germans for what they did in five and a half years of war. There is the memory of a murdered family in France that will not leave me. But if any Germans ever paid for their crimes, those in the Zone of Silence are doing so now.

2

The year 1948 was the *annus mirabilis* of the postwar era in western Germany. With the struggle for the country at its height and focused on Berlin, western Germany and especially the American-British Bizone suddenly began to recover economic health, and this process was accompanied by a small but significant increase in political activity and a genuine return to a national identity. For the first time since 1946, the Western Powers in Germany were given evidence that the German problem was more than defeating Communism in Germany, that the Germans and their country would become more and more important in Europe and the world. This discovery was greeted with enthusiasm by a few and with anxiety by the many. Those who hate and fear the Germans reflected sadly on the immediate postwar period when the German race was without influence or vigor. This was, to them, a halcyon period. Unfortunately for them, the Germans are a reality in Europe. In 1948 anxious eyes in the countries of western Europe and in the United States distorted that reality into an international danger. This was due partly to the swiftness of the economic recovery and partly to the terrible memories which the Germans have implanted throughout the world.

Cold figures tell the story of the economic revival. From the Statistical Annex to the United States Military Governor's report I have taken the following figures showing the increase in monthly production in January of 1949 compared to January of 1948 in units of a thousand metric tons:

	January 1948	January 1949
Steel ingots	304	651.4
Pig iron	265.8	544.5
Hard coal (gross cleaned)	6,624	8,204
Brown coal	5,421	6,150

The production of metal-working machines reckoned in metric tons was 1,367 in January 1948. A year later it was

3,766. The production of mining machinery and equipment rose from 4,449 to 11,096 metric tons. Western Germany produced 616 sewing machines for domestic use in January 1948. A year later production was 4,093.

Here are some other figures showing the increase in the number of items produced between the two months: agricultural tractors, 291 and 1,281; passenger automobiles, 1,273 and 4,928; radio receivers, 16,422 and 71,604; street and work shoes, 1,417,000 and 2,695,000.

The visual effect of this production jump was startling. Frankfurt on Main, for years a dismal, shattered city, suddenly came to life. As production increased from June onward under the impetus of the currency reform in the Bizone consumers goods, which most Germans had not seen since the middle of the war and had heard of only as being offered on the black market at prices far beyond their pocketbooks, began to appear. A good percentage of these stocks had been hoarded by merchants against currency reform. But thousands of the items which now took their places, shiny and new, in the shop windows were the product of the economic revival.

From Hamburg to Munich, construction began. Shops, factories, office buildings and homes, not enough homes, were built or rebuilt. At the same time restaurants which had won a precarious living since the war began to present German specialties, and in the British Zone the German burgher ate better than his conqueror when he patronized one of the restaurants which offered goose, pork, beef, potato pancakes, Wiener schnitzel and dozens of other specialties.

Life took on a new aspect. The nightmare memories of the war receded in men's minds. Business flourished. Businessmen and their wives took trips. Women bought new clothes. The *Autobahnen* long empty save for the trucks and cars of the occupation personnel now served German trucks and German passenger cars. The great industrial cities of the north resounded to the noise of new buildings going up and old ones being repaired. The great furnaces of the Ruhr lighted the night sky, and on a clear day from west of the Rhine the traveler could see the black pall of industrial haze hanging over the area just as it had done a decade before.

How far and how fast did the Germans come back in 1948?

The United States and British Military Governments use 1936 as the base year for estimating economic recovery.

The reasons for this are that this is the most recent year which can be considered "normal" since in 1936 war production had not yet begun to any great extent, yet the economy had already recovered from the worst effects of the depression of the early 1930's. Moreover the German industry census for that year makes available a large amount of data on production and value added by manufacture.

In January 1948 total industrial production of all areas in the Bizone was 47 per cent of the 1936 figure. This was an increase of 17 per cent over the January 1947 figure but it was still far from sufficient to supply the demands of western Germany or pay for the imports which maintained life. The American taxpayer had assumed the additional burden of $400,000,000 a year for the British Zone in December of 1947.

By June of 1948 when the currency reform in the western zones was carried out the total industrial production had risen four points to 51 per cent. From then on it rose steadily: July, 61 per cent; August, 65 per cent; September,

70 per cent; October, 74 per cent; November, 75 percent; December, 79 per cent, and January of 1949, 81 per cent.

In the year coal production rose from 73 per cent of the 1936 index figure to 90 per cent and in March of 1949 hit 96 per cent. Iron and steel output jumped from 27 per cent to 57 per cent and the production of nonferrous metals from 34 per cent to 73 per cent.

Small wonder that the French were worried. Small wonder that the Germans in the Ruhr late in 1948 said, "You see, we are the great industrial people of Europe. Give us the opportunity and we can supply ourselves with all we need."

Yet the French, the Germans and anxious watchers beyond the Atlantic have missed an important point. Industrial production, although it had jumped amazingly in the last half of 1948, had by February of 1949 begun to level off. This had been foreseen by American and British production experts in the Ruhr but their statements had been discounted as the wave of apprehension over German revival mounted. In the nineteenth century a Czar of Russia said to his aides, "Gentlemen, saddle your horses. France is a republic again." In 1948 people said in Paris, in New York, in Oslo, "Look out, German production is rising."

The U.S.-U.K. Coal Control Board has its offices in the huge, ugly Villa Hügel, once the home of the Krupp family which armed Germany for three wars. There late in 1948, Harry Collins, the burly, efficient Yorkshireman who heads the British section of the Board forecast the leveling off of production.

"Of course, I deal only with coal," he said, "but coal is the basis for the economy. And sometime next year we will reach the limit of production under the present plant and labor situation.

"Oh, we may go higher. Probably production will go well over 90 per cent of 1936. But it will be hard to keep it there. We need and will need more and more young miners, more electric power, more machinery. And if coal production levels off, so will steel, so will machinery, so will a dozen other things.

"The raw materials are here. The people are industrious, skillful workers. They may be able to restore the Ruhr to what it was. But it will take longer than many people seem to think. Meantime it's up to us to see that the production of the Ruhr is used for the good of the world."

By the end of 1949 Collins hoped that the Ruhr mines would be producing 400,000 tons a day, the 1936 average daily output. This, he noted, is not the maximum production. That was reached in peacetime 1938, when production averaged 448,000 tons a day.

First among the problems that confront the Ruhr is man power. This is especially true in the coal industry where there are not enough experienced miners in the younger age groups. In 1939 men of from thirty-one to thirty-five composed 21 per cent of the total labor force underground in the mines. Today they make up 8 per cent of the force. Lack of skilled miners is one reason why per capita production of all coal industry workers, exclusive of management and office help, remains just under a ton a day as compared with the prewar figure of 1.5 tons a day.

Not only were thousands of miners plucked out of mines by the Wehrmacht but many of those who survived refused to return to their old jobs and in Germany, as in England, the sons of miners are turning away from the mines.

Another factor which affects coal production in the Ruhr is the feeling among the miners that they are not getting their share of the new prosperity of western Germany. It is interesting to note, however, that in the early winter of 1948-1949 when this resentment was reaching alarming proportions, the miners had voted out of office all the Communist members on the board of directors of their union. Nevertheless, the resentment they felt was labeled "Communism" by some Military Government officials and German managers.

One afternoon in November 1948 I walked along a neat gravel path between two tiny vegetable gardens into the home of Hermann Bracht, one of the 135,000 men who work at the coal faces of the mines of western Germany. Bracht and his wife, his five children and one grandchild live in three rooms of a low, dank barracks which during the war housed the foreign laborers, mostly Polish, whom the Nazis brought to the Ruhr. At that he is lucky and knows he is lucky. Bombing destroyed the homes of 456,533 people in the Ruhr and severely damaged those of 800,000 more. Repair and reconstruction speeded up when the economic revival got under way but six months after currency reform ended it amounted to only about 2,400 houses a month and 300,000 people lived in air-raid shelters or ramshackle, insanitary housing.

The barracks in which Bracht lives lie in a hollow, a gray, forbidding place near Bochum, not far from the Zeche Carolinengluck mine in which he works. Bracht himself is a small, wiry man with rather narrow shoulders, a thin, high-nosed face, faded blue eyes and a complexion which seems to have taken on some of the grayness of the atmosphere of the Ruhr. He is forty-two and he has been a miner for twenty-four years. He looks sixty.

Although he has a roof over his head, Bracht is by no means contented with his lot. The reason is that although, as he admitted, he is reasonably well paid, the rise in prices prevents him from buying more than the essentials of life.

Bracht's pay sheet for one month showed that he had worked twenty-six eight-hour shifts in the month and earned 326 marks. A monthly allowance of twenty-eight marks for his five children boosted his earnings for that month to 354 marks. The official value of the mark is thirty cents so Bracht's salary is about $106 a month.

In the month under discussion the family budget was disjointed because Bracht had to pay eighty marks for a new leather jerkin to wear in the mine, where he operates a pneumatic drill at the coal face.

Rent is low. Bracht pays fifteen marks a month for his three rooms but "almost everything else goes to buy food."

Frau Bracht added, "Prices are terrible. Even for rationed foods they are too high, except maybe bread. But the rest is expensive and somehow it just doesn't reach the shops I go to."

The Brachts' supper that night was to be potatoes and cabbage stewed together. They keep a few chickens and when I visited them they were fattening a rabbit for the Christmas dinner.

"So we are alive and in good health," Bracht said. "Maybe it is foolish to complain. But look at the things in the shops."

Three miles away in a new, well-furnished shop turkey sold at nine and a half marks the pound and goose at eight marks and forty pfennigs.

"How can one feed seven people at those prices?" Bracht asked.

A can of beans weighing about a pound costs two marks eighty-five; canned pears three marks seventy.

Bracht and his wife live in one bedroom. The children

share two big beds which have been pushed together in a second room. The family's potato supply is heaped in one corner of this room. The coal is piled in a tiny bathroom.

Bracht threw open the door of a small cupboard. "Here are the family's clothes," he said, "all of them."

Bracht was a Social Democrat before Hitler came to power. When the Nazis took over he lapsed into that political anonymity granted to former Social Democrats who were important to the economy of the Third Reich and who kept quiet. Today he is a Social Democrat again, a much more belligerent and wiser one, I believe, than he was in 1932. I asked him how the Social Democrats had fought Hitler and the Nazis before the National Socialists won control of Germany.

His thin voice sounded a familiar refrain.

"What could we do?" he asked. "You work eight hours on a shift and go to a meeting. The party bosses or the union leaders say this is good or that is bad but you're too tired to care much. When you learn better, it is too late."

Bracht doesn't think German labor will make the same mistake again. "Today we know we must stay together," he said. "We intend to remain united. Neither the Communists nor the big business people can break us this time."

Bracht and Johannes Eckermann, a friend, fear neither the Russians nor the Communists in the Ruhr. When the war ended, they said, there was a good deal of sympathy for the Russians and the Communists in the area.

"We believed then that they really were interested in the welfare of the workers," said Eckermann. "Then we learned about the industry in the east, how the workers get even less than we do, how thousands of them are rounded up and sent to forced labor camps. My sister writes from the east zone and says her boy has disappeared, and can I send her food for the winter? And the blockade of Berlin—who feels that? People like us.

"So when Willi Agatz [the Communist leader in the Ruhr] comes around with his ———— about the solidarity of the working class I know where he can put it."

But although Bracht and Eckermann are strongly anti-Communist they are far from satisfied with the *status quo.* They want to see the Ruhr mines nationalized; they want new price controls which will bring good food into their price range; they want housing construction accelerated.

"Nowadays we read our papers and we listen to the speeches at the meetings," Eckermann said. "We don't want the Communists but we don't want the big bosses back again. And we want a little better life for our kids."

He laughed. "I am almost making an election speech. But anyway, tell them in America that we are not trying to make a war or make trouble here in Germany. I have had enough war and trouble to last me three lifetimes. But we are not going back to the old days."

Two other limiting factors should be mentioned in connection with coal production before we leave the economic revival and look at the people of western Germany and their society. At the end of 1948 the actual productive capacity of the thermal electric plants serving the coal industry was 775 megacycles, and it was estimated that it would take from eighteen months to two years to build boiler plants large enough and modern enough to raise the productive capacity to 1,000 megacycles. Before the war, the productive capacity of the electric plants serving the industry was about 1,400 megacycles.

In addition, a great deal of the plant and machinery now in

use is obsolescent or close to it. This is being replaced by current production, but much of the new machinery must be exported to other coal mining countries to help cover the cost of imports. Moreover coal mining is not as efficient an operation in the Ruhr as it once was due to the effects of bombing on transportation, freight yards and loading platforms. In the campaign to produce coal, the mines and the coking plants got the first priority in reconstruction. Today, the industry is getting around to repair and reconstruction of these facilities.

Will the miners work as hard under the International Authority for the Ruhr as for free German industry? I think so. But they will not work hard if they feel they are not sharing in the benefits of their labor, which is the basis for the Ruhr's economy, or if they believe that what Eckermann called "the big bosses," the Krupps and the Thyssens, are coming back. And sooner or later Germany will have to face the fact that a great many of the men who work in the coal mines and steel plants of the Ruhr want them nationalized.

In the Ruhr, which is situated in the *Land* North Rhine-Westphalia, one comes into contact with one of the major problems of the three western Zones of Occupation and any German government in that area: the refugee problem.

The American and British zones are the center of this problem. As of February 1, 1949, there were 4,411,100 refugees in the British Zone, and of October 1, 1948, there were 3,589,700 in the United States Zone or close to 20 per cent of the entire population. These German refugees come first from the Oder-Neisse territory, from Poland, Czechoslovakia, Hungary and other countries behind the iron curtain as a result of a provision in the Potsdam Agreement, and second from the Soviet Zone of Occupation and Berlin as a result of poor living conditions or persecution.

The population of the British Zone is 12.7 per cent higher than it was in 1939 and that of the American Zone 20.7 per cent higher according to the census of October 29, 1946. Since that census was taken the population has grown still more.

The refugees present both an economic and a political problem. Only in the Ruhr has any great number of them found steady work. In Bavaria where the urbanized, Protestant refugees are almost alien in a rural, Catholic country, thousands of them live from hand to mouth doing odd jobs for farmers and living miserably in bombed buildings, barns and rough shacks. Suspected and disliked by the Bavarians, they are full of bitter anger against their unwilling hosts, anxious to return home and easy prey to any demagogue willing to promise them a roof over their heads and a place in the community.

Surveys made by United States Military Government in 1949 show that over 90 per cent of both the refugees and the native Germans of the west believe that the expulsion of the refugees, or expellees, as Military Government calls them, in accordance with Potsdam was unjust. The same survey shows that the native Germans' attitude toward the prospect of living in harmony with the refugees is changing slowly. In 1948, most of the natives thought this was impossible. A year later, after the economic revival, they feel that it is possible.

A corresponding trend is apparent in the refugees' attitude toward their reception in western Germany. During the past year more and more of them found themselves satisfied with conditions, although in January of 1949 about 40 per cent were still dissatisfied with their treatment. Even now almost 100 per cent of the refugees want to return to their homelands.

The influx of refugees into the western zones and the rise in population resulting from this and other causes are reasons why, in the opinion of many Americans including General Clay, western Germany will never regain the standard of living it enjoyed in the late 1930's.

"Don't forget that the economy of western Germany is a sustained economy, helped by American funds through E.R.P.," Clay remarked shortly before he left Germany. "That help won't last forever. When it ends, the Germans will find that they'll have to work harder and longer than they are doing now and that the standard of living will not rise as they hope. That will be a difficult and troublesome period for the West German State and it would be to the advantage of those Germans who hope to run that state to point out that neither socialism nor nationalization nor any other quick panacea can solve the economic problem imposed by the rise in population and the fall in resources."

Western Germany is a political patchwork. It includes almost every shade of political opinion, from unrepentant Nazis whose only regret is their failure to serve "der schöne Adolf" as he should have been served, to honest democrats who sincerely believe that a democracy based on a combination of the American and British systems is Germany's only hope of survival. There are nationalists and internationalists, Communists and reactionaries who make the late Prince Bismarck look like a fellow traveler. Small parties burst into the open with a splurge of publicity, thrive for a month or two, then wither and die. Political "circles" grow up around a single leader who holds a weekly discussion group. There are even, in Bavaria, plenty of monarchists sighing beerily for the dear, dead days of the Wittelsbachs.

And yet, with all this, the political apathy which gripped the Germans in 1945 has not yet disappeared. This apathy measured in terms of knowledge about politics and interest in politics is, according to one official United States Military Government report, the "predominant" note in the American Zone. Farther to the north in the densely populated Ruhr the apathy is less evident.

There is a slight but important revival of interest in politics which coincides generally with the efforts to establish a German Federal Republic. But, early in 1949 just as early in 1946, six out of ten Germans in the United States Zone were willing to leave politics to others and 60 per cent also felt that they were not sufficiently informed about the political scene. In December of 1945 shortly after the start of the occupation only four in ten felt this way; the change may reflect the increased complexity of German politics today.

Nevertheless, as Report 175 of the Information Services Division, Office of Military Government (U.S.), points out, disinterest in politics does not imply a lack of opinion on political affairs, and whereas in 1945 Germans mumbled they "never bothered to think" about political subjects, today they are quick enough to talk about their political opinions even though they themselves eschew political responsibility or claim ignorance of "technical" political matters.

The report does not cover the British Zone where I have noticed that party allegiances appear to be stronger and the disposition to think along party lines more pronounced. In the industrial cities of the north I have encountered more of a feeling of political responsibility than, say, in the farming villages of Bavaria. One of the reasons for this probably is that industrialization in the north broke the old feudal attitude that the landowner, the priest or the village councilor would do all the thinking necessary and that the *bauer's* job was to get in the crops.

Two tendencies evident throughout the United States Zone of Occupation and in parts of the British Zone are first, the growing belief that the local German officials are doing a good job; and second, the consequent increase of the confidence in these officials. Confidence was fairly high in the first two postwar years, then it dropped and now appears to be on the upswing again. There are no figures at hand for the British Zone; my talks with Germans in the Ruhr give the impression that the continued housing shortage and the rise in prices have combined to produce distrust of the honesty and competency of town and *Land* officials there.

Although there is a multiplicity of political parties, "movements" and "discussion groups" in western Germany, the two leading parties, the Social Democrats and the coalition of the Christian Democratic Union and Christian Socialist Union, remain the largest and most important. However, their position is by no means so secure as it was in 1945 and 1946, and in Bavaria, once a C.D.U.-C.S.U. stronghold, the party's prestige has been challenged by the rise of the Bayern Partei or Bavarian Party.

It is symptomatic of the large potential vote which could be attracted to a third party that in the United States Zone there has been a steady rise in the number of people who like neither of the two leading parties or who withhold their opinions.

The C.D.U.-C.S.U. coalition in the United States Zone has lost favor with the electorate steadily, up to the middle of 1949, surveys show. In January 1946 about 35 per cent of the voters either belonged to it or preferred it. In February 1949 the percentage had dropped to about 18 per cent, according to Report 175. The Social Democrats, on the other hand, were preferred by 30 per cent of the voters in January 1946 and by about 27 per cent in February 1949, after slumping in the summer of 1948 to just over 20 per cent.

The Communist Party's showing at least has the virtue of consistency. In January 1946 it had the favor of about 2 per cent of the electorate and in February 1949 the figure was about the same. In the British Zone, where the Communists initially were much stronger, their position has fallen considerably although, if the housing and price situations are not solved, it may be assumed that the party's strength will revive to some extent.

Although American Military Government has tried to remain neutral in the struggle between the two political parties, its members have in most cases been drawn to the politicians of the C.D.U.-C.S.U. This, I believe, is due to two causes. First, the Social Democrats have been tougher in their dealings with American and British Military Government officials than the coalition party. To many high Americans the Socialists appear to be "troublesome" and even "dangerous." Second, since a great many of the Military Government officials are either professional soldiers or have had their political outlook molded by their years in the Army during the war they tend to confuse Communism and Socialism. Not long ago a rather senior officer of American Military Government told me he could not understand why the United States continued to "subsidize" the "Communist government in England." Political ignorance of this kind detracts from the increased prestige of the United States, in Germany and elsewhere on the continent, which has been one of the chief political results of the European Recovery Program.

Before we consider the ebb and flow of party politics in western Germany we must consider the most important, and perhaps the most alarming, factor in the present political situation in Germany. This is the revival of nationalism. This nationalism varies from the extremists who, despite the fact that Germany has not won a war since 1870, still dream of world domination, to the millions of people who are conscious of the fact that the punitive phase of the occupation of Germany is over and that the country has the opportunity of regaining at least an equal position in the councils of Europe.

What has happened generally is that the Germans have regained their national identity. If we take this as a working definition of what has actually happened during the revival of nationalism, I think we can avoid the extremist views of both the Germanophiles and Germanophobes in their estimates of what this revival will mean to Europe and to the world. I suggest, moreover, that the revival of nationalism neither confirms nor denies the growth of democracy on Western lines in the three western Zones of Occupation any more than it confirms or denies the return to power of the National Socialists. No future Germany, democratic, Fascist or Communist, situated in the heart of Europe between the two great political Powers of the day, the Soviet Union and the United States, can escape being nationalist in the sense that it will desire to think and act as a nation in defiance of the two great Powers.

The most forbidding factor in the situation created by the rise of nationalism is that in the United States Zone of Occupation the average German doubts his ability to carry on democratic self-government. Moreover, roughly six of every ten Germans in the zone have told Military Government surveys that they would choose a government offering economic security over one guaranteeing civil liberties if they were forced to make this choice. This is the choice which many Germans believed they made in 1932-1933 but I do not think their present attitude portends the revival of National Socialism as such. Rather it indicates the failure of United States Military Government to explain the value of civil liberties to the Germans, the economic insecurity which many still feel despite the revival of trade, commerce and industry in the last year, and the authoritarian potential remaining in the German electorate.

A great many Germans in the United States Zone—Report 175 puts the figure at four in ten—would be willing to yield specific civil liberties for economic security. The franchise and the freedom of the press, which are vital to democratic government, are the two rights which Germans appear most willing to sacrifice in return for economic security. Only small fractions of those Germans queried are ready to yield on freedom of speech, freedom to choose their jobs and freedom of education. Nevertheless the readiness to give up some freedoms is a melancholy reminder of how much more reorientation, as the Army calls it, must be done before Germany can be considered democratic.

In the American Zone the question was put: "Was National Socialism a bad idea, or a good idea badly carried out?"

The affirmative answers that it was a good idea badly implemented have risen steadily. In 1946 the figure was 40 per cent of those queried. In 1948 it was 55.5 per cent. These percentages apply only to the United States Zone. On a hypothetical choice between Communism and National Socialism, opinions since late 1946 have been turning from "neither" to National Socialism, the report shows. In November 1946, 17 per cent selected National Socialism. In February 1949, 43 per cent preferred it as against 2 per cent for Communism.

On the other hand more Germans in January 1949 than in November 1947 blame Germany for the outbreak of World War II and fewer of them claim that circumstances forced Germany to go to war.

Viewed in juxtaposition to the revival of nationalism throughout Germany and the probability that similar views are held in the other Zones of Occupation, these figures indicate that although some progress has been made toward the political re-education of the Germans, as a people they still are far from being the ardent democrats described by some enthusiastic Military Government officials.

To me the survival of authoritarian tendencies among the Germans seems more dangerous than the prospect of the revival of the National Socialists as such. As long as those tendencies survive, any authoritarian group or political party will appeal strongly to the mass of the people. Indeed many sound judges of German political trends believe that the relative success of the Social Democratic Party during the last three years can be ascribed to the appeal of that party's discipline and tight organization compared to the rather loose coalition of the C.D.U.-C.S.U.

The revival of nationalism has been accompanied by a general increase in sentiment against the presence in western Germany of the occupation forces. Here a distinction should be made between the feeling of the shoemaker or the farmer and those of Herr Dr. This or Professor That. By and large the present governing classes of western Germany see the retention of United States, British and French troops as a guarantee of the continuation of their own position and influence, although, for political purposes, they are seldom reluctant to assail the occupation. Moreover they are motivated by deep fears that at some future date Germany might be the subject of a *coup d'état* engineered by the Russians and the German Communists and they regard the occupation troops as insurance against such a development.

The average man is not concerned with these factors. He is concerned with high taxes, high prices and bad housing.

"I am still living in one room with my wife and children," a German newspaperman said in Frankfort recently. "But the Americans and the British, civilians and soldiers, have plenty of room. Don't you understand that by taking our best houses and our best buildings, you make us envious and bitter. We understand what you are trying to do, some of us at least. But must your officers live like kings to do it?"

In many cities of western Germany, the Germans are reducing their relations, official and personal, with Allied personnel. In the summer of 1948 an American friend of mine took a German businessman and his family, who had escaped to the United States Sector of Berlin from Leipzig, into his house and fed them until their air passage to western Germany could be arranged. Early in 1949 the American met the head of the family in the United States Zone.

"Of course," said the German, "you realize I cannot be seen

with you publicly any more. That is not popular in western Germany nowadays."

"It is all right for these damned women now," a German youth I picked up on the *Autobahn* said. "Let them get laid by the Americans. And the politicians are the same. Whores to the Americans, the British and the French. But someday this will all be German again."

This may reflect simply the conquered's dislike of the conqueror and the collaborator. It may symbolize the underground impulse for a violent reassertion of extremist nationalism when the occupation troops withdraw from Germany. Certainly pride in Germany, in Germany's history, in German ingenuity and ability are growing apace in the west.

"Of course the Americans can fly and the British are good on the sea," a German told an American recently, "but soldiers, no. You should have seen the Wehrmacht at its height. There was an army. I tell you it made a man proud just to be part of it."

Such observations usually are followed with the suggestion, "If you want to take your soldiers home and be secure against the Ivans, let us have an army here."

I must confess that these remarks sound frightening. But they are also the natural consequences of defeat. I remember hearing the same sort of thing from French officers and soldiers in Algeria and Tunisia in 1942 and 1943 and later in France in 1944.

The economic revival of western Germany had a powerful effect on nationalist sentiments. As the production figures mounted month by month, the Germans lost their doubts of their own ability and industry which had assailed them from 1945 to 1948.

There is a firm belief in German "know-how" throughout western Germany today. Germans tell you that the economic revival shows that "Europe cannot live without Germany" and that "we have demonstrated we are the foremost industrial people of Europe."

The new nationalism is compounded of all these sentiments. It can be a potential danger to Europe and the world. But it can also be a means whereby the mass of the Germans are jerked out of their present political apathy and made to realize that Germany has responsibilities toward the rest of Europe and the world which can be solved only by the assumption of individual responsibility. On the one hand there is the statement of a British general that "what we call nationalism in Germany is patriotism elsewhere." On the other hand there is the worst type of nationalism as seen in the League for German Revival and the German Right Party which preach a new authoritarianism laden with danger.

And beneath all is the abiding German belief that men are divided between the rulers and the ruled. One of the greatest mistakes American Military Government made in its initial approach to the German problem was to believe that the American concept of democracy as the highest form of political organization was shared by any large number of Germans. This is not so. It never has been so. Persistent questioning of intelligent, erudite Germans has led me to think that they firmly believe that the authoritarian form of government is best suited to the solution of the political problems of society in the world of today. This belief developed out of the old feudal system, the inability of the Weimar Republic to solve the economic problems of the 1920's and early 1930's and the geographical and ethnological position of

Germany in Europe. It is too old and too deeply rooted a belief to be shaken by four or five years of exposure to American democracy.

The failure of the American concept to win any vast number of converts does not reveal the weakness of Military Government efforts in Germany as much as it does the strength of German belief in another and, to us, distasteful form of state organization. No German government in the future, unless it is to be entirely supported by Western arms and soldiers, can long endure which does not recognize this authoritarian concept and its fundamental position in German political thinking.

Although political preferences divide the Germans, it is possible to enumerate certain basic national objectives which to some degree animate all political thought after four and a half years of occupation. Foremost among these is the unity of the country. Save among the members of the Bavarian Party, I have never met a German who does not look forward to the reunification of eastern and western Germany and few who do not believe that this is an essential to the restoration of Germany to something like her old position of prosperity and influence in Europe. The Russians and the German Communists, who have made many mistakes in Germany, have not been mistaken in choosing "German unity" as their principal slogan.

In western Germany wide differences exist on the price to be paid for unity. The leading politicians of the area insist that if any unity is to be won, no price must be paid. In other words, the eastern Zone of Occupation must join the three western zones and form a united Germany on terms laid down by the West. There must be, they say, "no Communist infiltration." My own belief is that if the eastern Germans are ever in a position to join the West freely, which means the removal of Soviet troops and the defeat of the Socialist Unity Party, "Communist infiltration" will be out of the question for there will be very few Communists left to infiltrate anything.

On the other hand, I have met a number of businessmen of the western zones who feel that western Germany, organized as a German Federal Republic under the Bonn constitution, will be strong enough economically and politically to make some concessions to bring eastern Germany into a German union and that the union is so essential for business purposes that such concessions should be made. Of course, until the middle of 1949 the business and commercial interests of western Germany did not exert the primary influence on the governing group there. That was exercised by the Military Governors. But with the establishment of a German government, the influence of these circles will grow, and their advocacy of the necessity for increasing commercial and ultimately political relations with East Germany can be expected to obtain a better reception among government circles. This will be true, I believe, even if the Social Democrats come to power. Should that party nationalize or socialize the Ruhr, it would not eliminate the need for economic ties with eastern Germany and the socialist managers who then would be running the Ruhr would be as anxious for trade with the East as any capitalist group.

In addition to these two influential but relatively small groups, there is the great mass of the people who earnestly although often inarticulately desire the unity of their country. Few of them wish that unity at the price of Communist or Russian domination. But few of them expect that, once Germany is reunited and the occupation forces withdraw, there will be much chance of this. In the middle of June 1949 when the Council of Foreign Ministers in Paris drew to a close, it was evident that nothing would be done at that session toward reuniting the country or withdrawing the occupation forces. In Berlin and in western Germany I encountered a groundswell of resentment against this.

On my way from Paris to Berlin I stopped at Frankfort where a German editor expressed his views. "You must understand that we feel this cannot go on forever," he told me. "We get many letters from readers asking why nothing should be done by either East or West to bring the two halves of Germany together and get rid of the occupation troops. I know why the Western Foreign Ministers refused to accept Vishinsky's proposal on a German peace treaty and the withdrawal of occupation forces, but it is difficult to explain to our readers who only see the lifting of a burden in his suggestion."

Again in Berlin a staunchly anti-Communist German said, "It looks as though the Allies began the occupation to protect Europe from the Germans and are continuing it to protect Europe from the Russians. Don't German wishes count?"

The general desire to see the last of the occupation troops naturally is closely connected with the desire for German unity. Some suggest it as the first step toward unity. Withdraw the occupation forces, they say, and we ourselves will unify Germany. Others suggest that Germany be united first and the occupation troops remain until the West is satisfied of the pacific intentions of the Germans and that the Russians do not intend to level a political attack on the new state along the Czech pattern. But in their approach to both questions in late 1948 and the first half of 1949, the Germans evinced a strong distaste for what they believed was the Western, particularly the American, tendency to use Germany and the Germans as pawns in the great power conflict over Germany without paying sufficient attention to the desires and wishes of the Germans themselves.

Of the two major political parties, the Social Democrats are the more interested in German unity. Although at the present they are the second strongest party in western Germany and although they are the best organized of the parties in the west, their hopes of winning a decisive election victory which would make them the dominant party rest to some extent on German unity. For the party always has been strong in eastern Germany, where today it forms part of the Socialist Unity Party. The expectation is that should German unity be achieved, the Socialists would emerge as a party strong enough to form their own government.

The elections for the Bundestag or lower house of the German Federal Republic on August 14, 1949 showed that the Socialists are not strong enough to win a majority in the three western Zones of Occupation and that in the last year there had been a steady swing to the right. As a result of the elections, the Christian Democrats, the Free Democrats, an assortment of German middle-class conservatives with slight liberal leanings and the German Party appeared late in August of 1949 to be moving toward the formation of a rightist coalition which would form the first government of the new republic.

The Socialists, possibly because of their better organization, have been swifter to grasp the political opportunities offered by the revival of nationalism than the C.D.U.-C.S.U. coalition. There has been a persistent emphasis on "German rights" and "German interests" since late in 1948 coupled with bitter defiance of the Soviet Union and German Communism.

Dr. Kurt Schumacher, the leader of the party, began its campaign for the elections for the Federal Parliament in June of 1949 with a sharp demand for the end of "interference by the Occupation Powers in internal German affairs" and a denunciation of the reparations policy of the Western Powers.

"Germany has an honest desire to pay reparations as far as this is possible," he said, "but she does not want to commit suicide by doing so."

He claimed that while big steel plants are destroyed in Germany, a new steel industry is constructed in France. He added, "To transfer the German steel-making capacity to France is not the way to build up political understanding between the two countries."

This and other speeches with demagogic overtones should not blind Americans to the ability and intelligence of this one-legged, one-armed man of fifty-four.

He impresses me as the most dynamic and independent of German politicians and certainly the toughest. His physical toughness is a legend. He is a man who has refused to die. But his mental toughness is great also. Although he is adept at all sorts of political stratagems and maneuvers, on the whole he has clung to his political beliefs despite Nazi torture or the not inconsiderable pressure placed upon any German politician by the occupation. Perhaps because he early realized that no German politician would survive the end of the occupation as an influential figure if he had enjoyed too close contacts with the Occupation Powers, Schumacher has remained aloof. Even at the height of the economic troubles of the winter of 1946-1947 when western Germany desperately needed American and British help, he never sacrificed what he believed to be his right as a German to criticize the occupation. He is a man whom it is difficult not to admire but equally difficult to like.

Far more likable is Dr. Carlo Schmid, the Social Democrats' delegation leader in the Parliamentary Council at Bonn which framed the constitution for the German Federal Republic. Schmid, a big bear of a man who looks like a tidy Heywood Broun, is more affable than Schumacher and more popular with the Americans and British. They regard him as a "moderate" although it is my feeling that this classification, springing from his ability to make compromises, is really a tribute to Schumacher's political shrewdness. If anyone in the party is to compromise with the Occupying Powers it will not be Schumacher who seeks to maintain his position as the defender of German rights and interests.

During the war Schmid was a German Military Government official in occupied France. His record there showed wisdom and restraint, so much so that when the tables were turned and the French were an Occupying Power, they brought Schmid into the government of the French Zone of Occupation. In his political thinking Schmid is much less parochial than Schumacher and he has a wider acquaintanceship with the modern world. His relationship to Schumacher is something like that of Aneurin Bevan and the other younger generation socialists in England to the veteran party wheel horses like Herbert Morrison.

Of all the German Socialist politicians I have met the most impressive as a man and as a political figure is Waldemar Von

Knoerrigen, the Social Democratic leader in Bavaria. He, too, is tough and has to be. For Bavaria is a political battleground where the Socialists do not enjoy the prestige or the party strength they have in the north and where the C.D.U.-C.S.U. coalition has always been strong. Moreover, the rise of the Bavarian Party, as we will see, has created problems peculiar only to this state.

Like Dr. Karl Gruber, the Austrian Foreign Minister, Von Knoerrigen looks as though he had stepped out of the ranks of an S.S. division. But like Gruber he has a fine record as an anti-Fascist in Germany before the war. He is also a convinced anti-Communist and hence is immune to the attacks usually leveled by Bavarian separatists and the coalition parties at Socialists as "Reds." During the war Von Knoerrigen worked in London on propaganda to Germany, and an Englishman who knew him then has told me, "He was the only refugee German I know that really made me feel there was some hope for Germany after the war."

Von Knoerrigen is tall with a mass of blond hair, sharp blue eyes and a firm chin. His hands are very large and when he talks they clench and open. He is continually assailed by the Bavarian Party and the right wing of the C.D.U.-C.S.U. as a "traitor to Germany" but he fights back convincingly.

"In my speeches, there is always someone who will break in and shout, 'The British hung Amery. We should hang you,' and such nonsense. I tell them that I did what I did for Germany, that Hitler did not represent the legitimate German government, and that in fighting him I was fighting for them and for all honest, decent Germans."

He added, however, that there were many disheartening elements in his work.

"To think that those who fought Hitler should be considered traitors, now four years after the end of the war," he told me in March of 1949. "This is what we have come to."

I asked him what the answer was.

"One must then go back over the whole history of the last twenty years and show the people that Hitler seized power illegally, just as the Communists would do today. One must make them realize that only when Germany is free from such actions, only when governments are made by the will of the people, can Germany be a nation among the nations of Europe."

Like a great many other politicians in western Germany, Von Knoerrigen feels that despite the surveys which show that many Germans regard National Socialism as a good idea which went wrong, the Western occupation has helped Germans think for themselves.

"Whenever I hear a farmer or a shopkeeper raise an objection to something the government is doing, I feel that some headway has been made. But we have got to conquer the idea that politics is only for the politicians."

The C.D.U.-C.S.U. coalition has been described variously as the "rightist" or "center" party of western Germany. As far as economic thinking is concerned it is essentially conservative, as a party which draws heavily on the German middle classes is bound to be. It naturally opposes socialization of industry, but it is as indignant as the Social Democratic Party about reparations removals and perhaps even more bitterly opposed to Allied measures which it believes are aimed at keeping Germany economically weak. Because it is the party of a great number of businessmen, it is often attacked by the Socialists as reactionary and for thinking more of economic conditions than political liberty.

My own impression is that a great many of the party workers are in fact as liberal on this standpoint as the Socialists. Certainly the party does not demand the strict obedience and discipline which the Socialists require. But perhaps because it is a coalition it does not plan as far ahead as its principal rival. The Socialists, for instance, have created within the party "shadow" departments which study questions of foreign affairs, internal security and public finance in anticipation of the day when an election is won and the party can present the people with a well-prepared government.

Dr. Konrad Adenauer, who as president of the Parliamentary Council is one of the Germans chiefly responsible for producing the constitution for the West German State, is at seventy-three perhaps the leading right-wing German politician.

He was Oberbürgermeister, or Lord Mayor, of Cologne from 1917 until he was dismissed by the Nazis in 1933. During this period he was an active member of the Zentrum or Center party and in 1923 during the Allied occupation he is supposed to have been involved in the schemes to establish a Rhenish republic. The Nazis twice arrested him, once in 1934 and again after the attempt on Hitler's life in July of 1944. When the United States First Army swept into Cologne, Adenauer was available, as he had been all his life. He was reinstated as Lord Mayor by United States Military Government but the British, when they took over control of the area, dismissed him. They found him too slow at carrying out their orders. For a brief period Adenauer was banned from all political activity by the British, but this ban was completely lifted on December 17, 1945.

Adenauer is tough, just as Schumacher is tough, but in a different way. Schumacher's quality is that of steel; Adenauer's of some tough old tree which bends but does not break before storms. Although at the beginning of the occupation he enjoyed immense prestige in the Christian Democratic Union in the north, this has dwindled somewhat, probably as a result of his close connection with the Occupying Powers, an association which grows less and less popular as German nationalism revives. Perhaps to counter the impression assiduously fostered by the Socialists, that he is only a tool of the Americans and British, Adenauer recently has begun to speak publicly and privately against what he terms the "excesses" of the occupation.

In debate Adenauer is like a good club fighter who has been around a long time and knows all the tricks of the trade. In the period between the wars he often aspired to a ministerial appointment and once even for the Reich chancellorship. Today he relies heavily on the prestige of his past and the dignity of his office at Bonn to carry him through stormy periods. As the Chairman of the Christian Democratic Union in the *Land* North Rhine-Westphalia he is probably the principal strategist of the coalition. This *Land* is the most populous in western Germany, and it is there that the rivalry between the Social Democrats and the Christian Democrats is at its fiercest.

Like too many leading German politicians, Adenauer is elderly. His appeal to the middle-aged businessmen and government functionaries of his party is strong, but he is not favored by the war veterans and the refugees. An old admirer of his recently described him as "an old and spiteful man." Whatever his errors in the past, western Germany found in this subtle, experienced figure the ideal man to compose the differences of the two great parties in the Parliamentary Council and guide the constitution to completion. I once asked a German editor at Bonn what Adenauer had. "Nothing but brains" was the answer.

Josef Mueller, the leader of the Christian Socialist Union in Bavaria, is in marked contrast to Adenauer's austere coolness. He is a little round man with a big round face who, according to report in Munich, worked for both German and American intelligence services during the war. Mueller might wish to stay aloof from the day-to-day political battle but in Bavaria this is impossible. He is adept, as his record shows, at keeping a foot in both camps and he is a singularly keen observer of political trends not only in his own *Land* but in all western Germany.

When I visited him in his apartment in Munich in the spring of 1949, the turbulent politics of Bavaria had taken an unexpected turn. Mueller himself was under fire in his own party. Various new parties like the Deutsche Union and the Bavarian Party were attracting voters from the coalition. The Social Democrats had been strengthened by the vast influx of refugees. Mueller was in danger of losing his political shirt but it was clear he would not lose his head.

Mueller's outlook is less parochial than that of either Adenauer or Schumacher. Bavaria's ties with western Europe through France always have been strong; to Mueller, Bavarian separatism or even the German isolation advocated by groups like the Nauheim Circle seems ridiculous. He is a "middle of the road" man, the type which the C.D.U.-C.S.U. coalition fosters throughout western Germany. His difficulty in Bavaria is that for a large number of the voters something more conservative than even the middle of the road is the objective. But whatever political storms envelop that tubby figure, my guess is that Mueller will survive.

Bavaria is not only the most conservative of the west German *Länder,* but also the home of German, or rather Bavarian, monarchism, of strong authoritarian tendencies and a restless, bitter group of about 2,200,000 refugees who make up some 23 per cent of the population.

Next to Prussia, Bavaria was the largest state of the German Empire that perished in 1918. Today the Bavarian Party, which is reactionary and contains a large percentage of monarchists, is the fastest-growing political party in the *Land* and probably in all Germany. The party is grounded solidly in Bavarian nationalism with monarchial overtones, and most of its members want Bavaria to remain outside the general course of German policy, as represented by the planned German Federal Republic, or, at most, to have only a limited connection with the West German State.

When one talks with men like Dr. Anton Donhauser, a young, sincere and vigorous exponent of the Bavarian Party's program—he is also head of the Bavarian Red Cross—the words "Bismarck's Germany" crop up continually. The party's program does picture a German confederation something like the old Empire with Bavaria maintaining an autonomous status within the confederation and with its own representatives abroad. The adoption of the Bonn constitution by the other states of western Germany has not reduced the party's appeal. For this is based on the strong and perhaps very natural desire of the Bavarians to sever the ties which have bound the state to Prussia, ties which in their view have been responsible for Bavaria's losses in two World Wars in addition to the end of its old semi-independent status.

Donhauser early in 1949 estimated that between 75 per cent and 80 per cent of the party members are monarchists who see in the return to a "constitutional throne" of the House of Wittelsbach the answer to the state's lack of political order.

In 1949 the Bavarian Party was winning voters away from the Christian Socialist Union and winning elections in the towns and villages of rural Bavaria. Should the party ever get enough votes to dominate the Bavarian *Landtag,* or state legislature, it would give Bavaria a government which one American intelligence officer predicted would be "strongly reactionary but with plenty of lip service to democracy—while we're here."

His words are borne out by the way in which the Bavarian civil service, a strongly reactionary and authoritarian group, and the rich farmers—Bavaria does not have a large industrialist class such as exists in the north—have flocked to the support of the Bavarian Party.

The party's leaders include some talented demagogues like Ludwig Lallinger and Dr. Jakob Fischbacher who warn the pure young men of Bavaria against the "dangerous Prussian women" who spend their vacations in the Bavarian Alps and who, according to these Huey Longs in leather breeches, swim naked in the lakes. They also are capable of bitter attacks on American occupation politics.

Antioccupation sentiment seems stronger in Bavaria than anywhere else in western Germany and reaction seems more firmly in the saddle. Nowhere are attacks against politicians who try to work with American Military Government officials fiercer and nowhere is the idea more widespread that a few lawyers, landowners and churchmen alone are capable of government.

I asked four experienced officials of Military Government

in Bavaria what would happen if the occupation forces and Military Government withdrew. Here is a summary of their answers:

(1) Land reform would end. The liberalization of education would end. The present constitution which is too "democratic" for Bavarian reaction would become a scrap of paper.

(2) The grip of the civil service and the hierarchies of the existing political parties on Bavaria's economic and political life would be tightened, political opposition stifled and economic affairs regimented. The reform of the Civil Service would be discontinued.

(3) All those Nazis not now in government who held government posts under National Socialism would be restored to their old posts, even, as one official said, "if they had to go out and search for them."

(4) Such racial and religious tolerance as Americans have introduced would disappear. So would freedom of the press and of speech.

In Bavaria it seemed to me that the basic tendency toward authoritarianism is more dangerous than the return of Nazis who in the past expressed that tendency.

Early in 1949, 83 per cent of the judges and 81 per cent of the prosecutors in the Bavarian courts were former members of the National Socialist Party. In the Ministry of Finance for *Land* Bavaria 61 per cent of the officials were former Nazis and in the Ministry of Labor and Social Welfare the figure was 22 per cent. All these former Nazis have been denazified and have promised to be good.

Now it is all very well to argue, as do able men like William Henry Chamberlin, that in a totalitarian state run by a single political party like Hitler's Germany, men of ability and intelligence were forced to make obeisance to the ruling party in order to keep their jobs, their homes and even their freedom.

This is quite true and I have never held that all Nazis of whatever rank must be excluded forever from public office in Germany. But the return of the Nazis to position in Bavaria is too overwhelming. It means that men who have been members of a party which, after all, was the most ruthless and cynical exponent of authoritarianism that Germany has ever seen are back in positions where that same authoritarianism can be exerted.

There is in Bavaria, in addition to the Bavarian Party and the rightist elements of the Christian Socialist Union, another disturbing development. This is the German Union, a somewhat loosely organized collection of former members of the Hitler Youth, young intellectuals and German refugees from Czechoslovakia and Hungary. Its leaders talk of a "crusade" for the restoration of Germany's internal order, and worship "order" as though it alone is the answer to all Germany's problems. This same admiration for order, with no "ifs" or "buts" from those ordered, is present in the thinking of the C.S.U., the Bavarian Party and the civil service.

The refugees who everywhere in western Germany provide a political problem are an incalculable factor in Bavaria. A number of them who were Social Democrats in Czechoslovakia have joined the party in Bavaria, thus strengthening it in its rivalry with the C.D.U.-C.S.U. and the Bavarian Party. But thousands of others, restless, dissatisfied and eager for revenge against the Russians who expelled them and the Bavarian Government, which they believe has failed to give them an economic or political chance in their new home, are ripe for the first demagogue who appears.

In the British Zone, where there are more industry and more jobs, the refugee problem has been somewhat easier. But not all the refugees, thousands of whom come from the Oder-Neisse lands (now Polish) and the Soviet Zone of Occupation, can be absorbed into the economy, and they too form a reservoir of discouraged and bitter humans. The *Land* governments of the north have tried their best to give the refugees political representation but during the first six months of 1949 there were signs that a League of German Refugees with its headquarters at Lippe was beginning, after many false starts, to be a political power in the zone.

Germany is made up of two geographical areas, each of which can and probably will become a country, and a city—Berlin. No examination of the Germany emerging from war and reconstruction and occupation is complete without discussion of that turbulent, vigorous city divided like the remainder of the country between East and West. For it is in Berlin that the heat of the struggle has been caught and confined, an action that for a year from June of 1948 to June of 1949 made the city the hottest spot in the struggle for Germany and even, for a few weeks, a candidate for that melancholy list of cities like Danzig and Sarajevo which have been the starting points for war.

To me the people of western Berlin represent the best hope of Germany, just as those of Bavaria are the most depressing. Despite the fact that the three sectors occupied by the Americans, British and French lie isolated in the midst of the Russian Zone, it is precisely in these sectors that the flame of freedom burns brightest in Germany, that there is some indication that across the barriers of history, tradition and language the free peoples of the West and Germans have made contact. Even granted the violence of anti-Russian and anti-

Communist feeling in Berlin, there are reassuring signs that in this shattered city the seeds of democracy have taken root. Berlin can be the birthplace of a new day for Germany, just as it can be the starting point for a new war.

The Germans, as Winston Churchill once said, are "a very brave race." But their bravery in the past has been the bravery of battle, not the less spectacular political bravery which has played so important a role in the histories of the United States and Britain. That resistance to domestic tyranny which lights the stories of the English-speaking peoples is not prominent in German history. There are Gunther Prins without number but mighty few Elijah Lovejoys.

The battle for Berlin was not fought by the Germans with planes, tanks or rifles. It was fought with political courage. The maintenance of the city by the Anglo-American Airlift was only part of the story. It would not have mattered how many thousand tons of food and coal the American and British fliers were able to bring into the city over the Russian blockade if the Berliners themselves had not resisted first the Soviet and German Communist inducements to be fed by the eastern sector of the city, and finally the threats and violence. There were brave men among the Berliners.

When in the autumn of 1948 it was decided to hold an election reaffirming the faith in the city's assembly felt by the people in the western sectors, the Russians and their stooges among the German Communists kept a careful check on the political activities in the western sectors. This did not affect the position of men like Ernst Reuter or Otto Suhr or Ferdinand Friedensburg. They knew their fate if the Russians ever won control of the city and found them. But it did affect the position of hundreds of little men, part-time party workers, shop stewards, civil servants who in political meetings all over the city stood up, knowing they were spied on, and spoke for democracy and against the Russians.

But this demonstration of courage and faith, which resulted in 86.4 per cent of the people of the western sectors casting their votes for the legitimate city government in defiance of the Russians, was equaled in some respects by that shown in the endurance of the ordinary men and women of the city. It was not an especially cold winter in Berlin in 1948 and 1949. But it is cold enough when a family huddles around a single stove and one scuttle of coal. It was dark, dank and misty much of the time. The two hours of electric power allotted to the Germans were varied in the different districts of the city so that a housewife in Schoeneburg might find that her lights were on from two to four in the morning. This meant that she got up, did her ironing and, if she had an electric stove, her cooking for the next day in those hours.

"So, it is bad, but better than to have light and the Russians," a housewife in the Tempelhof district told a friend. "No, there is not much grousing about the rationed foods," she added. "Of course, we are not used to dehydrated potatoes and many don't like them. But I shut people up when I hear complaints. I ask them if they want the Russians back again."

I do not want to give the impression that during the siege of Berlin democracy as we in the United States know it developed as the sole political ideal of the people. The government of the city which exercises control under Military Government over the western sectors is a Social Democratic one. Many of its adherents are convinced Marxists. What did develop in Berlin was an understanding that the essential freedoms of man must survive, in Berlin, in a mountain village in Greece, anywhere. Under tremendous pressure the people came to realize the value of what had been given them.

And of course the Occupying Powers helped.

"Perhaps it is a symbol of our basic weakness," said a German friend of mine, a mechanic in the Tempelhof area. "Now, as you know, I am a Social Democrat and I believe in our party's program. And there are hundreds of thousands like me in western Berlin, Socialists, Christian Democrats and Liberal Democrats. But I am afraid that when this crisis came last year we had to be led, we had to be shown we must stick together and hold out against the Communists. In the past when someone put pressure on liberal, free Germans they succumbed. This time we did not. Was it because the Americans and the British were here? I don't know.

"But it was because we didn't succumb just as much as because of the air bridge, that you and we are still here today," he added.

The position in which the Berliners found themselves during the blockade of the city gave them a certain dignity and pride. Oddly, the last time I remember encountering this attitude was among the Londoners in another winter, that of 1940-1941 when it was a proud thing to be a Londoner, to be in the forefront of a fight waged at that time against the Luftwaffe controlled from this same city of Berlin. And now the Berliners, resisting another tyranny in their shattered city, felt the same way!

As long as Germany is partitioned and Berlin remains a divided city geographically within the Soviet Zone of Occupation, it will be a trouble spot. For, while the Americans and British remain in Berlin, the Russians and the German

Communists cannot completely dominate the eastern zone and the rebels against their authority will draw secret sustenance from the presence of the West in the capital. So the Russians must try to get the Western Powers out or at least, by political stratagem, reduce the international political importance of the city to a point where its influence, or rather the influence of the Americans and British and the free Germans of the western sectors, will not affect their plans for eastern Germany.

But to give up Berlin and the Germans who have fought along with the West for its political soul would be madness on the part of the Western Powers and might well deprive not only the people of Berlin but large segments of the German population elsewhere of their faith in the fairness and trustworthiness of the United States and its allies. Berlin's chance of escaping from the heavy pressure of the Russians lies in the eventual achievement of German unity. When that day comes the city may well emerge as the leading exponent in Germany of Western democracy, and its political leaders will assume an influence over democratic thought in Germany which may be greater than that exerted by the political leaders of today.

Of these, Ernst Reuter, Lord Mayor of Berlin, is the stand-out personality both as a man and as a political leader. Like so many convinced Socialists he has been a Communist—he was "the young Reuter" to Lenin—but today there is no more convinced anti-Communist. Certainly no political figure in Germany has been so roundly abused by the Communist press. In his dealings with the German Communists and their Russian masters, Reuter's early training has helped him enormously. During the crisis of 1948-1949 he kept one step ahead; his own experience told him what the Russians would do.

At the luncheon table on January 31 he turned to me and said, "It's all over; the Russians know they cannot get Berlin by blockade. Soon they will start to find a way out. We have only to remain firm and they are beaten."

Reuter is a bulky, balding man with gray hair, an oval, melancholy face which reminds his political opponents of a disappointed bloodhound. He wears a beret as a sort of political trademark. He is deliberate in his speech and his thought. From 1935 until the end of the war he was in Turkey, where he advised the Turkish Government on municipal government problems, especially transport, on which he is an expert. Today he runs with a firm hand the involved finances, administration and police powers of the world's most explosive city and, simultaneously, directs the Berlin Social Democratic Party, a militant, aggressive organization which has enough toughs on its roster to hold its own in street fights with the Communists of the eastern sector.

"When there is no longer any need for that, it will be over," Reuter claims. "We Germans have had enough of violence."

CHAPTER NINE

IT WAS THE BELIEF OF MANY MILlions, in and out of uniform, that when in May of 1945 silence crept across a continent long noisy with guns and bombs "the German problem," which had overshadowed so many lives for so long, had at last been settled. The march of events since that memorable day, bathed in the sunlight of optimism, has shown us how wrong we were. The German problem remains; defeating Germany was not enough.

That problem has been hideously complicated by the great struggle for the soul of Europe between the United States and the Union of Soviet Socialist Republics. In that struggle the conquered of 1945 are the greatest prize. A Germany joined with Russia in an ideological and economic alliance would dwarf any western European association. A Germany taking its place as part of that association would add so much to its strength that the United States well might feel that western Europe was safe from chaos and Communism.

Although the tug of war over Germany with the Soviet Union has been the aspect of the German problem which has excited the greatest interest in the United States and demanded a great share of the energies of three successive Secretaries of State, it is not the only aspect of that problem. There remain the Germans and their own future hopes and ambitions. There is no guarantee in history that the present period of world political conflict between America and Russia will continue indefinitely. There is the possibility of war. There is the possibility of a general Russian retreat resulting from some earth-shaking political cataclysm within the Soviet Union. There is the possibility that a depression or even a national conviction of the futility of further efforts abroad will cause the United States to withdraw into its own continental limits. In each of these possibilities the position of sixty to seventy million virile, courageous and industrious Germans situated in the strategic heart of Europe is terribly important. I submit that it is as important to the future of the United States to estimate correctly the future direction of Germany in world politics as it is to estimate that of the Soviet Union.

Partition is the primary political fact in Germany; just as it is the primary economic fact.

Both the East and the West continue to talk hopefully of some future solution of Germany's partition. But by the end of the Paris meeting of the Council of Foreign Ministers it was clear that, as Mark Twain said about the weather, although everyone talked about partition no one did anything about it. From the standpoint of the four Occupying Powers, the reunification of Germany is remote indeed. And although four-Power talks will continue on the subjects of political and economic reunification, at the moment this is written the prospects for such action are dim. Among the Occupying Powers the division of the country is an accomplished fact. To the Germans it is an unwelcome by-product of the cold war, one which certainly will be the basis of fierce resentment as German nationalism strengthens.

At the moment this resentment is directed more toward the East than the West. But its very presence in German thinking affords the Russians an opportunity to make good their losses in Germany since 1945.

The partition of Germany certainly is welcomed by many in western Europe and in the United States, as a guarantee against a revival of German aggression or as a partial defeat of the Russian effort to win domination or achieve alliance with Germany. A rereading of the troubles that overtook eastern Europe as a result of the three partitions of Poland in the eighteenth centry should be an adequate answer to complacency over partition. Partition does not mean the end of the German problem. Nor does it guarantee that there will be no more German adventures in aggression; indeed it is most probable that in the long run the national spirit of Germany, which rightly terrifies so many, will be increased, not reduced, by partition.

For the moment, at least, the United States must deal with two Germanies. Its approach to eastern Germany must be made through the Ministry of Foreign Affairs in Moscow: an entry which has not proved to be particularly easy in the past. But in western Germany there is evolving a state with which the United States can deal openly, although, if I may venture a prediction, the course of relations between America and the German Federal Republic will not be a smooth one. The fact that the foreign policy of the United States was the leading motive force in the organization of that states does not automatically guarantee gratitude or co-operation. The Germans in the process of organizing their state and the Germans representing that state once it is organized will prove to be two very different kinds of people. There will be many periods in our relationship with the West German State when the German attitude will be so irritating, obnoxious and obdurate that there will be a natural inclination in the United States to wash our hands of the whole affair and to limit American interest in the state to those security measures which we hope will insure us against a renewal of German aggression. No course could be more disastrous.

At the outset we will have certain definite advantages in the West German State. In the future it will be the task of United States policy to see that those advantages are retained for ourselves and our allies. First the German Federal Republic politically is organized along the lines suggested by the United States, the United Kingdom and France. Those freedoms which Americans believe form the basis of strength in society are written into its constitution. Whether or not the protection of these human rights will continue and, if it does continue, the growth of freedom in western Germany will result, we do not know. At the moment, however, a state has been organized which cannot be denied entry into any association of western Europe nations on the grounds that its government is not based on democratic concepts.

The way has been made clear for the addition of a nation of nearly fifty million people to any such association. Whether we like it or not, and a great many people do not, such an addition would go far toward strengthening western Europe against military, political or economic attack from the East. Some people would find attractive a neat world in which Germany might have been left alone to consider her defeat and slowly and painfully rebuild her wrecked society while the rest of the nations continued hand in hand to fraternal brotherhood under the United Nations. Unfortunately we do not live in that sort of world.

The economic advantage of the West German State is

closely tied with the political. The German Federal Republic will be based on one of the most important industrial areas in the world, the Ruhr. I do not believe that the Ruhr will recover entirely any more than I believe that Germany ever can return, even if no restraints were placed upon it, to the pinnacle of power achieved a decade ago. But to the Europe of today, which, despite the tremendous recovery of production, is still to a great extent dependent on the United States, an economic entity like the Ruhr capable of producing, to name only one product, 400,000 tons of coal a day is a considerable reinforcement.

The principal difficulty which we must discuss fully later is the inevitable arrival of the day when the production of western Germany must find other outlets than the reconstruction of Germany's peaceful economy and the contribution to the general economic health of western Europe.

The advantages inherent to the United States in its political struggle with Russia through the establishment of the German Federal Republic can be retained, however, only if the United States realizes the political factors within that state and in its relationship to the rest of Europe which, in the end, may nullify those advantages.

One such factor is the too easy assumption that Communism has been defeated permanently in western Germany. Since 1945 it has received numerous setbacks partly as the result of the ineptness of the party leaders and partly as a consequence of the ruthless Russian attempt to seize control of Berlin in 1948. In western Germany as elsewhere Communism appears to have lost its old political evangelism; it is more interested in declaiming the wickedness of the American "imperialists" than in investigating the desires and needs of the people and promising their fulfillment. Since the summer of 1948 it has been on the defensive.

However, the fact that conditions exist in western Germany, especially in the Ruhr, which give scope to Communist organizers is one of the most important political factors in the country. There is a deep dissatisfaction with high prices, poor housing and the return, real or imaginary, of "old bosses" among the workers of North Rhine-Westphalia. Equally deep is the refugees' bitterness over the failure of most of the *Land* governments in western Germany to give them adequate employment and housing. Both groups form a potential for a Communist revival.

The Social Democrats believe that, given power, they will be able to deal with this dissatisfaction. Perhaps. The changes in the society of the western zones of Germany brought about by war, destruction and occupation will make it difficult for any government for years to come to meet these protests. Overcrowding, low real wages and the resentment against the influence of the managerial class, associated in the past with the great industrial barons of the Ruhr, will continue for some time. So will the grip of the middle-aged or elderly civil servants on the machinery of government.

And as long as these conditions exist there will be the opportunity for Communism among the workers, the refugees and the war veterans.

The West German State will be faced in international politics by a considerable disadvantage. The government of the Third Reich won itself the unenviable position, to which that of the Soviet Union has now succeeded, of being regarded as completely untrustworthy. Undoubtedly the government of the German Federal Republic and its future envoys abroad will be met with a suspicion which can be traced in part to the remarkable record in international double-dealing made by Hitler and his cronies. This attitude is not going to be affected by the political character of the government.

"I don't care if he is a Socialist," an English friend of mine once said of a prominent Berlin politician. "My international Socialism stops at the Germans. I don't trust any of them, Social Democrats, Christian Democrats or Communists." The same attitude is discernible in the relations between the French and the Germans. Generally the Americans in western Germany, having suffered less at the hands of the Germans in the past, are more willing to take the present leaders of Germany on trust. But it will take shrewder men than either Konrad Adenauer or Kurt Schumacher to convince the other nations of western Europe that the good intentions of the new German state can be trusted.

The leaders of the new state also must accept the fear of German economic revival in Europe. Usually this is expressed in the equation: German recovery in industry plus German nationalism equal German aggression. But although deep fears do exist over future German aggression, it also is clear that these fears are often used to mask a less creditable concern over the German economic challenge in world markets.

Britain must export to live. That life is sufficiently precarious today. What does Britain do if its markets are invaded by German production?

Recently a British production expert in the Ruhr said, "My God, here we are helping these bloody Germans to get things right again so they can get into our markets! Did you ever see anyone cutting his throat? Well, take a look."

This is a danger which is in the future rather than the

present. Some suggest that as long as Germany's merchant marine is controlled, German exports can be "localized" to western Europe. But is the consumption there sufficient? And won't the Belgians, the Dutch and the French, in defiance of Germany's need to export and the United States' endorsement of those exports as a means of paying Germany's way and thus lightening the load on the American taxpayer, erect tariff barriers against imports from western Germany? Despite the energy and ingenuity of the American E.R.P. representatives in western Europe, I believe there is a grave danger that the future may see a re-erection of those tariff walls which have cost Europe so dear in the past.

However, if we weigh the present advantages of the West German State against the future difficulties, we can see that at the moment that state faces West. The Communists and their allies, some of them unwitting allies, make much of the fact that the state is not a natural growth but a forced one. Granted that the three Western Allies did create the conditions for the establishment of the new state, why should they be expected to encourage the natural growth of an aggressive, nationalist state in western Germany? The last such state caused enough trouble.

At the moment the Western outlook of the future republic is affected by such factors as American aid to Germany under the European Recovery Program, the continued occupation of western Germany and, above all, by the fact that the controls instituted in Germany by the Western Powers, such as the International Authority for the Ruhr, are co-operative affairs in which Germans will share with representatives of the Western Powers.

But the Western outlook in the future cannot be localized

to either the United States or the United Kingdom. For it is by no means certain that the United States, despite the vast amount of money and effort it has put into Germany in the past four years, will have the strongest political influence on the new state. If Socialism in Britain survives the 1950 elections and a Social Democratic government eventually achieves power in the German Federal Republic there will be a strong political tie between the two countries, even though their economies may be in conflict for world markets.

If, on the other hand, the C.D.U.-C.S.U. coalition remains the leading party of the new republic, then its political outlook will be more sympathetic to Washington than to London.

In any case, if American aid to the state lasts until 1950 or 1951, the United States can be assured of strong economic ties although these will not restrain the Germans from political dispute with the strongest of the Western Powers. The Germans are not going to reduce the strength of the general sentiment for unity merely because the United States Government may have concluded that unity with the Soviet Zone of Occupation is impossible because of the aggressive character of Russian policy in Germany. And we must reckon that, with nationalism on the increase in western Germany, the appeal of unity will grow progressively greater.

The main focus of the struggle for Germany in 1948 was Berlin. After the establishment of the German Federal Republic it is probable that the struggle will center around the new state. In other words the Russians and the German Communists will do everything possible to divert the economic and political outlook of the republic from West to East.

In their efforts they will be assisted by the small but grow-ing number of Germans who greet both the Soviet Union and the Atlantic Powers with Mercutio's curse and seek neutrality. The Nauheim Circle in the United States Zone and the Bavarian Party both are motivated by a desire to cut themselves free from the East-West conflict and the evil they believe it has in store for Germany. The Nauheim Circle envisages Germany as part of a neutral belt between Russia and the United States and the nations of western Europe, act-ing with Sweden, Austria, Switzerland and Yugoslavia as a neutral cushion between the two great Power groups.

This idea, first circulated in the winter of 1948-1949, was welcomed by the Soviet political strategists. For a neutral Germany trading with both East and West is more adaptable to Russian plans than a united Germany or a Western German State with an almost exclusively Western outlook. In their coming struggle to draw the German Federal Repub-lic into the Eastern orbit, the Russians and the German Com-munists will do their utmost to present this idea of neutrality as an alternative to Germany's entry into any firm association with the nations of western Europe.

Before we consider Russian aims and means in the expected offensive against western Germany, we must consider that the establishment of the German Federal Republic, enforcing as it does the partition of Germany, also cuts off Western influence from eastern Germany except as that can be exer-cised from Berlin. The effect which the entry of Western ideas into eastern Germany would have had on the popula-tion there, if unity had been achieved, cannot now be real-ized. Similarly the frontier of Western democratic thinking, save always for Berlin, now is firmly established along the eastern border of the republic and we must accept a consequent reduction of its influence on the peoples of Poland and Czechoslovakia.

Berlin remains the only "missionary center" behind the Iron Curtain from which American ideas and ideals can be transmitted to the peoples of the East. In a partitioned Germany its importance as a propaganda center remains even though its value as a headquarters will decrease with the establishment of the republic in the west.

It can be accepted as certain that the Russians will direct an intensive political attack on the new West German State. Partition has not diverted Soviet foreign policy from its basic objective of winning political control of Germany; it has merely made it more difficult for the moment and forced a shift in the basic tactics. In a unified Germany, the German Communists could have directed their efforts solely at winning control of the central government. With unity out of the question and the shape of the new German Federal Republic already defined, strongly anti-Communist in political outlook and based on a firm economic foundation, the preliminary task for both the German Communists and for their Soviet mentors is to divert the western state from its present political tendency. Not until the republic's economic and political ties with western Europe have been matched, in part at least, by economic and political ties with eastern Germany and eastern Europe, not necessarily the Soviet Union, can the Russians hope to press home a successful attack on its government. The exception would be the creation of a "revolutionary situation" inside the western state— that is, a situation in which the Russians believed that the Communist Party would be strong enough to seize and hold power. There is, as I have pointed out, a possibility of a revival of Communism's influence in western Germany, particularly in the Ruhr, but this is by no means certain or imminent.

The best card in the Russians' hand in their dealings with the new republic of the west is the economic situation in which that state will find itself in the foreseeable future—that is, at the conclusion of E.R.P. assistance. At that time the German manufacturers of the west will be faced with the prospect of either winning markets back from the Americans, the British and the French, without a merchant marine and with mounting costs of production, or of re-entering the old markets of eastern Europe, including the eastern Zone of Occupation, which the Soviet Union's production cannot satisfy.

The production of western Germany has to be sold somewhere. Both the Russians and the Germans are aware of the value of the eastern market and of the value of the raw materials from that area to German production. The Soviet Union and any government established by it in eastern Germany are sure to make most attractive trade offers to the businessmen of Düsseldorf and Cologne and Frankfort. The latter are now and probably will be then staunchly anti-Communist. But it is doubtful if they will allow their political preference to prevent their turning an honest pfennig.

Seemingly, the Russians are aware of this. Long before the blockade of Berlin was lifted in May of 1949, German envoys from the Soviet Zone were in Frankfort picturing the advantages of renewed trade with the eastern zone and subsequently all of eastern Europe. They did not do this on their own, although certainly they were sympathetic to the idea.

They did it because the Russians know that once trade ties, in the form of pacts and agreements, are concluded between east and west Germany the task of drawing the German Federal Republic out of the Western orbit will be that much easier. In May of 1949 the representatives in Frankfort of the German Economics Commission of the Soviet Zone already had offered 171,000,000 marks' worth of goods for sale to the merchants of western Germany and were seeking the purchase of an even greater amount of machine tools, steel and finished products from the industry of western Germany.

The economic partnership of Germany and Russia is not new. In the years before the Russian Revolution, German economic writers saw it as the solution of Germany's export problem. The Russo-German pact of 1939, whatever its political significance, was an attempt to put that partnership in operation to serve the pressing economic needs of both countries. Today even the industrialization of the Soviet Union has not robbed the idea of economic partnership of its validity. The Germans know better than most peoples how much the Soviet economy needs their production. The Russians hope that a restoration of the economic partnership will lead eventually to political infiltration and domination.

Once the West German State is induced by its commercial ties with the East to assume a precarious neutrality in the political struggle, the job of the Soviet political strategists is half accomplished. What remains is to feed the enthusiasm for German unity which will continue as long as partition continues and to emphasize the willingness of the Germans of the east zone to reunite with their compatriots of the western state. There certainly will be voices raised in western Germany against reunion on anything but the republic's terms. The Russians, if they are wise, may accept those terms in exchange for a unity in which the Communist Party of eastern Germany, whether it is disguised as a "national front" or wears its present mask of the Socialist Unity Party, can spread from its bases in the eastern zone into western Germany. Moreover, any government of eastern Germany is certain to be dominated by the Communists, and union with the west inevitably would bring about the admission of some Communists or their tools into the united German government.

None of this can happen rapidly, if indeed it happens at all. But the Political Bureau plays a long, slow game. It plans not for next month or next year but a decade hence.

Altogether the attraction which the Eastern Power group can exercise on Germany would seem to be almost irresistible. There are plenty of historic precedents. The economy of the whole central and eastern European area appears to demand it. To many in Germany, intellectuals, ex-soldiers, businessmen, the thing seems inevitable. Yet at the moment western Germany appears to be safely won for the West.

In the American Zone of Occupation well over 50 per cent of its people with whom I have talked in the last year are in favor of a union of the states of western Europe including Germany. Both in the western sectors of Berlin and the British Zone of Occupation the percentage is far higher. Thus if nationalism is growing in western Germany, as it certainly is, there remain plenty of people who are willing to try internationalism as well.

A friend of mine, a manufacturer in Stuttgart, said he was both.

"Certainly I want to see Germany strong and united. Is

that a crime? If the government is not strong, how can we resist the Communists? If that is being a nationalist, then I am one. But also I want to see Germany in a European union. The old wars between the countries of western Europe are over. We must unite or be gobbled up one by one, like the Czechs and the others. I expect Germany will be one of the strongest states in a union, but won't that give added security to the others?"

The large majority of the people of the American and British zones regard the United States as the first Power in the world. Moreover they believe that the United States in the next ten years will have the most influence on world affairs and will use that influence to promote peace.

It is interesting that American possession of the atom bomb is not the only reason why the Germans look to the United States for power and influence. In every industrial area there is tremendous respect for American production, which most German veterans regard as the decisive factor in the war in the west. Perhaps this attitude is a variant on the old "stab in the back" theme which soothed the pangs of defeat in the 1920's and 1930's. However, I think not.

"Always the propaganda said, 'You are going to get new tanks, great new tanks faster and with bigger guns than the Americans' or even the Tigers. By next month there will be a thousand new fighters to protect you. Just hang on.' But when next month came there we were with the same old equipment with the 'Jabos' [fighter bombers] coming at us all day," said a veteran of the fighting in France and along the German frontier.

"Every day there were more American tanks, more guns, more planes. Your artillery would fire as much in a day, even an hour, as ours in a week. We had been proud of our equipment early in the war, but I can see now it was nothing compared with what the American Army had in 1944 and 1945. And now I know that at the same time you had a big navy in the Pacific war and a big air force also. It is a scale of production we find hard to understand."

Most of the Germans I have talked with believe there will be war between the United States and the Soviet Union. Their respect for the production of the United States makes them believe America would win such a war. But I have nowhere found any overwhelming eagerness at the prospect of war. The story which we have heard so often since the last war, that the Germans are doing their utmost to stir up a conflict between the Soviet Union and the United States, seems highly exaggerated to me. Many have sought to divide the victors of 1945. Certainly there is a large group of ex-officers and former regular soldiers who would welcome a return to their old trade. But even they do not believe Germany would get anything out of a war.

"Certainly I would fight for the Americans," an ex-pilot told me. "I hate the Russians for what they have done to Germany. But I know that a war would finish us completely. Look what has happened already. And this time Germany would be the big battleground. There's little enough left now. After another war it would be just a wasteland."

I believe that the basic cause why so many Germans are interested in the idea of a western European union is that they see in it some insurance against war. There is enough of the old arrogance left to encourage the idea that in such a union Germany would be the outstanding Power and would exercise great influence on the policies of the union. But I,

personally, never have heard a German speak with any satis-
faction of either the prospects for war or Germany's chances
of retrieving its fortunes through war. Nor do I believe that
the pride with which many Germans refer to German feats
of arms in the second World War should be accepted as proof
that there is an overwhelming desire to start another war.

On the other hand, no one should discount the latent dangers of German militarism. There certainly are hundreds of
thousands who could be induced to "try it again" either from
a desire for revenge, hatred of the Russians or the Americans
or simply because they know no other trade than war. There
still are Germans who do not realize what has happened to
their country as a result of two world wars, bombing and
occupation. These men believe in Germany's destiny as the
dominant continental Power. Pride in Germany's martial
powers still exists.

It is not difficult to find ex-officers who will show you how,
with just a few more guns at El Alamein or a few more tanks
at Stalingrad, the war could have been won. The mass repu-
diation of Hitler and his gang, which struck the conquering
armies of the Western Allies so forcibly in 1945, came not
from any rejection of the hideous philosophy of National
Socialism but resulted from the simple fact that Hitler lost
the war. Indeed shortly before this book was completed
Franz Halder, former Chief of the General Staff of the Supreme Command of the Germany Army (OKH), published
a book the main objective of which seems to be to prove what
a bad general Hitler was and how he lost the war.

This may, as some Americans suggest, serve a useful purpose in pinning responsibility for the defeat on Hitler and
thereby further blackening his name in the minds of the Ger-

man people. I doubt, however, if this is necessary. Hitler lost the allegiance of the present generation of Germans when it became evident that his government was losing the war. Meanwhile the book maintains the legend of the General Staff's intelligence and efficiency, both of which were very high. It would have been a far tougher war if it had been run by Von Brauchitsch, Von Rundstedt and Halder from 1941 onward.

Hitler lost the war and consequently the admiration and confidence of the present generation of Germans. But this does not mean the end of the Hitler legend. As long as German nationalism survives, the memory of the man who led Germans to their greatest conquests will survive. As Germany recovers from the effects of the war, the fact that Hitler also plunged the country into its greatest defeat will be forgotten. All the disasters which overtook the German arms in and after 1942 will appear to a new generation not as a senseless waste of life to feed one man's ambition, but as a Homeric epic of German courage and devotion. In ten years I believe we will see in Germany a Hitler legend as popular and as influential as that which developed in France after the death of Napoleon at St. Helena.

In his day Napoleon was hated and feared quite as much by his own compatriots and his enemies abroad as Hitler was in his. Yet so well balanced and liberal a man as Thiers wrote of Napoleon after his death: "How wonderful was this man's destiny, to be the greatest writer of his age as well as its greatest commander, legislator and administrator!" Thiers had forgotten the secret police, the censorship, the long agony of 1812 and the colossal downfall at Waterloo. So in a decade will Germans have forgotten the Gestapo, the concentration camps, the destruction of German cities and the final, complete humiliation of 1945.

The latent militarism of many Germans, the development of the Hitlerian legend, the arrogance of a defeated people, all these will make the Germans difficult partners in any western European association. These are not things that can be conjured away by pious statements about German democracy. They are going to remain part of the German character for the foreseeable future. The task is to see that these characteristics never again are fused into a single political party. The fact that they exist should not force us to turn away from the Germans now or in the future. For if that is done, we will be handing Germany back to the extremists.

At present all the signs point to an increasing co-operation between the west Germans and the peoples of western Europe and the Atlantic Nations. Self-interest in the event of war between East and West, the belief that only through co-operation with western Europe can Germany be saved from Communism and the clutches of the Russian colossus, the idea that within a western European union Germany could regain some measure of her old power and influence all attract Germany to the West.

Why, it may be asked, after four and a half years of occupation does the question even arise? The United States has poured millions of dollars into Germany, sent educators, editors, lawyers and experts on government to Germany by the planeload to "build democracy." The Marshall Plan has been extended to Germany to give democracy there a solid economic basis. These should be enough to assure German resistance to Eastern influences. Unfortunately they will not be enough in the future.

The economic outlook, as I have explained, is toward the east. Will Belgium, to which the Germans exported 197,000,000 marks' worth of produce in 1937, admit anything like that amount in 1957? If the West German State is to import wheat from Poland, the wheat must be paid for ultimately by German exports to Poland.

The reasons for disquiet over western Germany's political orientation after four and a half years of occupation are less tangible but equally alarming. The basis for them is the fact that four and one half years of occupation, during which the strength of Military Government especially in the United States Zone has been reduced steadily, are not enough to insure that there is a general German conviction of the essential rightness of democracy. The authoritarian and totalitarian state still holds its appeal for millions of Germans and, although at present the country is strongly anti-Communist, ten or fifteen years from now a Communist leader and party promising a revival of Germany's power in a reunited country, and the end of internal disorder, which the Communists would have fomented, would, in my opinion, stand a very good chance of success.

This is not a blanket indictment of Military Government, American, British or French. It is an admission that the occupation has not been long enough or numerically strong enough to make an impression on the thought habits of centuries. Some hundreds of hard-working American and British officials have succeeded in chipping a few bits off the mass of authoritarian thinking in Germany. The political parties have been encouraged to take firm stands on civil liberties. There has been a minor development of respect for such aspects of political democracy as free speech and freedom of assembly. The glorification of war and conquest in education has been fought although it has not been entirely eliminated.

Since its beginning Military Government and occupation policy have been the subject of "sound and fury."

"From the letters I get," a Military Government officer in Hesse said recently, "every s.o.b. in the United States knows more about my job than I do. Maybe I don't know too much, but at least I am here and I've been here for two and a half years. I guess ignorance is bliss at that.

"One day I get a letter telling me to watch out because they're rebuilding the German Army around here. The next day there's a letter from someone else telling me I'm being too hard on the Germans."

The impression remains in the United States that Military Government is really a rather simple operation in which the Americans give the orders and the Germans carry them out. This might have been so at the beginning of the occupation, although personally I never saw anything so uncomplex as that, but it most emphatically has not been so since 1946. Today, the punitive phase of the occupation is over. Any analysis of the faults and virtues of American military occupation in Germany must be preceded by the acknowledgment that this was and is a vastly complicated business and perhaps the most important work abroad which has ever engaged the energies of Americans in peacetime.

To my mind the principal fault to be found in American military occupation and the one which stands in close relation to concern over the future political orientation of Germany is that, almost since the start, it has placed the main emphasis on the economic rather than the political side of occupation. This has been because to Americans in Germany, and in Washington, this phase of occupation seemed more immediately important and also because of the belief that, after a thorough purge of overtly Nazi influences from government, educational system and information media, democracy would thrive automatically.

It is easy to understand the motivation of those soldiers who in 1945 said, "By God, we've got to get things moving again." They were Americans—which means they were builders and movers, men who wanted to see the wheels turning again. Moreover they saw in the appalling state of the empty and stagnant Germany that lay before them the promise of trouble with the Germans. And in 1945 it was the Germans, not the Russians, whom most people in Military Government worried about.

They did not believe that the Germans would continue their stolid acceptance of military rule. Why should they? And they foresaw that, unless there were food and some shelter, the people who now seemed so eager to please them might in a year or eighteen months be equally eager to kill them. The reader may say that such fears were exaggerated. At the time I thought they were. But how could any officer take the chance?

There was a stronger pressure than this exerted on the economic aspects of the occupation. It came primarily from the need for increased German production to fulfill the needs of western Germany itself and to pay for some of the imports to the area, thus lifting some of the load off the American taxpayer. This pressure already was being exerted long before the Marshall Plan took form. From the outset the British called for greater industrial production in Germany to relieve their own budgetary expenditures. And American economic experts were not far behind in their advocacy of a raised level of industry.

At the same time the countries beggared by the war and German occupation rightly claimed that they share in any production of a revived German economy. And as the European Recovery Program took shape it was obvious that the great industrial potential of Germany should be added to the efforts to rebuild economic security in western Europe. But well before E.R.P. the Americans and the British, fearful of rising costs in the support of western Germany, had made the first moves toward the establishment of the Bizone.

The charge is frequently made by those who in their sincere anxiety to prevent another world war wish to hold Germany down, that the economy of the western zones has been revived without any benefit to those countries which bore the first onslaught of German aggression. Statistics do not bear out this assertion.

According to the Statistical Annex to the Report of the Military Governor for the Office of Military Government (U.S.) for Germany the total dollar value of the exports from the Bizone in March of 1949 amounted to $86,072,000. The exports of coal alone were valued at $27,119,000 and of iron and steel, including scrap, at $10,881,000.

Seven countries, Belgium, Denmark, France, Greece, the Netherlands, Norway and Yugoslavia, absorbed $34,745,600 of these exports. It is notable that France, a country where protests against the revival of German industry have been fiercest, bought $13,669,200 worth of exports in March alone and in that month and the preceding one was the Bizone's best customer.

Whatever other criticisms may be made, the present export figures show that the recovery of production in western Germany has made a significant contribution to general European recovery, although production in the Bizone still lags behind production in other countries of western Europe compared to prewar figures. In addition the amount of money spent in Germany by the United States is slowly being reduced although the reduction is neither so fast nor so great as officials of Military Government wish.

There are two valid criticisms of the manner in which the economic aspects of the occupation have been emphasized.

From the beginning of occupation there was a tendency among the "production," as differentiated from the "political," officials of both American and British Military Government to employ either former National Socialists or supporters of the Hitler regime in industry. The excuse presented, that the former Nazis or Nazi-supporters were the only people capable of doing the work required, had a sound basis of fact. There were mighty few anti-Nazis among the managerial class of the Third Reich. Military Government erred, nevertheless, in failing to train recognized anti-Nazis for such jobs, perhaps because they were informed by the Germans that So-and-So, although he might be anti-Nazi, was "really a Communist."

During the last six months of 1948 a number of men who had held important managerial or administrative posts in the coal-mining and iron and steel industries under the Hitler regime returned to positions equal or only slightly inferior in importance to those they had held under National Socialism.

By December of 1948, thirty-three such officials had been restored to positions of importance in the coal-mining industry alone. At that time fifty-eight applications had been made to the U.S.-U.K. Coal Control Board for reinstatement. Nine of the applicants had been rejected and the applications of sixteen others still were under consideration.

Otto Springorun is a good example of the type of man who had been reinstated. Under the Nazis, Springorun was chairman of the Vorstand or board of management of two major coal combines. From September 1945 to April 1947 he was interned as a "leading industrialist." A German denazification tribunal classified him as a Category Four offender, which gave him the right to apply for re-employment at his old post or some similar post. He returned to the coal industry as a member of the Vorstand of a single mine, a less important post than he held under the Nazis.

Erich Sauerbrey was a commercial director on the board of management of one of the Hugo Stinnes companies before Germany's defeat. In December of 1948 he had been reinstated to a similar post but not in a company formerly owned by the Stinnes interests.

Bernhard Dreyer, also interned as a leading industrialist, is one who, unlike Springorun, failed to come back. Before the war Dreyer was the superintendent of a small group of mines. After he had been released from internment he applied for reinstatement. But his application was rejected because his reinstatement would have meant the replacement of another German of unblemished political record.

Men such as these earned between fifty and sixty thousand marks a year before the war. Some, but not all, owned stock in the corporations for which they worked. None of them was a large stockholder.

Why are any of them back in industry? Essentially because the basic directive given the Coal Control Board by Military Government was "maximize coal production." Men like Springorun and Sauerbrey have spent their lives in the industry and the board believed they could help it reach the goal set by American and British policy makers.

The principal danger inherent in the return of these men and others like them to positions of power and influence in their industries is not so much the immediate abuse of that power and influence in favor of German rearmament or German economic war, but their connection with former owners of Ruhr industry. At the moment the accounts of the big industrialists are blocked and there is no question of their exerting openly any of the rights of ownership.

But in the Ruhr it is commonly believed that liaison has been established between the owners of the industries and their former employees of the managerial class and that meetings are held to discuss policy matters.

"You see, it's all so damned easy," a British intelligence officer said. "They can get together over the dinner table or pay each other friendly visits. Such visits take place, I'm certain. But what can you do about it? These people aren't in jail. And you can't arrest people because they invite old friends to dinner."

Generally I have been impressed by the awareness of British intelligence of the potential danger in the restoration of the old ownership in the Ruhr, both as it applies to the peace of Europe and, in a narrower sense, the peace of mind of the workers of the area. There is a general feeling that control over the Ruhr through the International Authority should be maintained for at least another decade.

Sometimes the point is made that the managers and executives who return to their old jobs or similar ones in the Ruhr are not "political"; that they are working just as hard for the Americans and British as ever they did for Hitler. The answer to that is that they probably would work as hard for a new Fascist government in Germany or a Communist government. That is the core of the whole problem of re-employment of Nazis and Nazi-supporters. A man like Schumacher who would die, and very nearly did, rather than submit to National Socialism is, in the long run, a better instrument in Germany than the highly efficient technical expert who will work for anyone.

I have noted the deep opposition among the workers of the Ruhr to the "old bosses." Many British and American Military Government officials in the area believe that this sentiment is so strong and the trade unions which voice it so powerful politically that any present misuse of managerial power is impossible. In November 1948 even Willi Agatz, the Communist boss in the Ruhr, shared this view in private although in public he was forced by the tenets of his faith to bewail loudly the reappointment of "Nazis and Fascists" to "the control of Ruhr industry."

There remains the blunt fact that the economic revival of the Ruhr does mean that the war potential of Germany has been increased for future use by Germans or perhaps by the Russians. Unless the United States had been willing to adopt the Morgenthau Plan, this was inevitable. Coal is war potential. So is steel. So is a steel plant. So, if the proposition is reduced to absurdity, is a factory which makes shoestrings which can lace a miner's—or a soldier's—brogans.

Ultimately such discussions all come back to the original question of whether or not the safeguards established by Military Government such as the Military Security Board and the International Authority for the Ruhr will prevent German industry being used for war by Germans in the future. These are the only safeguards, because, in our anxiety to lighten the tax burden, to provide coal and steel for the rest of Europe and to prevent unrest in Germany by increasing production, we have neglected the political side of the occupation, specifically the political re-education of the German people.

Due to the depth of German feeling for authoritarian government, this admittedly is an enormous task. But it is also an important one. Had eight Germans out of ten told the American Military Government survey that National Socialism was a bad idea rather than 55.5 per cent saying it was a good idea badly implemented, there would be less need of controls in the Ruhr and elsewhere.

A second general failing of Military Government, which in the long run may prove as costly as the emphasis on economic rather than political reconstruction, has been the steady quantitative and qualitative decline of personnel. This has been accompanied by a decline in emphasis on the German political problem. There are many able and intelligent men in Military Government in the United States Zone, but, perhaps inevitably, the sense of urgency has disappeared. It is a job, not a mission. And there is far too much willingness to "trust the Germans."

From the beginning of the occupation, the great mass of the American soldiers lacked any critical facility in dealing with the Germans. There was a great pother about this in the summer of 1945. There was deep resentment over fraternization and the fact that in many parts of Germany G.I.'s and their officers were living on terms of the greatest friendship with their recent enemies. As late as the summer of 1948, a woman correspondent lately arrived in Germany from the United States was tiresome over the fact that the American soldiers, whom she had talked to, did not seem able to distinguish between Germans and Displaced Persons.

On the whole she and other Americans expect too much from Johnny Doughfoot, the man who does the killing and the dying in all wars. Four years before, she had encouraged the American Army to destroy the Germans. Four years later, she could not understand why riflemen in an infantry division were unable to differentiate between one foreigner and another. There are mighty few T. E. Lawrences or Stendhals among the men who dress by the right.

At the start, despite the amount of fraternization which went on from buck privates on up into the rarefied strata of the Army hierarchy, there was a pretty sure realization, on the part of the combat troops at least, of the essential character of the Germans. They never had it so good, they said. Pretty young blondes with big breasts, nice old women who would cook their rations and mend their socks, warm farmhouses when the winds blew. But in the back of the doughfoot's mind, the man who had fought his way across France and Germany or up through Italy, was the memory of what he had seen or heard on the way.

But by the end of 1946, although the blondes, the motherly old women and the farmhouses were still there, the first somewhat shopworn by now, the beribboned veterans of St. Lo and Anzio and Aachen had departed. The new army, the shy, awkward young men who had not yet been fitted into the military frame and who stood terribly lonesome and homesick in the Red Cross clubs, had arrived to represent the might, majesty and dominion of the sovereign people of the United States of America.

These boys fell even harder for the Germany they were offered. With no memories of El Guettar or Gela or Easy Red Beach or the weeping women in French towns, they accepted the Germans as promiscuous, harmless and hospitable people. When in 1934 the first dreadful stories of Dachau began to drift across Europe like the stench of a burning ghat by the Ganges, most of these boys were only kids in grammar school. The nameless terrors of the Gestapo were more unreal to them than the adventures of Dick Tracy. The little band of men who sent death in black boots and breeches stalking over Europe for six years were to them a rather humorous gang including a fellow with a funny mustache, a little man with a big head and a club foot, and a big, fat guy. The rather dreary sergeant who lectured on current affairs said this gang had raised plenty of hell in its time—but who took him seriously?

This is not very creditable to the Army or to the educational system which is supposed to mold the boys who came overseas after the war. But it is unwise to look for too much in infantrymen. If you find a boy who will get up out of a hole when the whistle blows and move forward you have done pretty well. Leave the thinking to someone else. It would be fine if every rifleman was a political theorist and a fighting man beside. But we have not got to that stage yet. So it is easy to understand the kids who went for the big blondes and the schnapps in the kitchen on a winter night and to forgive them. But in forgiving them it must not be forgotten that they are the people on whom the occupation ultimately rests and that their friendship for the Germans made it more difficult for the Military Government officers who had a more austere and skeptical view of the native virtues of the conquered.

"That guy, he's screwy," the G.I.'s would say. "He thinks these Krauts are a bunch of gangsters. Look at old Herman over there. Some gangster, eh?"

With these sentiments permeating the rank and file of the occupation army, it is not strange that a change took place on the next highest level of the occupation, the Military Government officials in the field.

At the start this group had included some of the most earnest and thoughtful officers of the Army, men who had seen great evil in their time and who viewed their assignment in Germany as an opportunity to eradicate the bases of that evil. To them it was a mission. Many of them because of age or physical infirmities had not been on the firing line. But they were honest and on the whole efficient public servants, although, as I have indicated earlier, they were baffled by the confusion which existed on the upper levels of Military Government.

Today the Germans claim that there were too many "enemies of Germany"—a cool phrase—among the original Military Government officers. There were also a great many men of German-American families who understood the language of the country, believed it could be converted to democracy on the Western style and labored long and hard for their beliefs. Many of them left Germany disillusioned. Some who had come to fight Fascism found that the professional soldiers who were their commanders did not know what the word meant or knew all too well. Others who had come with the same objective found that their only allies were Commu-

nists and that in any case the Army seemingly was not interested in eliminating Fascism or authoritarianism in Germany
but in rebuilding bridges and restoring production.

Newspapers, elections and denazification didn't mean
much, they were told. The thing to do was to get production
started again; this, they were told, "is basic."

Increasingly they found that it was unpopular to worry
about the Germans. From 1946 Russia has been on the minds
of the professional officers, and quite rightly since Soviet aggression is far more dangerous in the mind of a regular soldier than German aggression ten or twenty years in the
future. When you place a man in uniform and tell him his
job is to put out international fires you should not be surprised if he pays more attention to those already lighted than
those which may be burning a decade hence.

It is well that in 1948, when the struggle for Germany between East and West was at fever pitch, the United States
Army was alive to the dangers of the situation. But the tendency of the Army to forget all sources of trouble save the
Soviet Union is not a healthy one. Nor was the unbalanced
exaggeration of Russian strength wholly to the credit of the
representatives of the finest army in the world. In the first
six months of 1948 the attitude toward the Soviet Union of
army wives and army hangers-on in the American Zone was
almost disgraceful.

"Once they clamped that blockade on Berlin, the people
around here thought there would be war any minute," an
old friend of mine in the First Division told me. "Not the
G.I.'s, you know. The civilians who manage things for the
Army and the wives were the worst. Why, one night last
July the fire alarms sounded here and a hell of a lot of people

were all set to light out for Switzerland. They thought the war had started. It wasn't very encouraging."

Gradually, because there were better opportunities at home, because they felt they were getting nowhere, because they received no encouragement from the higher echelons, a great many of the original Military Government officers returned to the United States. The replacements, in my opinion, have not been up to the originals. Each group has made mistakes. But the men and women who first tackled the enormous job of occupation at least in most cases had a deep desire to do something about Germany. Certainly there were "empire builders" and "deadheads" among them. But the average was pretty high. And of course the problem was new and challenging.

Among them were a large number of professional soldiers. Although many of these Army men lacked any basic knowledge of Germany or saw the German problem on anything but an engineering basis, they did work. Many criticisms can be leveled at the soldiers in the original Military Government organization, but laziness is not one of them. Germany and the Germans have benefited tremendously from their labors to "get this country going again," as they themselves put it. But their political limitations prevented them from making any great contribution to what should have been the first consideration of the occupation—the future political stability of Europe.

Their industry would be welcome now. There are notable exceptions but in the American Zone of Occupation I am always shocked by the amount of leisure. In Bavaria, a state brimful of all the political tendencies which Americans should seek to outroot, there are too many shooting parties, too many leaves for week ends in Austria or Switzerland, too much of a "colonial" atmosphere.

I have never subscribed to the idea that people on the public pay roll work less than those in private industry. I have known too many Army officers and civil servants who literally have worked themselves into the grave in the interest of the United States. But it is my firm conviction that in Germany too many of our officials, softened by the ease of their life, by the number of servants available and, above all, by their position as the representatives of the conquering Power, have not and are not devoting enough of their time to their jobs.

Curiously when the occupation started there were many hard things said about the "colonial" attitude of the British toward the occupation. It was truly said that the British in their Zone of Occupation had established communities isolated from the Germans, that one could walk into an officers' club in Düsseldorf or Hameln and meet an atmosphere not much different from that of an officers' club at Aldershot. This was not the way to do it, said the Military Government officers of 1945. Of course it was not.

But today there are "Little Americas" throughout the United States Zone of Occupation—lunchrooms on the *Autobahnen* where the German waitresses speak "G.I. American" and studiously copy American culture as purveyed by the movies; officers' clubs where on a rowdy Saturday night you can close your eyes and believe yourself in any tavern in the United States.

The charge is made that the occupation force and Military Government have been conquered by the Germans. As I have shown, that is partly true. But there has been also a general withdrawal on the part of too many officials from the roots of the German problem. It is easier to listen to what Bürgermeister Schmidt or Herr Dr. Hoffman has to say about German problems than to go out among the people and dig for the answers.

American Military Government has much to answer for in the way it has been impressed by the Bürgermeister and the Herr Doktor. The Germans have laid on flattery with a trowel. They have been confiding and friendly in private. Most of these Germans, I am convinced, do not want another war. And they have been at pains to point out that the Russians are a much worse people than the Germans.

At a dinner party in the American Zone recently I was promised that at table I would sit next to a countess, "a real lady, real old regime." The lady turned out to be a rather tedious personification of all the German arrogance and bigotry which has revolted the world for the last eighty years. She had just returned from a holiday in Switzerland.

"It really was wonderful," she told me. "All the women were very chic and the men most courteous and well turned out. They were Spaniards, I think."

She leaned her pretty, empty head close to mine.

"And do you know," she said, "there were no Jews. It was such a relief!"

The personnel problem is not one of unrelieved black. Since the start Military Government has commanded the services of men who would be outstanding in any job. I know an American intelligence officer in Bavaria who for brains, courage and understanding of the general problem cannot be matched anywhere in Germany. There are several men in the lower levels of the Information Services Division who are aware of the tremendous importance of the job to be done in Germany in sustaining the idea of a free press. Scattered throughout the Military Government organization are men who could be making twice their present salaries in the United States but who believe in the importance of what they are doing and are making a personal sacrifice to do it.

At the top United States Military Government has been singularly fortunate. In General Clay it had a man of courage and resource. Combined with those characteristics was a sort of antique probity, the thing we always expect and so seldom find in our public men. At the time General Clay was leaving Germany, I came across some words of Woodrow Wilson written about Grover Cleveland which seemed to fit the retiring Military Governor.

"Men have said," wrote Wilson, "that he was stubborn because he did not change and self-opinionated because he did not falter. He has made no overtures to fortune, has obtained and holds a great place in our affairs by a sort of inevitable mastery, by a law which no politician has ever quite understood or at all relished, by virtue of a preference which the people themselves have expressed without analyzing."

The words fit Clay. That was the sort of man he was. His virtues permeated the Military Government organization encouraging the falterer and rewarding the worker. His retirement robbed the American Government of a great and unselfish public servant whose continuing services to the organization he headed were as great as those more spectacular and more widely publicized ones he rendered to the cause of the West in the Berlin crisis of 1948.

General Clay overshadowed his co-workers to such an extent that most of their names are unknown or, if they are known, will be quickly forgotten. He had great personal loyalty and he is a kindly man, so that he suffered many a deadhead to remain in office long after the man's usefulness had ended. But he also encouraged young men, gave them high positions and his full trust. It should be noted, too, that he was saddled with many a governmental misfit sent to him from Washington.

Yet all Clay's ability, the hard work and intelligence of some of his subordinates, the planning and the surveying and the anxious consultations did not suffice in the first four years of the occupation to shift the political attitudes of the German mass mentality. Partly this was because the emphasis was on economic reconstruction. Partly it was because there was a steady reduction in the quality and quantity of Military Government. Partly it was because, from 1946 on, the immediate threat of Russia and German Communism was a greater concern than the long-term threat of renascent German nationalism.

We must, I believe, take it for granted that the Germans with whom the United States will have to deal in the future are not much different basically from those it has fought and defeated. This is an unpleasant conclusion. But it must be faced and dealt with. We know now that we cannot eliminate Germany. We know now that Germany will assume a great place in the affairs of Europe. We know now that the days of Germany's complete impotence and surrender are over. How then do we fit the Germany of today into the world of today?

W HEN, ON THAT SUNNY MORN-
ing which now seems so long ago, the weary Neville Cham-
berlain announced to his countrymen their entrance into the
second World War, he told them they would be fighting
"evil things." The subsequent actions of the German Government and its armies, air forces and navy proved him right.
In the years between September 1939 and May 1945 the Third
Reich aroused all over the Western world and in the Soviet
Union distrust, fear, suspicion and hate. The evil that men
and governments do lives after them. The distrust, fear, suspicion and hate evoked by the Nazis must be eliminated before any German state will be accepted as a true partner in
the affairs of western Europe.

One of the most singular things about the entire German
situation is the fact that the basic attitude of the countries of
western Europe toward the Germans is not understood in
Germany. If it were, the chances of a true reunion of Germany with the West and perhaps of democracy in Germany
would be improved.

"Of course the French hate us," a German shopkeeper told
me. "We defeated them in 1940. You don't love people who
conquer you."

I asked her if she didn't think the forced labor, the cruelties
inflicted on the French by the retreating Germans in 1944,
the massacres of whole villages by the S.S. troops in retalia-
tion for *maquis* resistance had anything to do with it.

She shrugged her shoulders. "Oh, we've been hearing all about that since the end of the war. Perhaps a few of our troops did behave badly. But their discipline was very good and I don't believe it was so bad as the French and the propagandists say. Besides, look what the Russians have done in Germany."

Thus we come back to the Russians. The actions of the Soviet Army in Germany in 1945 and to a lesser degree thereafter have had the peculiar effect in Germany of excusing in many German minds the excesses committed by their own troops in the Soviet Union or elsewhere. Listening to the tales of rape, arson and murder in the eastern zone and to the long list of deportations from the zone to Russia, most Germans feel their own guilt transferred to the Russians.

Nor can I find much German realization of the anxiety with which western Europe views any revival of Germany's industrial power. "Yes," Germans admit, "we went to war in 1939. But we were led to war. And we have had enough of war. Look around, if you doubt."

If Germany understood the revulsion which concentration camps, the Gestapo and the whole hideous story of Nazi brutality awaken in the minds and hearts of the people of western Europe and the fear with which they watch each German step on the road to recovery, it is possible that they would attach greater value to American efforts to introduce democracy in western Germany. Sometimes, reading the speeches of German political leaders and American Military Government officials about the beauties and glories of democracy, I think that each sees democracy in his own image. For most of the German politicians democracy means something on which the Americans are insistent and which can be successfully counterfeited while the Americans are there, by elections and all the other trappings, but which will not change the essential idea that in each town and each state the educated experts and the well-to-do will make the rules.

For the Germans do not realize that only when a true democracy is in operation in western Germany will the fears of the rest of the world subside.

American thinking on Germany is conditioned by the record of the Nazi regime just as is the thinking of western Europe. But sometimes I feel that the hate aroused by the Nazis is stronger today in the United States than it is in, say, Holland or France. Certainly it is more vocal. And a number of people appear concerned with maintaining the hatred and arousing new fears of Germany. Americans, both individually and as a people, have plenty of reason to fear a German revival and to hate a regime which, in the past, stood for everything to which an American should be opposed. But the emotional approach to the German problem which sees the Germans either as sixty million devils or as an equal number of friendly, warm-hearted people led astray by a Mephistophelian Austrian, is not the best guarantee for an intelligent foreign policy.

We cannot expect to get the sort of Germany we want unless we try to encourage its emergence. We should be ready to show friendship to any German government which proves its respect for the freedoms on which our own society is based. It is quite probable that one of the early governments of the German Federal Republic will be a Social Democratic one. The fact that the government of the republic is Socialist should not prevent us from helping and encouraging that government, so long as the essential freedoms are honored, no matter how distasteful Socialism as a political ideology may be to us as a people.

Conversely we cannot allow any encouragement of neo-Nazism or neo-Fascism in Germany. The Russians have a nasty trick of so twisting the meanings of words that they become meaningless. The word "Fascist" is one of these. The fact that the Russians apply the term to everyone from Cardinal Spellman to General Clay should not blind Americans to the fact that there were Fascists in Germany and Europe, that a decade ago they seemed to many impressionable Americans the coming power group and that before they were defeated the combined might of the United States, the British Commonwealth and Empire and the Union of Soviet Socialist Republics was mobilized.

There are too many Americans at home and abroad who, overfrightened by the Soviet Union, are willing to condone relations with men whose black past is forgotten merely because they are anti-Communist. This is almost obscene when you think of the long rows of graves. It is also bad tactics.

For Communism will never be defeated by imitation. To defeat totalitarianism what is needed is not a Fascist imitation, in Germany or anywhere else, but a reassertion of belief in democracy. Democracy *can* defeat Communism in a cold war or a hot one, but only if it breathes freely. It can never win if it imitates the totalitarians. And each time it seeks a dubious ally through what it deems "necessity," American democracy loses some of its prestige with the people of the world.

I have written at length in this book of diplomacy and propaganda. But essentially wars, hot or cold, are won by peoples. The peoples of Europe can be our greatest ally. Let us not force them to turn elsewhere by making friends with those they believe are their enemies.

But if we are to be vigilant against the revival of Fascism and Nazism in Germany, we must not make the mistake of attacking every new manifestation of patriotism as a Nazi revival. There are degrees in German nationalism. It would be the height of folly to assail every German who wants to see his country prosperous and united as a neo-Nazi or a tool of the Communists. In dealing with Germany in the future we must see the Germans as they are, not as we would like them to be. We must recognize that it will take a long time to change the Germans from their present political habits and that money spent to that end is well spent.

The task is difficult but not hopeless. We should continue to spend money on exchange scholarships for German students, for reading centers in German towns, for the circulation in Germany of news about the United States. But we must never attempt to force the Germans into acceptance. The attitude of a lot of American officials toward democratization of the Germans has been that of the father at Jones Beach who slapped his child and said, "I brought you down here to have a good time and by God you're going to have it!"

You can't slap happiness or democracy into people. And we must remember that democracy—which to us is a natural, simple thing—to the bulk of the Germans is a new and complicated procedure to which they must become adjusted.

Finally I believe Americans must see Germany as she is today and not as she was a decade ago. We should never lose sight of the terrible drain which two great wars impose on a nation's vitality and resourcefulness. There is always the chance that new Hitlers will rise in Germany. But never again, I am convinced, will a German dictator, a Communist or Fascist, have at his disposal the same powerful industrial machine that was the basis of the Third Reich. Nor do I believe that such a dictator would ever again be able to command a nation so bellicose and confident as that which went to war with Poland a decade ago.

Germany will come back. But I do not believe she will come back all the way. I am aware that men said this in the 1920's and were proved wrong. But today Germany after a second World War and four and a half years of occupation is a far different country from what it was in 1922. And, whereas after the first World War, France and Britain were exhausted, Russia was torn by internal strife and the United States had turned its face from Europe, today all four Powers keep a close watch on Germany, and two of them, the United States and the Soviet Union, have assumed positions of power and influence in the world so great that they would appear to preclude any re-emergence of Germany as one of primary Powers of the world.

There does not appear any real hope that the great political contest waged by the United States and the Soviet Union will abate for years to come. There is a possibility, no more than a possibility, that when Stalin dies the government of Russia and of the Communist Party of the Soviet Union will be convulsed by a great struggle for individual personal power. Whether or not such a struggle spills out of the Kremlin and engulfs the people of the Soviet Union, who know as much about what goes on inside those red-brick walls as a gull does of coal mining, the struggle almost certainly will halt the actions of Russian political strategists from Berlin to Shanghai.

For it is one of the grave weaknesses of totalitarianism that when the guard is changed in the palace, no official, no matter how obscure, dares move until the face of the new order is revealed. The period after Stalin's death may be the West's great opportunity in Germany. Certainly until then there is no prospect of a respite from the cold war there.

At the moment our position in Germany is much better than that of the Russians. We have not been able to lead a unified Germany into the comity of western Europe. But we have overseen the planning of a West German State which can be added to any association of the states of western Europe. If this is done, then western Europe is strengthened against Communism by the addition of a nation of fifty million people and one of the great industrial areas of the world. Certainly Russian policy, which has failed so often in Germany, failed terribly when it prevented German unity and thus gave the West the opportunity to shut Russia out of western Germany.

On the whole, the Western Powers have done better in their political appeals to the German people than have the Russians. I believe that, slow though our progress has been, there are more Germans today who accept the democratic ideology of the Western nations than Stalinist Communism.

Superficially our progress in western Germany appears to be balanced by the survival of extreme nationalism and the emergence of neo-Fascism. But these same tendencies are evident in the Soviet Zone of Occupation. The difference is that there the Nazis and the rampant nationalists are admitted into the Socialist Unity Party, while in western Germany they are forced to come out into the open where they can be watched. In the end it will prove to be the Russians who are taking the risks, not the West.

Nor is there any real progress toward the solution of the Russians' basic political problem: the abiding fear and hatred of Russia which exists throughout Germany, even, I am convinced, among members of the Socialist Unity Party. In western Germany the occupation forces may be disliked, but they are not the objects of savage hatred as are the Russian troops beyond the Elbe.

From the economic standpoint the West German State will be stronger because it will be freer than any government established by the Soviet Military Administration in the east. The standard of living in the west will not return to that of prewar days, but it will be infinitely higher than in the Soviet Zone. That in itself will be a major political factor in the contest of attraction between east and west Germany.

The danger lies, I repeat, in the promises of markets and raw materials which the East can offer the West and the prospect that the Soviet political strategists might use such commercial arrangements as a basis for political infiltration. We must plan on the assumption of an eventual reopening of trade between eastern Germany—perhaps eastern Europe— and the West German State. The period after that trade is reestablished will be the critical one in the future struggle. How are we to hold Germany to the West?

It will be necessary, I believe, to include Germany in all political and economic planning for the nations of the West. This means German entry into international trade agreements and political associations. There is no valid reason why, after a long period of probation, Germany's entry into the United Nations should not be considered. There should be no distinction made against the kind of government in Germany, Socialist or Capitalist, so long as it is freely elected and guarantees the essential freedoms.

At all costs we must prevent the growth in German minds of the idea that their country is a pariah, that every man's hand is against it. If that idea does develop, the Russians will use it to draw Germany toward the East.

We would be unwise if in the next decade we were to relax the controls we have imposed on Germany. But mechanical controls are not enough. The Germans must be told why they have been imposed, and what conditions we wish to see in Germany before they can be relaxed. Ultimately the efficacy of all controls rests on the basic attitudes of the German people. If in a decade the West is satisfied that the relaxation of these controls will help democratic Germany, they should be relaxed. And never should we begrudge the money spent to bring the Germans into closer contact with Western ideas on politics and economics.

There always will be opposition to the idea of freeing Germany from the bonds imposed on her by defeat and occupation. But the Western Powers never should assume a position in which they have nothing to promise the Germans in the future. Certainly one of the principal points of Russian propaganda in western Germany from now on will be that in a united Germany on a Russian plan the Germans again will control the Ruhr.

There are three basic political possibilities in Germany's relationship to the rest of the world. The most unlikely, in my opinion, is that the present partition of the country will continue for an indefinite period with two German states, the western of which will be attached to a western European association and the eastern of which will continue as a satellite of the Soviet Union.

The second possibility is that within a decade Germany

will be reunited and, as a united country, assume a position within the Western community of nations. This implies the withdrawal of Russia's influence from the Elbe to the Oder and the acquiescence of the Kremlin in a united Germany facing West rather than East.

The third possibility is that a united Germany will enter into an economic and ideological alliance with the Soviet Union, becoming the most powerful of the satellite states. In that case prepare for war.

I believe continued partition is unlikely because in the long run neither East nor West in Germany will be able to resist the growing German demand for its end. Any German government of the future will use the national demand for unity to play East off against West and vice versa. No German government five years from now will be able to reject the overwhelming demand which by then will have developed. These are dangers but the less so because they are foreseeable.

It should be clear that in the period before the demands for reunification become so strong that they must be met or the structure of the West German State will be imperiled, that state must be so strengthened that in any reunited Germany it is the dominant area politically and economically. The unification of Germany will not be accomplished without arousing the gravest fears throughout the Western world. But these fears can be lessened by making sure that the dominant area in the new Germany is the West German State. For if democracy thrives there in the intervening period, the peoples of western Europe can feel that they have some safeguard, first against the reassertion of German aggression on a German basis, and second against a Communist *coup d'état* which might produce a government no less aggressive than that of Hitler and unreservedly backed by the resources of the Soviet Union.

So Western efforts to draw the German Federal Republic into the Atlantic community today may result tomorrow in the inclusion of a united and democratic Germany in that community. This is the second possibility and it is the one which seems to guarantee the greatest security for the West. Unfortunately it also presupposes that the Russians will have the sense to cut their political losses in Germany and withdraw from a united German state. This is possible.

Some good judges of Russian political strategy believe it is more than that. They hold that ultimately the Russians will not wish to hold part of Germany as long as they are convinced they cannot, at the moment, get all of Germany and thus will make a strategic withdrawal to the east. After all, they point out, even if the Russians withdraw from Germany, by the nature of things they will continue to exert great influence on the country.

It is only forty miles from the eastern limits of Berlin to the Oder and the western frontier of the Communist empire. Only a German government whose independence is guaranteed by the Western Powers will be able to resist the influence of this simple geographical fact. Unless such a guarantee is given, the actions of future German governments in Berlin always will be affected by the brutal fact that the Russians are only an hour's drive from the capital.

Today it is evident that the mass of the Germans believe their own interests are identical with those of the Atlantic nations and that a united Germany allied with those nations would be able to resist Soviet pressure. Part of the American task in Germany will be to stress continually to the Germans the advantages of their association with the West.

For, to swing Germany eastward, the Russians will offer much: in the economic field—markets, raw materials, low prices; in the political field—a joint political and military alliance and ostensible equality within the Eastern bloc. There is always the possibility that the Russians would not at first attempt to establish a Communist state in a united Germany. They would count on the long-term effect of their economic and political association to bring Germany into the Russian camp. Eventually, of course, by the nature of Communism, the German state would have to become Communist.

This brings us to the third possibility, unity and a Communist Germany. It is a gloomy picture, the more so because of the responsibility the United States would bear. At the moment it appears the most remote of possibilities. But unfortunately the conditions for political chaos exist in western Germany. In five or ten years we may get a Communist revival; we are much more likely to see a neo-Fascism which in the long run would be easier for the Russians to deal with than either a Capitalist or a Socialist democracy.

If a neo-Fascist state is organized in western Germany, the transition from it to a Communist state will be swift indeed. It would be far more vulnerable to an outright political attack by the Communists than a Capitalist or Socialist state, for nothing would incense the German workers more than the return of the conditions they believe ended in 1945.

There is another aspect to Fascism in western Germany and the struggle for that country between the Soviet Union and the United States. This is that the Soviet political strategists might be able to swing a Fascist Germany away from the West without first attempting a political revolution. A Fascist Germany will be a nationalist Germany, and to such a state the Russians will make seductive offers: control of the Ruhr, the return of the Saar, perhaps even the return of the Oder-Neisse lands.

Any Fascist government which comes to power in western Germany will achieve popular support only if it promises to attempt the territorial revisions mentioned above plus the unification of Germany. Only the Soviet Union, shut out of western Germany, will be interested in gaining the friendship and support of that sort of Germany.

Once it has swung the Fascist state into its orbit, Russia can then begin to develop a political attack upon its leaders. Such men are vulnerable to the Russian challenge. In a small way we have seen how the Fascists and survivors of National Socialism are joining the Socialist Unity Party because the party promises them most under Communism: position, martial trappings, authoritarianism. The same process could be carried out on a larger scale if a Fascist or semi-Fascist western Germany joined the Communist eastern Germany. For Russia, and Russia alone, would be in a position to offer the neo-Fascists what they want.

The second method by which a united Communist Germany could be achieved is the melancholy pattern of depression, dissatisfaction and Communism. A world depression similar to that of the early nineteen thirties will help Communism everywhere; the Kremlin has been waiting for a depression since 1945. Nowhere do the Russians hope to gain more from it than in western Germany where the economic hardships would be heightened by the general feeling of resentment and dissatisfaction among the refugees and the war veterans. There is a Communist potential in western Germany and the Russians know it.

For, curiously, if a Communist and united Germany is to emerge from that country, the main impetus must come from western Germany. The eastern zone can and will supply the trained police units, the party organizers and the propaganda. But after four and a half years of occupation it cannot supply the measure of popular support which national Communism must have. No factory worker in Leipzig will be fooled by the talk of the workers' democracy, although, if a depression comes, it is quite probable that an unemployed steelworker in Düsseldorf or a refugee textile worker in Ingolstadt will swallow it hook, line and sinker.

It is evident, I think, that should a united Germany become a Communist state allied with the Soviet Union, war, which is now a possibility, would become a probability. That is why we must not lose in Germany.

For the war which would develop would in truth be the last war of all.

Germany is our problem. A good deal of the rest of our lives will be spent thinking or worrying about developments there. But we cannot evade our responsibilities in Germany now that we have assumed them. Those responsibilities are heavier even than the burden of occupation. They entail a close and constant connection with Germany from today onward.

Like most of the direct responsibilities Americans have assumed this was unsought. Moreover our attitude toward Germany is complicated by the fierce emotions many of us feel toward the Germans. But in the end, whether we approach the struggle for Germany in the heart or in the mind, the task remains. For today Germany is not just an international criminal with a bad record, or an erring brother to be brought back into the fold. Germany is the center of the struggle for Europe.

There are indications that a western European association in alliance with the United States can halt the western expansion of the Soviet Union. But I submit that such an alliance is not complete, is not powerful unless it includes Germany, or as much of Germany as we have managed to hold for the West. Certainly there will be efforts to keep Germany out of such an alliance and these will be pushed with the utmost vigor by pressure groups in the United States and abroad. It will be said that this is against the national interests of France or Britain or Norway.

But finally the United States is the leader of the West. With due regard for the contributions which other states have made in the past and may make in the future it is on the United States that the penalty for defeat in the cold war, which ultimately means armed conflict, will fall. Let us have no misconceptions. If another war comes, the United States will not weather it as it did the second World War. We will be in the next one from the start and to win it we will have to pour forth the blood and treasure amassed in a century and three quarters of independence as we never have before.

Therefore it is in the national interests of the United States to tackle the German problem with regard for those interests. The penalty exacted for listening to the desires of other states for Germany's continued inferiority may not be war,

THE STRUGGLE FOR GERMANY

but as long as there is a possibility that it will be war, then the government should be free to act in the interests of its own people.

Let us look at the problem one last time in its essentials. Here in Germany, east and west, we have about sixty-five million people. They have, whether they know it or not, suffered a decisive defeat. This defeat coming as it did twenty-seven years after an earlier defeat, accompanied by bombing on a hitherto unknown scale and followed by occupation, has drained the essential strength of the nation. The country is divided. There is no easy road to unity. And all Germans are beset by political problems and tortured by political choices on which the lives of those who choose may depend. The German people have spawned some of the most wicked men of modern times. They have also produced great writers, musicians and thinkers. And although we cannot condone, and God forbid we ever should, what went on at Dachau or Belsen, we must not make the error of believing that Germany is the only home of cruelty.

Now we are engaged in a great contest with a totalitarian Power whose sources of strength are greater than those of Nazi Germany. The last four years have taught us, if they have taught us anything, that there is no retreat. The consequences of defeat are before us in eastern Europe. One of the ways in which victory can be won is to bring Germany back into the Western community of nations. But this Germany cannot be the Germany of Hitler. A Fascist Germany is a false reinforcement to the democratic Powers.

We must make two efforts. The first is to see that the Germany which develops in the next five or ten years is a democratic Germany which we can trust. The second is to insure that this Germany does not through our own mistakes fall to Communist pressure and ally itself with Russia.

This struggle will not be easy. It will be complicated by all the nuances of a situation in which we are fighting two battles—one against the age-old authoritarian instincts of the German people, and another against the Russian drive to take advantage of those instincts and mold Germany into an authoritarian Communist state. This struggle will be complicated by our own and other nations' fears of Germany. It will not end with the establishment of a German Federal Republic; indeed it will enter into its critical phase once there are eastern and western German governments. It is a struggle we dare not lose.

THE END

INDEX

Adenauer, Dr. Konrad, 230, 231, 249

Adorf, 18, 188

Agatz, Willi, 89, 116, 209, 269

Agitation and Propaganda Committee of the Central Committee of the Communist Party of the Soviet Union, 88

Allied Control Council, 32, 62, 64, 65, 69, 70, 94, 95, 96, 97, 98, 101, 109, 131, 133, 142

Allied Co-ordinating Committee, 142

Allied Reparation Commission, 30-31, 65

Allied Trizonal Administration, 167

Anglo-American Airlift, 122, 238. *See also* Berlin Airlift

Anglo-American Coal Directorate, 27

Article 18 (Ruhr Authority), 185-186

Article 20 (Ruhr Authority), 186

Attlee, Prime Minister Clement, 49, 50, 67

Atlantic Powers, 252

Austria, 16, 64, 252

Baden, 34

Bavaria, 33, 34, 44, 59, 155, 211, 213, 214, 228, 232, 233, 234, 235, 236, 275

Bavarian Party, 54, 59, 174, 214, 228, 232, 233, 234, 236, 252

Bayern Partei, *see* Bavarian Party

Bechler, Bernhard, 87, 198

Belgium, 21, 142, 265

Benelux Powers, 82, 144

Berlin, headquarters of Control Commission, 29, 69; declaration of

Berlin—*Continued*
1945, 32; blockade, 115, 129, 151, 152, 153, 254, 274; refugee problem, 211; democratic "hope of Germany," 237, 238, 253, 256; living conditions, 239-241; crisis of 1948, 247, 251, 278

Berlin Airlift, 59, 121. *See also* Anglo-American Airlift

Bevin, Foreign Secretary Ernest, 49, 50, 94, 103, 112, 139, 140, 156, 158, 161, 162, 163, 192; quoted, 159, 160

Bidault, Foreign Minister Georges, 94, 104

Big Three, 51

Bipartite Board, 164

Bizone, *see* Bizonia

Bizonia, 24, 97, 102, 103, 106, 110, 111, 138, 140, 157, 163, 164, 165, 180, 183, 200-202, 203, 265, 266

Bochum, 172, 206

Bohlen, Charles E., 136

Bonn, 16, 151, 227, 231, 233

Bracht, Hermann, 206-208, 209

Brandenburg, 120, 190

Brauchitsch, von, ———, 260

British Foreign Office, 161

British Labor Party, 155, 168

British policy in Germany, 158-159, 160-161, 162, 163, 179

British Zone of Occupation, 52, 69, 94, 97, 101, 107, 131, 132, 133, 144, 156, 163, 166, 167, 168, 169, 179, 210, 211, 213, 214, 215, 237, 256, 257, 276